CLASSROOM

DIVE INTO Close Reading

Diane Lapp, Ed.D., Barbara Moss, Ph.D.,
Maria Grant, Ph.D., and Kelly Johnson, Ed.D.

Foreword by Lori Oczkus, M.A.

Contributing Authors

Stephanie Herweck Paris
Jennifer Prior, Ph.D.

Publishing Credits

Corinne Burton, M.A.Ed., *President*
Conni Medina, M.A.Ed., *Managing Editor*
Nika Fabienke, Ed.D., *Content Director*
Emily R. Smith, M.A.Ed., *Project Consultant*
Sara Johnson, M.S.Ed., *Project Consultant*
Monique Dominguez, *Graphic Designer*
Valerie Morales, *Assistant Editor*

Image Credits

p.146 and 222 illustrations by Timothy J. Bradley; all other images iStock and/or Shutterstock.

Standards

Shell Education
A division of Teacher Created Materials
5301 Oceanus Drive
Huntington Beach, CA 92649-1030
www.tcmpub.com/shell-education
ISBN 978-1-4258-1557-8

Table of Contents

Acknowledgments

We want to acknowledge all the teachers who believe that being literate is the inalienable right of every student. Their daily instructional actions indicate their actualization of this right.

We also want to thank Sara Johnson for her initial belief in this program and Kristina Mazaika, Emily Smith, and Nika Fabienke who shepherded it to the finish line. We appreciate each of you.

Diane, Barbara, Maria, and Kelly

Foreword

At last, close reading is demystified and made practical in this fabulous resource, put together by the respected team of Diane Lapp, Barbara Moss, Maria Grant, and Kelly Johnson! The authors bring their rich classroom experiences and knowledge of the reading process to this useful tool, designed especially for grades 3–5. The movie title of *Dive into Close Reading: Strategies for Your 3–5 Classroom* could be *Everything You Wanted to Know About Close Reading But Were Afraid to Ask!* Whether you already teach students to read closely or are new to the term, *Dive into Close Reading* is for you! This useful and classroom-tested resource is jam-packed with grade-level specific ideas and detailed lesson samples to use all year long. Whether you read *Dive into Close Reading* on your own or if you study close reading in a professional learning community in your school or district, this is a wonderful book!

In my work around the country as a literacy consultant, I find that the definition of close reading varies as well as the practices related to it. The authors of this text aptly define close reading as an approach for all students to develop deep comprehension of complex texts, including English language learners and below-level readers. They add that, "In close reading, students act as investigators, gradually uncovering the meaning of short pieces of literature or informational texts. Through the process of reading, questioning, focusing, and rereading the texts, students uncover the 'bones,' or main ideas, of the passage." The authors claim that rereading to delve deeper into texts is at the heart of close reading.

Today, teachers still ask lots of questions regarding the implementation of close reading and what models work best. The authors of *Dive into Close Reading* address the issues and problems teachers share when incorporating quality close reading lessons in their classrooms. Here are some of the current concerns teachers may express with close reading:

- What is the definition of close reading?
- How can I make close reading relevant to my students so that they will do it on their own?
- What types of texts, including complex texts, should I use in my lessons?
- What are some ways to motivate students to reread during close reading lessons?
- How can I teach close reading using the materials I already have in my classroom?
- What are some lesson formats that fit different types of texts and genres?
- What is the most effective use of text-dependent questions during lessons?
- How can I make time for close reading?
- How does close reading differ from other familiar reading approaches?
- What is the best way to teach students to annotate text?
- How can I use close reading to promote better comprehension and critical thinking?

Foreword *(cont.)*

Dive into Close Reading is chock-full of not only research-based how-to questions and answers but also includes sample texts and lessons that engage students in the close reading process. Teachers will welcome the easy-to-read format and concrete examples. *Dive into Close Reading* has a unique format that is really a two-in-one professional book, plus a rich sample lesson treasure trove. The authors have taken the guesswork out of creating close reading lesson plans that really work!

Dive into Close Reading features:

- ➜ Rubrics for evaluating texts based on:
    - what the text says
    - how the text works
    - what the text means
- ➜ Grade-specific text-dependent questions charts for grades 3–5 that teachers will want to use every day!
- ➜ Suggestions for scaffolding tools, such as partner texts, realia, or illustrations.
- ➜ Concrete ideas for performance tasks that are grade-level specific. For example, at 3rd grade, role playing with two characters; or 4th grade, creating posters; or 5th grade, making audio podcasts that critically examine a topic.
- ➜ Concrete strategies for helping struggling readers and English language learners grasp concepts.
- ➜ Very specific sample lesson plans and strategies for literary texts for each grade level 3–5.
- ➜ Very specific sample lesson plans and strategies for informational texts for each grade level 3–5.

Join me in congratulating the authors Diane Lapp, Barbara Moss, Maria Grant, and Kelly Johnson for their brilliant exploration of close reading and their generous gift of a practical guide to illustrate the approach. Teachers everywhere will want copies on their desks to use all year long as they help students *Dive into Close Reading*!

—Lori Oczkus

Literacy Consultant and Coauthor of the *Close Reading with Paired Texts K–5* series

Section 1: Close Reading Introduced

A Short Scenario

In Mrs. Marquand's fourth grade classroom, students are tackling a standard that involves looking at energy and fuels derived from nature and natural resources. Mrs. Marquand selects a section from the text, *The Next Wave: The Quest to Harness the Power of the Oceans* (Rusch 2014), to use for a close reading. In most circumstances, this text might have students rolling their eyes and putting their heads down. For example, a sentence such as "Despite these overwhelming challenges, the work of these ocean energy pioneers is finally reaching a crest, with an array of amazing machines proving their worth in the water" could easily lose students' attention. After all, this sentence includes technical language (ocean energy), academic language (despite these overwhelming challenges), and even a pun (use of the term *crest*, which is both a high point in the research discussed and a part of wave anatomy).

How can a teacher guide students to notice and comprehend such subtle yet important intricacies of text? That's the question asked by thousands of teachers as they sit down to craft meaningful lessons that involve reading complex texts.

Fortunately, there is an answer to this question—an effective, thoughtful, research-based means of implementing close reading that can be personalized to meet the needs of any teacher's students. The key is to guide students to unlock meaning through strategically crafted text-dependent questions.

Let us return to Mrs. Marquand's fourth grade class to see how she does this.

Mrs. Marquand begins by asking students to read the two paragraphs she has designated for this close reading and to think about the question *What is this text about?* Students are also instructed to use the annotation markings of their choosing to note key words and ideas, confusing concepts or questions, and connections between elements.

Annotations: symbols, notes, comments, and other markings that help readers remember their thinking. For more information about annotations, see Table 3.2 (page 61).

Fourth graders David and Max feel confident in their skills. They have practiced with Mrs. Marquand for weeks now. Following the first close reading, the students chat and share their thoughts, first as partners, then as a whole group.

Max: I think this is about how hard it has been to get energy from the ocean.

David: Yeah, because the ocean is strong and has big waves and stuff.

Max: Right. Also, I was confused about some of the words, like *harness*. Do you know what that means?

David: Uh-uh. I don't know what *harness* means either.

Mrs. Marquand (to the class): Focus on the sentence that has this phrase, "It must *harness* the power of the waves and convert it into electricity." What clues does the author provide to help you understand that sentence?

As she teaches the close reading lesson, Mrs. Marquand uses student annotations and partner talk to guide her next steps. She offers appropriate text-dependent questions to help students unlock meaning for themselves. She guides students by strategically directing their attention to specific areas in the text. In doing so, she empowers them to use their insights and those gained from conversing with their peers. Her instruction includes close assessment of student performance, fostering independence, and building self-esteem. This is evident as Max and David continue to talk after Mrs. Marquand's questioning.

> **Max:** So, there are two parts to that sentence. It has to harness power and then convert it.
>
> **David:** It says harness the power *of the waves*. So, maybe it means *get*, like *get the power*.
>
> **Max:** Right, it has to get the power from the waves and then change it into electricity.
>
> **David:** That makes sense. We figured it out!

As this scenario illustrates, students begin to feel capable when they learn to read complex texts on their own, which is a teacher's dream. This book serves as a guide to teachers as they follow Mrs. Marquand's lead—teachers like you, who are teaching students to closely read complex texts by challenging them with appropriate text-dependent questions that build reading skills, deepen comprehension, and foster independence.

The Close Reading Approach

Compare today's modern, dynamic classrooms to the educational system in place 50 years ago, and it is obvious that huge improvements have been made in the teaching profession. As a frontline educator, you have never before been so well positioned to serve the ever-evolving needs of an increasingly diverse student body, but there are still areas that need attention. Every year, new techniques and buzzwords swirl around, each one promising to open the world of knowledge and critical thought to your students. Some live up to their promises, and some fizzle, only to be replaced by the *next big thing* the following year. You must carefully evaluate new techniques to ensure that they will be of actual benefit to students. No one denies that students need strong preparation for college and future careers. The question is, and always has been, *how* can we best provide students with the skills they need to lead productive, successful lives? The close reading approach described in this book is a terrific place to start.

Close reading is a powerful, useful, and successful approach for teaching reading comprehension and critical-thinking skills. The lessons and strategies described in this book have been piloted and refined by classroom teachers, are backed by current pedagogical research, and are aligned with college and career readiness standards from around the country. Using the close reading approach simply means building upon current practices. Table 1.1 lists useful definitions for terms used in the close reading approach.

Table 1.1 Useful Definitions for the Close Reading Approach

Term	Working Definition
annotation	the process of marking a text with information and questions for further study; may include highlights, symbols, notes, and comments
chunking	breaking a text into smaller pieces, or chunks, numbered for ease of reference and study
close thinking	a sister approach to close reading, where students think deeply about texts that are read aloud to them, as opposed to texts they read independently; is especially useful technique for when students do not yet have the decoding skills necessary to tackle a particular text
guided reading	a small-group reading approach in which a teacher supports developing readers through pre-loading and individualized scaffolding; is frequently used as an intermediate step between shared and independent reading
qualitative	unable to be defined numerically; factors include things such as student experiences with a topic, author purpose, and language features
quantitative	can be defined and assessed numerically, such as by grade level, number of words per page, and word length
scaffold	support for a student's learning; a tailored teaching practice used with the intent of helping the student achieve his or her learning goals
shared reading	an interactive reading experience in which the teacher models the skills of a fluent reader
text-dependent question (TDQ)	a question that is based on the text itself, rather than personal experiences, and can only be answered by someone who has read a particular text selection
text complexity	a measure of the level of challenge presented by a particular text selection for a student at a given level
thinking aloud	technique of speaking the thoughts that occur in the mind while approaching a particular reading challenge; a process that can be used to model or assess a particular skill

Frequently Asked Questions

What does the close reading of complex texts really mean?

When a fluent reader approaches a text, he or she does more than simply decode the words. The fluent reader thinks about a dozen different things before beginning to read: *What do I know about this? Who wrote this? What do I know about that person? When was it written? Is this a book, a pamphlet, an excerpt, a magazine article, a newspaper article, an advertisement, or some other kind of writing? What sort of font is being used, and what does that imply about the writing?* Once the reading begins, this mental questioning process continues, and the reader looks for answers within the text. The fluent reader may reread sections or, if the selection is very short, an entire passage, as understanding of the piece evolves. A truly rich and complex text may be revisited many times over a lifetime, with the reader making new and interesting discoveries with each rereading.

Close reading is a structured approach that enables all students, including English language learners and below-grade-level students, to develop this deep comprehension of complex grade-level texts. In close reading, students act as investigators, gradually uncovering the meaning of short pieces of literature or informational texts. Through the process of reading, questioning, focusing, and rereading the texts, students uncover the "bones," or main ideas, of the passage. Students return again and again to the text, becoming ever more adept at identifying and interacting with the language, context, structure, and layers of embedded meaning. This emphasis on returning to the same text repeatedly to gradually acquire a comfortable and deep relationship with it is at the heart of the close reading approach.

Why do today's standards require the close reading of complex texts?

Comprehension of complex texts is linked to success on high-stakes assessments of college and career readiness and to actual success in college and career. Today's standards require instruction and supported practice with close reading of complex texts.

A study by the college readiness testing company ACT (2006) evaluated the results of 568,000 ACT reading tests taken by eighth, tenth, and twelfth grade students. These test results were compared with a benchmark level of "college readiness," a standard meant to predict college acceptance, retention, and the achievement of a 3.0 GPA. Next, the researchers analyzed the student responses with the goal of identifying which factors were indicative of success. Students who were able to read and comprehend the most complex texts were the ones most likely to have high

> The Partnership for Assessment of Readiness for College and Careers determined that "A significant body of research links the close reading of complex texts—whether the student is a struggling reader or advanced—to significant gains in reading proficiency and finds close reading to be a key component of college and career readiness" (2011, 7).

scores on the college-readiness standard. The ACT researchers found that "Students who can read complex texts are more likely to be ready for college. Those who cannot read complex texts are less likely to be ready for college" (2006, 5).

Additionally, there is a significant gap between the complexity of texts being used at the twelfth grade level and those being utilized in career and college settings. In his 2006 study, Gary L. Williamson reported that there is a gap greater than 1.5 standard deviations between the level of these texts, a larger difference than that between typical fourth and eighth grade texts!

At what grade level should we begin using the close reading approach?

Today's reading standards require students of all ages to take a much more critical look at the texts they read. The earlier students begin to closely read, the better. The close reading approach should be introduced to even the newest readers. In this way, close reading will become a habit of mind when tackling challenging texts (Boyles 2012). Emphasizing the need to repeatedly return to a text in order to uncover evidence for perceived meaning is an essential skill, which can and should be applied in all areas of academic study. Introducing this concept as early as possible can improve students' academic performance throughout their careers.

Why should close reading replace tried and true reading approaches?

It shouldn't! There is nothing about close reading that precludes the use of other approaches that work well for you and your students. You can and should continue to use successful approaches, such as guided reading, shared reading, book study, and collaborative groups. Close reading is an approach that will support your students in deeply and critically analyzing all types of complex texts. It is not meant to be the sole approach or strategy for literacy development in your classroom. Think of it as an additional powerful tool in your teaching toolbox. As every craftsperson knows, it is important to use the right tool for each job. The close reading tool is exceptionally useful when teaching students how to approach, analyze, and deeply connect with complex literature and informational texts.

How does close reading differ from other familiar reading approaches?

Close reading focuses on short, complex texts or self-contained sections of texts that are visited and revisited multiple times. Before the reading, teachers *do not frontload information* for students. Unlike guided, shared, or read-aloud sessions, it is not recommended that teachers model skills and strategies or preteach background information before students read or listen to a text during the close reading. There is, however, nothing to preclude a teacher from inviting students to closely read a subsection of a text or a stanza of a poem that is already under study or, in the early years, that has been previously shared as a read aloud. However, during the actual close reading, students are encouraged to independently *have a go* at a text selected for its complexity and placement in their appropriate Lexile band. During the first reading, students should read or listen to uncover the big ideas and key details of the text. Students engage in repeated readings of the text to access deeper meaning, including how the text works, by scrutinizing the author's craft and the meaning of the text. Student annotations should illuminate their thinking as well as their points of confusion, any unknown vocabulary, and other questions or points of interest they wish to pursue more deeply.

At every juncture, the main role of the teacher is to assess student performance and provide scaffolds to support text analysis. This happens, for example, while listening to conversations to determine the direction to take in the next read, asking students what they are looking for in the read, and reassessing student needs. The major scaffold teachers provide is through the continuous questions they ask: *What does the text say? What evidence can you find for that? How is the information conveyed? Can you find that in the text?* Purposeful questions help students resolve the complexity and uniqueness of each text.

Close reading lessons are also unique in planning. Preplanning of text-dependent questions is essential to the success of a close reading lesson. Unlike other reading instruction approaches, however, close reading cannot be completely preplanned. Although you may craft an initial set of questions before students begin reading the text, tailoring questions and dialog to the issues and questions that arise during students' reading is powerful and authentic. Close reading experiences occur organically and can never be recreated. Each encounter with the text should, however, push students to a deeper level of understanding.

What do I do after a close read?

Close reading experiences should conclude with performance tasks that encourage students to demonstrate their learning. These tasks may include writing, slide shows, reader's theater, art projects, or any other assessment activity designed to further extend students' learning and provide them with opportunities to share their mastery of the learning goals for the lesson. If students are still struggling or are unable to competently demonstrate their knowledge, reteaching may be in order. See pages 67–78 for assessment and reteaching ideas.

Close Reading Management

The easiest way to manage the scheduling of close reading is to encompass other literacy practices within the close reading session. For example, if you use shared reading regularly, try using a close reading approach, which involves a shared reading component. Similarly, close reading can be easily rotated into your guided reading lessons. As students' proficiency with close reading increases, it becomes easier to incorporate it throughout your curriculum.

Generally, we believe that students should have opportunities to engage in close reading on a daily basis. However, these experiences should ideally be spread out across all areas of study, not just with specified language arts lessons. A student might engage in close reading for a math lesson on Monday, a social studies lesson on Tuesday, and a language arts lesson on Wednesday. It is essential that students have ample opportunities to make close reading a deeply ingrained habit so that they can depend on these skills to propel them beyond surface reading for the rest of their lives.

The close reading approach is structured for whole-group instruction and partner work. However, when students struggle, small-group scaffolding becomes necessary. In those cases, a small group can be pulled together while the rest of the students are engaged in independent or small-group work that does not require teacher attention.

Table 1.2 illustrates how one teacher incorporated close reading in her classroom over the course of a week.

Table 1.2 Incorporating Close Reading

Content Area	Monday	Tuesday	Wednesday	Thursday	Friday
Language Arts	close reading: *Tom Sawyer* pp. 40–41	read aloud: *Tom Sawyer* chapter 5	close reading: *Tom Sawyer* p. 101	read aloud: *Tom Sawyer* chapter 6	read aloud: *Tom Sawyer* chapter 7
Science	lecture and shared reading: *Galileo and the Starry Messenger* pp. 4–6	close reading: *Galileo and the Starry Messenger* pp. 7–9	constellation activity	close reading: *Galileo and the Starry Messenger* pp. 10–15	build your own telescope activity
Social Studies	finish final project on the Dark Ages	groups present final projects on the Dark Ages	close reading: *The Italian Renaissance* (textbook chapter intro)	lecture and class discussion of Renaissance changes	Renaissance art
Mathematics	review: graphing	assessment: graphing	small-group work: graphing and measurement review	lecture: finding volume	close reading: *Count Like an Egyptian: A Hands-On Introduction to Ancient Mathematics* pp. 1–2
Other	practice for spring assembly performance	close reading: visual literacy lesson on Van Gogh's *The Starry Night*	practice for spring assembly performance	little buddy time with kindergarten partners	begin Renaissance stained glass art project

Organization of this Book

We have created this resource with some very specific goals in mind. First, we want to support other teachers in implementing close reading in ways that demonstrate intentional, explicit instruction. In other words, we want to take the guesswork out of the process and provide a research-supported approach that can easily fit into classroom lessons. Secondly, we want to provide instructional examples of close reading that demonstrate how it can be used to address other important classroom goals, such as general reading and writing goals, the development of academic language, inquiry learning, use of technology, deep thinking, and reading across disciplines.

Finally, it is important to us that we provide a close reading toolkit that includes sample texts, sample student activities, sample performance tasks, and other supports teachers can use to create close reading lessons. A close reading resource is only truly useful if it includes the tools needed to incorporate the approach into every area of the curriculum. For this reason, we have decided to present the majority of this book in a format that supports your efforts to create close reading lessons for classroom use.

Digital Download

The planning templates, appendix resources, and sample lesson passages included in this book are available as Adobe® PDFs online. A complete list of the documents is on pages 273–274. Additionally, the file names are referenced throughout the book. To access the digital resources, go to http://www.tcmpub.com/download-files and enter the following code: 54740083. Follow the on-screen directions.

Guide to Book Sections

Section One has presented an overview of the close reading approach. In previous sections, the structure of close reading, useful terms, and frequently asked questions were reviewed.

Section Two presents the process for planning a close reading lesson. This is the section you should turn to as you are thinking about how to make initial planning decisions for a close reading session. Close reading requires careful preparation on the part of the teacher. There are several crucial decisions to be made. First, it is necessary to select an appropriate text. You will also decide which standard or standards to address and identify the areas of complexity for your students. Lastly, you will plan text-dependent questions and additional scaffold questions. It is important to note that the text-dependent questions can and should evolve during the course of the lesson. You may anticipate that students will struggle with the main idea (and, therefore need additional scaffold questions), but upon viewing their first read annotations, realize that they instead struggled with a challenging vocabulary term. In that case, you might modify your initial text-dependent questions to include text-dependent questions that lead students to clarify the challenging term. Section Two will walk you through each of these steps explicitly.

Digital Download
A digital download with planning templates, appendix resources, and sample lesson passages accompanies this book.

Section Three presents the process for teaching a close reading lesson. This section includes detailed descriptions of how to scaffold the lesson for students of all reading levels. Throughout a close reading lesson, there are several more decisions that need to be made to determine how to scaffold the instruction for students. *Who will be doing the reading? How many times should students revisit the text? How will the lesson be chunked? What annotations should be used? What types of student resources are needed?* At every stage, remember that you may choose to "take back" the reading. If you find that students are struggling too much and becoming unfocused or frustrated, your choice for independent reading may be replaced by a new choice to read aloud and model the thinking and reading skills of a fluent reader. Each of these is addressed more fully in Section Three.

Section Four presents simple step-by-step techniques for assessing and extending close reading lessons. This section includes specific guidelines, activities, templates for anecdotal records and performance tasks, and suggestions on how to reteach information to students who have not fully grasped a lesson. The final set of decisions for a close reading lesson surround the specific ways to assess students' understanding. You should create and use both formative and summative assessments to determine what, if anything, must be retaught.

Section Five and **Section Six** present a collection of close reading lessons. For each grade level, there are three literary and three informational texts with corresponding lessons. These lessons address a range of college and career readiness anchor standards, specifically key ideas and details, craft and structure, and integration of knowledge and ideas.

Finally, the **Appendices** are designed to help you scaffold lessons for a diverse group of students. Appendix B is a glossary of reteaching ideas, and Appendix C lists the graphic organizers and templates that are provided in the **Digital Download**. For example, there is a character web graphic organizer and a plot chart to be used for teaching text structure. There is also a T-chart and a guide for identifying figurative language to assist with vocabulary development.

The sections of this book are organized around the decisions to be made at each stage of planning and teaching a close reading lesson. Table 1.3 provides an overview of the decisions made at each stage.

Table 1.3 Close Reading Stages and Decisions

Close Reading Stage	What Decision Must Be Made?
Preplanning	• Identify a standard and lesson purpose. • Select a text. • Determine the areas of complexity. • Create text-dependent questions.
Teaching	• Determine how to scaffold the close read. • Who is doing the close reading? • How many times do students revisit the text? • Does any minor frontloading need to occur after the first reading? • How should the text be chunked? • What types of annotations should be used? • What types of student resources are needed?
Assessing and Extending	• How do I assess student understanding? • How do I assess student understanding during the lesson? • How do I assess student understanding after the lesson? • What do I do for students who, at the end of close reading, have not totally comprehended the text? • What do I do to reteach the students who did not understand?

Try It!

Directions: Using Table 1.2 (page 13) as a model, identify potential places in which you can incorporate close reading into your instructional schedule. Write on the table below, or use a digital copy of the table in the Digital Download (incorporatingclosereading.pdf).

Incorporating Close Reading

Content Area	Monday	Tuesday	Wednesday	Thursday	Friday
Language Arts					
Science					
Social Studies					
Mathematics					
Other					

Section 2: Planning Close Reading

Close reading is a unique instructional approach in that it cannot be strictly preplanned. The teacher designs the overall outline of the lesson, and the carefully selected text influences much of the learning. However, with each dive into the text, the discussion and learning follows student needs. During a successful close reading lesson, you will be both prepared and flexible. Table 2.1 lists the areas of planning and decision making. The shaded areas will be addressed in Section Four of this book.

Table 2.1 Planning for Close Reading

Planning	Date:_____ Grade: _____ Discipline:_____ Purpose(s):_____ Standard(s):_____ Text Selection (literary or informational):_____ Performance Assessment: _____ Materials: _____		
Text Selection	Title:_____ Author:_____ Page(s) or section(s):_____ How should this text be chunked?_____ _____		
Areas of Complexity	Lexile Level:_____ Meaning or Purpose:_____ Structure:_____ Language Features:_____ Knowledge Demands:_____		
Text-Dependent Questions	1._____ 2._____ 3._____ 4._____ 5._____		
Performance Task	_____ _____ _____ _____	Differentiation	Additional Support: _____ _____ Extension:_____ _____

Identifying a Standard and Lesson Purpose

The first step in any lesson is to decide what to teach and why. Begin by considering the standards that will be addressed, the skills on which to focus, and the knowledge of language students already possess. For our sample lessons, we have selected and built them around the applicable standards from the Common Core State Standards for English/ Language Arts (2012) to meet the expectations of college and career readiness and built the lessons around those learning goals. Many state standards parallel these expectations. If the standard chosen is particularly challenging, you may opt to focus the lesson entirely around that one. However, often it is useful to bundle several standards into one lesson. The five steps to take in preparing your lesson purpose(s) based on the standards chosen are listed below.

Steps for Identifying a Standard and Creating a Lesson Purpose

1. Choose a standard from the college and career readiness standards or state standards.
2. Create a lesson purpose in kid-friendly language.
3. Share the lesson purpose with your students.
4. Post the lesson purpose where all students can easily view it.
5. Translate the lesson purpose into an "I Can" statement that helps student self-assess.

Once you have selected your standards, they should be translated into a lesson purpose to be shared with your students. The purpose statements, also known as learning goals or intentions, should be thought of in two ways: *what* students are learning and *how* they are learning it. The goal of writing purpose statements is to make explicit, for students and teachers, what learning is occurring and how they can demonstrate that learning. Avoid writing purpose statements that are solely task or activity oriented. This might lead students to mistakenly think that learning is achieved through writing lists, completing graphic organizers, or presenting orally. Instead, purpose statements that describe the actual learning teach students that by writing lists, completing graphic organizers, or presenting orally, we can demonstrate our understanding of the content.

All lesson tasks will be tied to the lesson purpose, so it is important that it clearly articulates what the teacher is trying to teach and is general enough to encompass all the learning goals. For example, imagine your class is reading a text about Mars. You have identified several pertinent standards including summarizing by determining the main idea of a text and how it is supported by key details. For the students, you can articulate *what* they will learn by writing the purpose statement: "You will understand the features of the planet Mars." Additionally, you can share with students *how* they will demonstrate their learning with the purpose statement: "List five key details in a summary paragraph."

Lastly, the purpose statements can be translated into "I Can" statements. These are student-generated sentences that students use to state what they are able to do. If the purpose of the lesson was for students to understand the features of the planet Mars and students will demonstrate their learning by listing five key details in a summary paragraph, the "I Can" statement might be, "I can list key details about the features of the planet Mars." At the end of the lessons, students assess themselves and decide if they can truthfully make this statement.

By sharing the learning targets with your students, you provide them with contexts and goals around which to structure their own reading. It encourages them to stay focused. Post the purposes in front of the classroom so that both you and the students can reference them often and have visual reminders of the current learning goals and how to achieve them.

Examples of Student-Friendly Purpose Statements and "I Can" Statements

- **WHAT:** Understand how the respiratory system works.
  HOW: List the parts of the respiratory system.
  I CAN: I can list the parts of the respiratory system.
- **WHAT:** Analyze a character.
  HOW: Describe the personality of Huck Finn in two paragraphs.
  I CAN: I can describe the personality of Huck Finn.
- **WHAT:** Recognize insect classification.
  HOW: Compare and contrast bees and wasps.
  I CAN: I can compare and contrast bees and wasps.
- **WHAT:** Examine how figurative language shapes a reader's understanding.
  HOW: Explain three idioms from the text in your own words.
  I CAN: I can explain idioms in my own words.
- **WHAT:** Understand how setting helps us deepen our understanding.
  HOW: Draw a map of Mr. Looper's farm.
  I CAN: I can draw a map of the setting of a story.
- **WHAT:** Recognize the author's purpose for writing about a particular character and setting.
  HOW: Write an argumentative essay about whether Harry Potter would have been a good fit for Slytherin.
  I CAN: I can write an argumentative essay about a particular character and setting.

Selecting a Text

The next step is to select the text. In many cases, you may wish to plan a close reading lesson focusing on a short, complex sub-section of a larger text already being studied. In others, you may wish to seek out and select a text specifically to engage in a close reading experience. In either case, it is important to evaluate the selected text for appropriate complexity and length. The close reading approach can be used for any lesson that involves a short passage that is of sufficient complexity to offer a challenge for your students. Additionally, it can also be used to closely examine charts, graphs, graphics, cartoons, or other visual elements. However, we will focus on texts for our examples. Feel free to extrapolate the method to work with other kinds of reading material. If a text does not feel easily accessible to your students, then it is a perfect opportunity to engage in the close reading approach.

> Research has shown that in order to be effective, texts selected for close reading should be "compact, short, self-contained ones that can be read and reread deliberately and slowly" (Coleman and Pimentel 2012, 4).

You might notice that it is repeatedly mentioned that the close reading approach is best for short texts. This is because it is an intensive and deep reading approach. The goal is that students will use the skills gained during the close reading experiences in your classroom whenever they are faced with a challenging text of any length, either in school or on their own. However, to tackle a larger text in a classroom setting can become unwieldy and daunting. That is definitely not the goal! The classroom use of close reading should provide students with an opportunity to develop and practice skills that will be useful to them for a lifetime. Thus, upon choosing texts, keep in mind the time requirements and make sure to not overwhelm yourself or your students.

There are several questions to keep in mind when selecting a text.

- Is it a text that is worthy of deep study and critical analysis?
- Is it relevant, interesting, and engaging? Does it support the topic or theme being studied?
- Does it fall within the range of students' abilities, plus a little more? Will it make students stretch to gain full understanding?
- What are the demands of the text? (e.g., language, structure, knowledge)
- What scaffolds may be needed when tackling this text with the class? (e.g., Will there be students who will benefit from small-group instruction? Is it necessary to partner this text with another less complex text to build background knowledge and language as scaffolding for struggling students?)
- Does the text address the identified standard?

Determining Areas of Complexity

When evaluating text complexity for students, there are three aspects to consider: the quantitative text attributes, the qualitative text attributes, and the reader/task attributes.

Quantitative Text Attributes

Quantitative text attributes are those that can be measured using numeric evaluations. These include sentence length, number of syllables, word length, and word frequency. The quantitative attributes of a text can be calculated using computer programs and reported with numeric designations. In the past, they were generally reported with grade level designations, such as 4.6 (fourth grade, sixth month). However, there are several analysis systems that have come to favor and provide more information than simple grade level designations, such as the Lexile® Framework for Reading.

The Lexile text measurement evaluates text complexity and represents the quantitative attributes of text with a numeric designation. There is no absolute mapping of the Lexile scores with specific grade levels; instead, students are expected to read within a Lexile range or "Lexile band." For example, students in second grade should be comfortably reading within the 450L–730L band. Those same students should be challenging themselves to read within the 420L–820L "Stretch" Lexile band. See Table 2.2 for a complete Lexile band chart.

Table 2.2 Lexile Band Chart

Grade Band	Current Lexile Band	"Stretch" Lexile Band*
K–1	N/A	N/A
2–3	450L–730L	420L–820L
4–5	640L–850L	740L–1010L
6–8	860L–1010L	925L–1185L
9–10	960L–1120L	1050L–1335L
11–CCR	1070L–1220L	1185L–1385L

*Common Core State Standards for English, Language Arts, Appendix A (Additional Information), NGA and CCSSO 2012

Other common leveling systems include DRA Levels, and Fountas & Pinnell's F&P Text Level Gradient™. Each of these systems attempts to provide graduated, quantitative assessment of text difficulty. Table 2.3 shows the levels common to each grade.

Table 2.3 Other Leveling Systems

Grade Level	DRA 2 Level	Fountas & Pinnell
Kindergarten	A–4	A–D
1	6–18	E–J
2	20–28	K–M
3	30–38	N–P
4	40	Q–S
5	50	T–V
6	60	W–Y

Leveling systems are good tools for evaluating the quantitative attributes of texts, but they cannot reflect the content of the text. For example, what if a text requires understanding of historic context to illuminate its subject? What if there is symbolism, a weighty central theme, or a challenging social dynamic at play? These attributes cannot be reflected in a quantitative metric. Therefore, it is essential to go beyond the quantitative elements when evaluating text complexity for students and delve into qualitative text attributes.

Qualitative Text Attributes

Qualitative text attributes are those text attributes that cannot be easily measured using a numeric value. These include text structures, author's purpose, language attributes, and the meaning of the text. The level of challenge included in these features of the text must be carefully analyzed and evaluated before the text is chosen for a group of students. Just because a text uses simple words does not necessarily mean that the text is not complex. Certain authors are known for choosing accessible language to convey nuanced topics. For example, pick any book by Ernest Hemmingway or John Steinbeck, and you may discover that simply by looking at its quantitative attributes, it is simple enough to be read by most elementary students. In fact, Hemmingway's *The Sun Also Rises* has a Lexile level of 610, which means that it should be easily decoded by an average third grader. But when qualitative attributes such as author's purpose and meaning are considered, the text is revealed to be much more complex.

Another important consideration included in qualitative text attributes is the *knowledge demand* or amount of background knowledge a reader must have in order to discern the full meaning. For example, in reading a text on the Underground Railroad, a student must have a relatively deep knowledge of cultural concepts before beginning: *What is slavery? What is a railroad? Who were the abolitionists? What were the dangers for escaped slaves and those who helped them? What prevented escaped slaves from traveling through normal modes of conveyance?* Even if the text gives a lot of support and context, a reader lacking at least some familiarity with the time period and issues involved may find an otherwise simple-seeming text deceptively challenging.

Authors write with audiences in mind. As we write this text, we envision it being read by professional educators who are engaging students in close reading practices. As we write, we target the information and tone to our audience—you. If you are not a member of our expected audience group, this book may be extremely challenging, indeed! We have not included a detailed summary of modern educational practices to place the close reading approach in context. If we did, our actual target audience would become impatient and bored. Authors of every genre must balance the knowledge demands of their writing.

If the author provides less support, the reader must put in more effort to attain a proper understanding. This struggle can be very healthy and rewarding and should not be universally avoided. But if the struggle becomes unproductive or frustrating, it can become difficult for a reader to stay motivated to stick with the reading. Unfortunately, there is no numerical value one can assign to the knowledge demands of a text. To adequately analyze text complexity, it is imperative to consider the specific students who will be reading it.

The next qualitative aspect to consider when evaluating a text is its structure and organization. For narrative texts, consider whether the piece is written using a linear plotline or if it utilizes flashbacks, flash-forwards, or other non-linear storytelling techniques. For elementary students, a straightforward, linear approach is usually easier to navigate. When evaluating informational texts, look closely at how the information is presented. Informational texts can utilize a number of structures, such as cause/effect, sequence, compare/contrast, and problem/solution. A text that sticks to one approach is typically less complex than one that includes a few. For example, consider a book that sequentially describes the process of a seed growing into a tree. All other things being equal, that book will be less complex than a text that starts out sequentially describing the seed growth process, jumps to cause and effect of the rainy season on seed growth, compares and contrasts the growth rates of a variety of seeds, and then tackles the problems and solutions of human encroachment on rainforest biomes.

Visual layout and visual support features play another part in determining the complexity of a text in terms of structure. There is sometimes a tendency to discount these features as outside the realm of "reading," but every aspect of a document factors into its complexity. Clarifying charts, maps, illustrations, and diagrams serve to simplify or extend the information already presented in the narrative. Likewise, font and layout choices made by the author or publisher affect the reader's comprehension. Clear, simple, uncluttered visual features tend to make even a complex text accessible. Busy fonts, multiple-column layouts, and ambiguously placed visual support features actually obscure the meaning of the text and make reading more challenging. Even a particularly sophisticated or hyper-informative map or chart can complicate an otherwise simple text.

The way the text handles relationships among ideas is an important component of the text organization that affects text complexity. Consider relationships between characters, plots, and subplots in narrative texts. For informational texts, relationships exist between main ideas, facts and details, or abstract and concrete concepts. When these relationships are simpler, the text is likely to be simpler. When the relationships increase in complexity, so does the text.

Another major area to consider when evaluating qualitative text attributes is how various language features affect the complexity of the text. As a general rule, a more conversational writing style will make a text more accessible and less complex. More formally written textbooks, while essential parts of students' educations, often increase complexity with their less familiar language styles. Likewise, when narrative texts utilize metaphors, similes, descriptive language, onomatopoeia, personification, and other literary devices, this can make a text's meaning more obscure and less comprehensible.

Vocabulary plays multiple roles in the complexity of a text. Words can be easily evaluated quantitatively based on length, number of syllables, and frequency of use in the English language. However, there are cultural aspects of vocabulary that clearly require qualitative evaluation. *Are these words commonly and currently used in this geographical area and in this way?* should be a question that goes through one's mind. Archaic, author-created, or culturally unfamiliar vocabulary can significantly increase the complexity of a text, providing layers of meaning and interest, while forcing the reader to return repeatedly in search of context clues. Dr. Seuss books are well known for their creative use of language, and, in fact, their creation of language. For example, consider this excerpt from *The Lorax*.

The Lorax

by Dr. Seuss

"Sir! You are crazy with greed.
There is no one on earth
Who would buy that fool Thneed!"
But the very next minute, I proved he was wrong.
For just at that minute, a chap came along,
and he thought that the Thneed I had knitted was great.
He happily bought it for three ninety-eight.

As is evident, the use of author-created words, such as *Thneed*, as well as the archaic/British term *chap* can increase the text complexity in ways that quantitative analysis might miss. However, these linguistic oddities also create layers of interest and depth in the passage. The various ways that authors choose to present and play with language creates a more meaningful and enjoyable experience for readers, but they also serve to add complexity to the text.

The meaning of the text and the author's purpose in writing it are two other important qualitative attributes to consider. The meaning of the text refers to the sophistication of the ideas and how overtly they are laid out in the writing. For example, *Watership Down* by Richard Adams is, on its surface, the adventures of a group of rabbits. However, when one takes into account its allegorical themes, one realizes that the story is much more nuanced, deeper, and more meaningful than a superficial assessment might expose. Despite the rabbit on the cover, this text is appropriate for a secondary classroom. Before using a book in a classroom, you need to fully evaluate the layers of meaning for your given text choice.

Like meaning, an author's purpose may be clearly stated, implied, or even intentionally hidden. When evaluating how the author's purpose affects the complexity of a text, one of the most important factors to consider is how, or if, this purpose is expressed. This can be particularly critical in informational texts where the author may be overtly or slyly trying to influence readers' opinions on a topic. It is important to remember that every author has a perspective and an agenda, and sometimes these can be particularly important when building an understanding of a text. When the author's purpose is subtle, uncovering it may be challenging, and thus, the text may prove to be more complex than one in which the author divulges up front his or her reason for writing the text. See Table 2.4 for an example of one teacher's evaluation of the first page from C. S. Lewis's *The Lion, the Witch and the Wardrobe* for a close reading lesson.

Table 2.4 Sample Qualitative Evaluation: First page of *The Lion, the Witch and the Wardrobe*

Qualitative Measures	Degree of Difficulty	Explanation
Meaning or Purpose	Medium	The passage explicitly states the main ideas, but certain details require inference to fully understand
Structure	Medium	The structure of the passage is conventional and chronological but utilizes dialog, which increases difficulty.
Language Features	High	The language is descriptive, sometimes idiomatic, and a bit archaic. The text assumes familiarity with some terminology associated with England during WWII (e.g. air-raid).
Knowledge Demands	Med-High	The text assumes cultural knowledge about WWII in England and the practice of sending children away from cities to keep them safer. This concept is stated matter-of-factly up front but may be questioned and misunderstood by students unfamiliar with the practice.

Tables 2.5 and 2.6 (pages 26–32) provide scoring rubrics, which help in evaluating the qualitative attributes of literary and informational texts.

Table 2.5 Qualitative Attributes Scoring Rubric for Literary Texts

Qualitative Rubric for Literary Texts

What Does the Text Say?				
Dimension	**Consideration**	**Scoring = 1** **Easy or Comfortable Text**	**Scoring = 2** **Moderate or Grade-Level Text**	**Scoring = 3** **Challenging or Stretch Text**
Meaning or Purpose	**Meaning**	The text contains simple ideas with one level of meaning conveyed through obvious literary devices.	The text contains some complex ideas with more than one level of meaning conveyed through subtle literary devices.	The text includes substantial ideas with several levels of inferred meaning conveyed through highly sophisticated literary devices.
	Main Ideas and Key Details	Main ideas and key details support the story theme and character development.	Main ideas and key details weakly support the story theme and character development.	Main ideas and key details that should support the story theme or character development are not apparent; much is left to the interpretation of the reader.

Table 2.5 Qualitative Attributes Scoring Rubric for Literary Texts *(cont.)*

Qualitative Rubric for Literary Texts *(cont.)*

What Does the Text Say?				
Dimension	**Consideration**	**Scoring = 1** **Easy or Comfortable Text**	**Scoring = 2** **Moderate or Grade-Level Text**	**Scoring = 3** **Challenging or Stretch Text**
Structure	**Organization**	The text follows a simple conventional chronological plot pattern with few or no shifts in point of view or time; plot is highly predictable.	The text organization is somewhat unconventional; may have two or more storylines and some shifts in time and point of view; plot is sometimes hard to predict.	The text organization is intricate and unconventional with multiple subplots and shift in time and point of view; plot is unpredictable.
	Visual Supports and Layout	Text placement is consistent throughout the text and includes a large readable font. Illustrations directly support text content.	Text placement may include columns, text interrupted by illustrations, or other variations; uses a smaller font size. Illustrations support the text directly but may include images that require synthesis of text.	Text placement includes columns and many inconsistencies as well as very small font size. Few illustrations support the text directly; most require deep analysis and synthesis.
	Relationships Among Ideas	Relationships among ideas or characters are clear and obvious.	Relationships among ideas or characters are subtle and complex.	Relationships among ideas or characters are complex, embedded, and must be inferred.
	Vocabulary	Vocabulary is accessible, familiar, and can be determined through context clues.	Vocabulary combines familiar terms with academic vocabulary appropriate to the grade level.	Vocabulary includes extensive academic vocabulary, including many unfamiliar terms.

Table 2.5 Qualitative Attributes Scoring Rubric for Literary Texts *(cont.)*

Qualitative Rubric for Literary Texts *(cont.)*

What Does the Text Mean?				
Dimension	**Consideration**	**Scoring = 1** **Easy or Comfortable Text**	**Scoring = 2** **Moderate or Grade-Level Text**	**Scoring = 3** **Challenging or Stretch Text**
Structure *(cont.)*	**Author's Style and Tone**	The style of the text is explicit and easy to comprehend, and the tone is conversational.	The style of the text combines explicit and complex meanings, and the tone is somewhat formal.	The style of the text is abstract, and the language is ambiguous and generally unfamiliar. The tone may be somewhat unfamiliar to readers, such as an ironic tone.
	Author's Purpose	The purpose of the text is simple, clear, concrete, and easy to identify.	The purpose of the text is somewhat subtle, requires interpretation, or is abstract.	The purpose of the text is abstract, implicit, may be ambiguous, and is revealed through the totality of the text.
	Theme	The author explicitly states the theme or message of the text.	The theme or message of the text may not be stated directly but can be inferred by the reader.	The theme or message of the text is not stated directly by the author and must be inferred through careful reading of the text.
	Point of View	The story is told from a single point of view (first, second, or third person) throughout.	The story is told from more than one point of view and may incorporate multiple characters' points of view that are identified by the reader.	The story is told from multiple points of view, including the viewpoints of different characters, and is not always easily identified by the reader.

Table 2.5 Qualitative Attributes Scoring Rubric for Literary Texts *(cont.)*

Qualitative Rubric for Literary Texts *(cont.)*

What Does the Text Mean?				
Dimension	Consideration	Scoring = 1 Easy or Comfortable Text	Scoring = 2 Moderate or Grade-Level Text	Scoring = 3 Challenging or Stretch Text
Language Features	Use of Language	The author uses a limited amount of symbolism or figurative language; language is explicit and can be literally interpreted.	The author conveys the meaning through some use of figurative language, including imagery, metaphor, symbolism, simile, and personification, but also includes examples and explanations that support interpreting the meaning.	The author conveys the meaning through extensive use of figurative language and provides very limited explanation.
	Standard English	The text is written using a language register and/or form that is familiar to the reader (as opposed to an unfamiliar form, such as Old English or extensive uses of dialect).	The text is written using a language register and/or form that contains some language conventions and vernacular that are not familiar to the reader.	The text is written using a language register and/or form that includes extensive variations of standard English that are uncommon to the reader.
Knowledge Demands	Background Knowledge	Experiences portrayed are common life experiences; everyday cultural or literary knowledge is required.	Experiences portrayed include both common and less common experiences; some cultural, historical, or literary background knowledge is required.	Experiences portrayed are unfamiliar to most readers. The text requires extensive depth of topical, historical, or literary background knowledge.
	Cultural Knowledge	Content addresses common cultural and historical knowledge that is familiar.	Content addresses some cultural knowledge that may not be familiar.	Content includes heavy references to cultural or historical knowledge that is not readily familiar to those from other cultures.

Table 2.6 Qualitative Attributes Scoring Rubric for Informational Texts

Qualitative Rubric for Informational Texts

What Does the Text Say?				
Dimension	**Consideration**	**Scoring = 1** **Easy or Comfortable Text**	**Scoring = 2** **Moderate or Grade-Level Text**	**Scoring = 3** **Challenging or Stretch Text**
Meaning or Purpose	**Meaning**	The information is clear, and concepts are concretely explained.	The information includes complex, abstract ideas and extensive details.	The information is abstract, intricate, and may be highly theoretical.
	Main Ideas and Key Details	Key ideas and details that support the central theme are explicitly stated.	Some key ideas and details are explicitly stated, but others must be inferred.	Key ideas and details that would support comprehension must be inferred.

Table 2.6 Qualitative Attributes Scoring Rubric for Informational Texts *(cont.)*

Qualitative Rubric for Literary Texts *(cont.)*

What Does the Text Mean?				
Dimension	**Consideration**	**Scoring = 1** **Easy or Comfortable Text**	**Scoring = 2** **Moderate or Grade-Level Text**	**Scoring = 3** **Challenging or Stretch Text**
Structure	Organization	The text adheres primarily to a single expository text structure and focuses on facts.	The text employs multiple expository text structures, includes facts and/or a thesis, and demonstrates characteristics common to a particular discipline.	The text organization is intricate, may combine multiple structures or genres, is highly abstract, includes multiple theses, and demonstrates sophisticated organization appropriate to a particular discipline.
	Visual Supports and Layout	Text placement is consistent throughout the text and includes a large readable font. Text features such as simple charts, graphs, photos, tables, diagrams, and headings directly support the text and are easy to understand.	Text placement may include columns, text interrupted by illustrations or other variations, and a smaller font size. Text features, such as complex charts, graphs, photos, tables, diagrams, headings, and subheadings, support the text but require interpretation.	Text placement includes columns and many inconsistencies as well as very small font size. Text features, such as intricate charts, graphs, photos, tables, diagrams, headings, and subheadings, are not supported by the text and require inference and synthesis of information.
	Relationships Among Ideas	Relationships among concepts, processes, or events are clear and explicitly stated.	Relationships among some concepts, processes, or events may be implicit and subtle.	Relationships among concepts, processes, and events are intricate, deep, and subtle.
	Vocabulary	Some vocabulary is subject-specific, but the text includes many terms familiar to students that are supported by context clues.	The vocabulary is subject-specific, includes many unfamiliar terms, and provides limited support through context clues.	Vocabulary is highly academic, subject-specific, demanding, nuanced, and very context dependent.

Table 2.6 Qualitative Attributes Scoring Rubric for Informational Texts *(cont.)*

Qualitative Rubric for Literary Texts *(cont.)*

What Does the Text Mean?				
Dimension	**Consideration**	**Scoring = 1** Easy or Comfortable Text	**Scoring = 2** Moderate or Grade-Level Text	**Scoring = 3** Challenging or Stretch Text
Meaning and Purpose (Vocabulary, Craft, Style)	Author's Style and Tone	The style is simple and conversational and conveys a casual tone. It may incorporate narrative elements with simple sentences containing a few concepts.	The style is objective, featuring passive constructions, highly factual content, some nominalization, and compound or complex sentences. The tone is generally formal but may have some conversational aspects.	The style is specialized to a discipline, contains dense concepts and high nominalization, and features compound and complex sentences. The tone is distant, extremely formal, and written in third person.
	Author's Purpose	The purpose of the text is simple, clear, concrete, and easy to identify.	The purpose of the text is somewhat subtle or abstract and requires interpretation.	The purpose of the text is unusually subtle or abstract and requires extensive interpretation
	Theme	The author states the theme or message of the text explicitly.	The theme or message of the text may not be stated directly but can be easily inferred by the reader.	The theme or message of the text is not stated directly by the author and must be inferred through careful reading of the text.
	Point of View	The author's perspective or point of view about a topic or issue is clearly stated within the text.	The author's perspective or point of view about a topic or issue may not be stated directly but can be easily inferred by the reader.	The author's perspective or point of view about a topic or issue is not directly stated and must be inferred by the reader through careful analysis of the text.

Table 2.6 Qualitative Attributes Scoring Rubric for Informational Texts *(cont.)*

Qualitative Rubric for Literary Texts *(cont.)*

What Does the Text Mean?				
Dimension	**Consideration**	**Scoring = 1** **Easy or Comfortable Text**	**Scoring = 2** **Moderate or Grade-Level Text**	**Scoring = 3** **Challenging or Stretch Text**
Language Features	**Use of Language**	The author uses common discipline related language that is explicit and can be literally interpreted.	The author uses language that is related to the discipline but less familiar to someone new to the discipline. Examples and explanations that support interpreting the meaning are included.	The author conveys the meaning through extensive use of highly sophisticated, discipline-based language and does not include supports for interpretation.
	Standard English	The text is written using a language register and/or form that is familiar to the reader.	The language used contains some language conventions and vernacular that are not similar to the reader's.	The language used includes extensive variations of standard English that are unfamiliar to the reader.
Knowledge Demands	**Background Knowledge**	The content addresses common information familiar to students.	The content addresses somewhat technical information that requires some background knowledge to understand fully.	The content is highly technical and contains specific information that requires deep background knowledge to understand fully.
	Cultural Knowledge	Content addresses common cultural and historical knowledge that is familiar.	Content addresses some cultural knowledge that may not be familiar.	Content includes heavy references to cultural or historical knowledge that is not readily familiar to those from other cultures.

Reader/Task Attributes

A final element of text complexity to evaluate when looking at a potential text for use in the classroom isn't about the text itself. It is about the students in the classroom and their readiness for approaching the chosen text and its associated learning and performance tasks. The reader/task attributes describe elements of text complexity that are specific to a reader (i.e., reading experience, background knowledge, and motivation) and specific to the tasks for which the text will be used (i.e., recording basic facts, enjoying a narrative, or deeply understanding nuance). If the reading task is to identify and sequence the events leading to the American Revolution, the reader may be successful using a wide range of texts. However, a more nuanced task, such as comprehending multiple perspectives and motivations leading to the American Revolution, would require a more careful match of reader and text. Likewise, a history buff who has acquired a lot of background knowledge on the American Revolution is likely to successfully comprehend an American Revolution text that seems to be just out of his or her reach according to quantitative measures.

Close reading lessons and the role of the teacher during those lessons will be significantly different depending on the readiness of students. If students have a strong background in close reading, obviously the teacher will need to do less modeling and will be able to tackle more complicated tasks throughout the lesson. On the other hand, if students are unaccustomed to the demands of close reading—perhaps they are used to skimming for content, skipping over unknown words, moving forward without fully understanding the content of what they have read—then it will be important to slow down the process and guide students to develop the necessary skills.

There are four areas to evaluate when considering the readiness of students for the close reading of complex texts: reading and cognitive skills, prior knowledge and experience, motivation and engagement, and specific task concerns. Let us consider each of these areas with the following short poem.

Bed in Summer

by Robert Louis Stevenson

In winter I get up at night
And dress by yellow candle-light.
In summer, quite the other way,
I have to go to bed by day.
I have to go to bed and see
The birds still hopping on the tree,
Or hear the grown-up people's feet
Still going past me in the street.
And does it not seem hard to you,
When all the sky is clear and blue,
And I should like so much to play,
To have to go to bed by day?

Reading and cognitive skills describe both the literal comprehension skills and the deeper-level thinking skills needed to approach the chosen text and dig fully into its depths. Think about the level of decoding that students display. Consider their ability to focus on the details and make inferences. Different students and different classes will require varying amounts of scaffolding to achieve full comprehension of a challenging text. In "Bed in Summer," students may understand that the child in the poem is frustrated by having to go to bed while the sun is out. However, they may need scaffolding to fully gather from the context clues that this child lives in a city during a time period without electric lights.

Prior knowledge and experience includes what students have lived and studied. Have students had experiences with close reading before? Are they familiar with the type of writing, topic, and style of the text chosen? In "Bed in Summer," students will probably be familiar with this rhyming couplet form of poetry from nursery rhymes. Also, the subject of longer days during summer and shorter during winter should be a common experience for students in most of the world. However, if students grew up near the equator, or are from a subculture that does not require children to sleep before sundown during the summer, there may be experience gaps to bridge while delving into this poem.

The area of motivation and engagement addresses affective needs. Sometimes students can be put off by the format of a text or the subject matter. For example, many students can find the poetry format initially off-putting. "Bed in Summer" is both short and accessible, but it will be necessary to closely consider your students' reactions to poetry in order to determine if they need reassurance and assistance in engaging with a poetic text. Subject matter can also draw students in or push them away. Knowing topics of interest can increase student motivation and engagement because they allow students to enjoy the process of close reading any type of text.

Specific task concerns include the impact of the tasks students are being asked to complete. Even if students are ready for a particular piece of text, it is important not to underestimate the challenge of the associated tasks. Let us suppose the task in this example is to describe the perspective of the narrator using prose. It is unlikely that every student in the class will be able to accomplish this task without some scaffolding. However, if you provide a graphic organizer for students to record specific ideas and details from the poem, the task becomes more manageable for all students.

Creating Text-Dependent Questions

Once you have determined the areas of complexity of a text, it is time to start thinking about the types of text-dependent questions to ask that help students hone in on the learning goals for the lesson. Your text-dependent questions will be based upon the areas of complexity you have identified. Text-dependent questions are great scaffolds for guiding students to use the text to uncover meaning. Text-dependent questions do not rely on a student's relationship to the topic but instead tap into what the author embeds in the text itself. A simple way to identify a text-dependent question is that students who have not read the text, or had the text read to them, cannot answer the question. Students cannot rely primarily on general life knowledge or personal connections to the topic to answer these types of questions.

Text-dependent questions are *not* all low-level literal inquiries for regurgitated knowledge. To the contrary, they can push students to dig incrementally deeper at each stage of reading. They require students to analyze and critically review the text and facilitate a deeper relationship with the text as students engage with the text repeatedly. So how do teachers get started in creating them? They

- ➜ begin by identifying key ideas in the text;
- ➜ consider what questions might focus students on the gist of the text;
- ➜ orient students toward key vocabulary and text structure used in the text (e.g., compare/contrast, problem/solution, cause/effect, or sequential);
- ➜ craft questions that link to the purpose of the lesson;
- ➜ determine and focus on the most challenging segment of the text based on the text complexity rubric;
- ➜ look at standards and derive questions that will focus students toward those goals.

To help get you started, we have provided some example question stems in Table 2.7 (page 38). It may also be useful to peruse the questions embedded in the lessons in the Lesson Section. It is important to note that although you will create text-dependent questions as you plan each lesson, you will also revise, add, or delete any of the proposed questions that do not meet your students' needs. Furthermore, it is essential to frame questions for narrative texts differently from informational texts. For example, questions about plot, setting, and characters will likely not apply to informational texts. Think of the text-dependent questions as starting points. As you proceed, your lesson becomes a living and breathing experience, molded and shaped to meet students' needs. You will direct your questions to areas of the text they are struggling to clarify, giving them the most meaningful, purposeful experience possible and maximizing their learning.

Table 2.7 Common Question Stems for Text-Dependent Questions by Grade Level

Question Stems

When trying to lead students toward information embedded in a text, it is important not to begin with too much focus. It is better to start with the most general questions, then ask more and more pointed ones if they become necessary. Here are some examples:

EXAMPLE 1: What does the character mean? (general)

- What language does the character use? (more specific)
- What does the word ________ mean? (even more specific)
- How does using that word help us understand what the character means? (quite specific)

EXAMPLE 2: Why did the author write this? (general)

- Look at the language the author uses. How does this help you understand why he/she wrote it? (more specific)
- Look at paragraph #_____. Find the word that tells what the author's opinion might be about this topic. (even more specific)
- How do the words ________ and ________ that the author used in paragraph #_____ help us to understand his or her purpose? (quite specific)

EXAMPLE 3: Why did the author use this structure? (general)

- How does including the chart help us understand the main idea? (more specific)
- Look at the chart. Find information in the chart that helps support the main idea of the text. (even more specific)
- How do ________ (fact 1) and ________ (fact 2) from the chart help us understand that ________ (main idea of the text)? (quite specific)

3rd Grade Text-Dependent Questions

Where appropriate for each TDQ, state, "How can you tell?" or "Give specific examples from the text." or "Use specific words and phrases from the text in your response."

What Does the Text Say?	
Main Idea/ Theme	• What is the theme/main idea (are the themes/main ideas) of the text? • How does the ___________ (paragraph/sentence) relate to the main idea/theme? • How does the information in paragraphs/sentences ____ and ____ help you understand the theme/main idea? • The main idea is not stated. How do you know what it is? • How is the idea of ___________ introduced in the text? Use the text to support your response. • What is the moral of the text?
Key Details	• What are the essential details in this text/story? How are they necessary to understand the main idea? • Why does the author put the supporting details in this order? How would it change if the text were in a different order? • What details in ____ (paragraph/page) help to support the main idea? • What is the relationship between the details in paragraphs ____ and ____? List one key detail from each paragraph/sentence. What do they tell us when you look at them all together? • Identify the important details about the characters in the text. How do these details influence your feelings about the characters? Offer support from the text.
Summarizing	• Summarize the text in your own words. • Retell the story by listing the key details in order. • What is the main event in the text/story? Use the text to identify the most important details about the main event. • Summarize the sequence of events. How is the order of events important?

Table 2.7 Common Question Stems for Text-Dependent Questions by Grade Level *(cont.)*

3rd Grade Text-Dependent Questions *(cont.)*

How Does the Text Work?	
Text Features	• What is the purpose of the __________ (text feature)? What does the author emphasize by using it? • What information can we learn from __________ (text feature)? Why is this important to the text/story? • Review the headings. How do they help guide the reader through the text? • Explain how you can use the table of contents/index to research __________ in the book.
Text Structure	• What is the genre of the text? How is it helpful for a reader to know this? • Consider how the author tells us about the setting and characters. Why does the author choose this text structure? Provide evidence from the text. • How does the author use dialog in the text? What effect does it have? Give examples. • How does the way the author begins the text affect the middle and the ending? Does this structure contribute to your understanding or enjoyment of the text? • Who is narrating the text? What would change if someone else narrated the text? • Think of the order of events. Why does the author choose that order?
Setting	• What is the setting of the text/story? Use words from the text in your answer. • What role does the setting play in the text? Support your answer with the text. • What impact does the time period have on the text? Support your answer with the text.
Plot	• How does __________ (event) bring about a turning point? Explain using words from the text. • How does __________ (event 1) relate to __________ (event 2)? • How does __________ (event) affect __________ (character)? • Describe how the events in the text build on each other. • Why does the author use flashbacks/foreshadowing/flash-forward/multiple narrators? How does this affect the plot? • What is the significance of __________ (event)? Provide evidence from the text. • What is the climax of the text?

Table 2.7 Common Question Stems for Text-Dependent Questions by Grade Level *(cont.)*

3rd Grade Text-Dependent Questions *(cont.)*

How Does the Text Work? *(cont.)*	
Characters / Individuals	• Describe ___________ (character/person). What words does the author use to help you get a picture in your head? • How does ___________ (character/person) change during the text? • How does ___________ (character/person) feel when ___________ (event) happens? What words tell you? • What does the author want us to know about ___________ (character/person)?
Point of View	• Who is narrating this text/story? Provide evidence from the text. • Describe the different points of view for each character. What specific words help you determine each? • How does the author show ___________'s point of view over time? Does it change? Explain. • How does the author's point of view affect the way the text is presented? • Why does the author choose to have multiple narrators? • Does the author show more than one point of view in this text? How? • What culture does this text/story come from? How does that affect the way the text is presented?
What Does the Text Mean?	
Tone	• What emotions do you experience while reading this text/story? What words does the author use to create these emotions? • Is the text positive or negative? How do specific words create this tone? • Does the author use a formal or casual tone? State specific words or phrases that help achieve this tone. • What is the author's opinion of (subject/character)? What words in the text tell you? • Is the author an expert on ___________? What specific information in the text makes you believe this?
Author's Purpose	• What is the author's main purpose in writing this text? • What question is the author trying to answer in the text? • Why does the author ___________? • What does the author want the reader to understand? • How, specifically, does the author try to achieve his or her purpose?

Table 2.7 Common Question Stems for Text-Dependent Questions by Grade Level *(cont.)*

3rd Grade Text-Dependent Questions *(cont.)*

What Does the Text Mean? *(cont.)*	
Language Usage	• The word ___________ has multiple meanings. How can you tell which meaning it has here? • Which words in the text/story show ___________? • Why did the author choose the word/phrase ___________ to describe ___________? How does this word help a reader understand more about ___________? • What if the author used ___________ instead of ___________? How would this change the text? • Reread paragraph # ____. What words do you remember? Which words stand out? Why are they important?
Figurative Language	• Why does the author use ___________ (personification/metaphor/hyperbole/literal and nonliteral words)? How does it help the text? • Which words does the author use to appeal to your senses in the #____ paragraph/sentence? • Why does the author compare ___________ to ___________? How does this help the reader better understand the text? • Which examples of figurative language help you imagine ___________?
Making Inferences	• Why does ___________ (character) feel ___________? Include specific words and phrases from the text in your answer. • What can you infer by the end of the #___________ paragraph? • Reread sentence #____. How does it help you predict what will happen next? • What can you infer from the dialog on page ____? Use evidence from the text to support your ideas. • What does the author want us to infer from ___________? How can you tell? • How does the narrator think/feel about ___________? How do you know? • In the #____ sentence, the author uses the word ___________. To what does this word refer?

Table 2.7 Common Question Stems for Text-Dependent Questions by Grade Level *(cont.)*

4th Grade Text-Dependent Questions

Where appropriate for each TDQ, state, "Which specific words or phrases support your answer?", "How does the author communicate this?", or "Include specific examples from the text."

What Does the Text Say?	
Main Idea/ Theme	• Considering the events in the text, what is the theme/main idea (are the themes/main ideas) of the text? • How does the ___________ (paragraph/sentence) relate to the main idea/ theme? • How does the information in paragraphs/sentences ___________ and ___________ help you understand the theme/main idea? • The main idea is not directly stated in the text. How do you know what it is? • How is the idea of ___________ introduced in the text? Use the text to support your response. • What message does the author want readers to take away from the text? • Explain how the events on page #____ (paragraph #____) relate to the theme of the text.
Key Details	• What are the essential details in this text/story? How are they necessary to understand the main idea? • What are the findings described in paragraph #____? How do these support the main idea of the text? • Why does the author put the supporting details in this order? How would it change if the text were in a different order? • What details in ___________ (paragraph/page) help to support the main idea? • What is the relationship between the details in paragraphs #____ and #____? • List one key detail from each paragraph/sentence. How do these details relate to each other? What do they tell a reader when considered as a whole? • Identify the important details about the characters in the text. How do these details influence your feelings about the characters? Offer support from the text.
Summarizing	• Summarize the text in your own words. • Summarize the story by listing the key details in order. • Summarize the main events in the text. Use the text to identify the most important details about the main events. • Summarize the sequence of events. How is the order of events important? • Summarize the main events of the story without including personal opinions.

Table 2.7 Common Question Stems for Text-Dependent Questions by Grade Level *(cont.)*

4th Grade Text-Dependent Questions *(cont.)*	
How Does the Text Work?	
Text Features	• What is the author's purpose for including the __________ (text feature)? What does the author emphasize by using it? • What information can we learn from __________ (text feature)? Why is this important to the text? • Review the sidebars or graphics. What specific information do they provide? • Review the headings in the text/story. How do they relate to the structure of the text? • Provide specific examples of how a reader might use the table of contents/index to research __________ in the book.
Text Structure	• How does this text differ from one that gives information about __________? • What is the genre of the text? Why is it important for a reader to understand the genre? • Is this a piece of literature or informational text? How does this text differ from a text that provides facts or a story about __________ (the topic)? Give specific examples from the text. • Consider how the author introduces readers to the setting and characters. Why does the author choose this text structure? Provide evidence from the text. • How does the author use dialog in the text? What effect does it have? Give examples. • How does the way the author begins the text affect the middle and the ending? Does this structure contribute to your understanding or enjoyment of the text? • Who is narrating the text? What would change if someone else were narrator? • How does the author manipulate time in the text? How does this affect the reader?
Setting	• What is the setting of the text? Use words from the text in your answer. • What role does the setting play in the text? Support your answer with the text. • How does the setting affect the overall tone of the text? Support your answer with the text. • What is the historical significance of the setting of the text? • What impact does the time period have on the text? Support your answer with the text. • How would the story change if it took place in a different setting?

Table 2.7 Common Question Stems for Text-Dependent Questions by Grade Level *(cont.)*

4th Grade Text-Dependent Questions *(cont.)*	
What Does the Text Mean?	
Plot	• How does ___________ (event) bring about a turning point? Explain using words from the text. • How does ___________ (event 1) relate to ___________ (event 2)? • How does ___________ (event) affect the development of ___________ (character/characters)? • Why does the author focus on the events of __________ (chapter/paragraph #)? • Describe how the events in the text build on each other. • Why does the author use flashbacks/foreshadowing/flash-forward/multiple narrators? How does this affect the plot? Use evidence from the text. • What is the significance of __________ (event)? Provide evidence from the text. • What is the climax of the text? Support your answer with specifics from the text.
Characters/ Individuals	• What do ___________ (character/person)'s actions reveal in the ___________ (paragraph/page)? What can you infer about _____ (character) from these actions? • How does the author show __________ (character/person)'s growth/change over the course of the text? • What does the author want readers to understand about ___________ (character/person)? • What are ___________ (character 1)'s feelings regarding ___________ (character 2)? Use the text to explain. • What does the dialog between ___________ (character/person) and ___________ (character/person) reveal about these characters? How does it relate to their personalities?

Table 2.7 Common Question Stems for Text-Dependent Questions by Grade Level *(cont.)*

4th Grade Text-Dependent Questions *(cont.)*

What Does the Text Mean? *(cont.)*	
Point of View	• Why did the author choose this character/these characters to narrate the text/story? Provide evidence from the text. • Describe the different points of view of each character. Use specific words or phrases from the text to support your answer. • How does the author show ___________'s point of view developing over time? • How does the author use different points of view to develop the theme/main idea/characters? Cite evidence from the text. • How is ___________ (character's) viewpoint expressed through dialog in the text? • How does the author's point of view affect the way the text is presented? • Why does the author choose to have multiple narrators? • Why does the author use first/third person perspective in this text? • What culture does this text come from? How does that affect the way the text is presented? • What conflicting viewpoints are presented in this text? • How does the author respond to evidence that conflicts with his or her viewpoint?
Tone	• What emotions do you experience while reading this text/story? What words does the author use to create these emotions? • Is the text positive or negative? How do specific words create this tone? • How does the tone affect your perception of the text? • Does the author use a formal or casual tone? State specific words or phrases that help achieve this tone. • What is the author's opinion of (subject/character)? What specific words in the text support this idea? • How do the characters' dialog and actions contribute to the tone of the text?
Author's Purpose	• What is the author's main purpose in writing this text? • What question is the author trying to answer in the text? • What specific language does the author use to persuade the reader? • Does the author achieve his or her purpose in the text? Explain using evidence from the text. • Why does the author ___________? • What does the author want the reader to understand? • How, specifically, does the author try to achieve his or her purpose?

Table 2.7 Common Question Stems for Text-Dependent Questions by Grade Level *(cont.)*

4th Grade Text-Dependent Questions *(cont.)*	
What Does the Text Mean? *(cont.)*	
Language Usage	• What is the meaning of the word ___________ as it is used in paragraph #____? What other words could the author have used here? • What part of speech is the word ___________? How can you tell from the context of the sentence? • What emotions do the characters experience in paragraph/chapter #____? What words convey these emotions in the text? • Which words in the text show ___________? How can you tell? • Why did the author choose the word/phrase ___________ to describe ___________? How does this word help a reader understand more about ___________? • What if the author used ___________ instead of ___________? How would this change the text? • Reread paragraph #____. What words do you remember? Which words stand out? Why are they important?
Figurative Language	• How does the author's use of ___________ (personification/metaphor/hyperbole/similes/idioms/adages/proverbs) enhance the reader's understanding of ___________? • Which words does the author use to appeal to your senses in the #____ paragraph/sentence? • Describe the figurative language the author uses in the text. How does this language add to a reader's understanding of the ___________ (theme/characters/setting/plot)? • Why does the author compare ___________ to ___________? How does this help the reader better understand the text? • Which examples of figurative language help you imagine ___________?
Making Inferences	• Why does ___________ (character) feel ___________? • Reread sentence/paragraph #____. What is stated explicitly, and what is implied? • What can you infer by the end of the ___________ paragraph? • Reread sentence #____. How does it help you predict what will happen next? • What can you infer from the dialog on page #____? • What does the author want us to infer from ___________? How can you tell? • How does the narrator think/feel about ___________? How do you know? • In sentence #____, the author uses the word ___________. To what does this word refer?

Table 2.7 Common Question Stems for Text-Dependent Questions by Grade Level *(cont.)*

5th Grade Text-Dependent Questions

Where appropriate for each TDQ, state, "How does the author communicate this to the reader?", "Cite specific textual evidence to support your answer.", or "Offer support from the text."

What Does the Text Say?	
Main Idea/ Theme	• What is the theme/main idea (are the themes/main ideas) of the text? • Describe the multiple themes of the text. How are these themes interwoven throughout the text? Justify your answer with specifics from the text. • How does the ___________ (paragraph/sentence) relate to the main idea/theme? • How does the information in paragraphs/sentences #____ and #____ help you understand the theme/main idea? • What is the main idea of the text? Build a case using textual evidence. • How is the idea of ___________ introduced in the text? • What message does the author want readers to take away from the text? • Explain how the events on page #____ (paragraph #____) relate to the theme of the text. What evidence supports this idea?
Key Details	• What are the essential details in this text/story? Use textual details to explain how they are necessary to understand the main idea. • What are the findings of the study described in paragraph #____? How do these support the main idea of the text? • What is the relationship between the key details in the text and the order in which they are presented? • How do the key details in the text support the main theme? • What details in ___________ (paragraph/page) help to support the main idea? • What is the relationship between the key details in paragraphs ___________ and ___________? • Identify one key detail from each paragraph/sentence. How do these details relate to each other? What do they tell a reader when considered as a whole? • Identify the important details about the characters in the text. How do these details influence your feelings about the characters? Offer support from the text.
Summarizing	• Summarize the text in your own words. • Summarize the central idea, and identify the specific details that support it. • Summarize the main events in the text. Use the text to identify the most important details about the main events. • Summarize the sequence of events. How is the order of events important? • Provide an objective summary of main events. Be careful not to reveal your personal opinions or judgments.

Table 2.7 Common Question Stems for Text-Dependent Questions by Grade Level *(cont.)*

5th Grade Text-Dependent Questions *(cont.)*	
How Does the Text Work?	
Text Features	• What is the author's purpose of including the ___________ (text feature)? What does the author emphasize by using it? • What information can we learn from ___________ (text feature)? Why is this important to the text? • Review the sidebars or graphics. What purpose do they serve in the text? • What features help a reader scan for particular information? • Review the headings in the text/story. How do they relate to the structure of the text? • Provide specific examples of how a reader might use the table of contents/index to research ___________ in the book.
Text Structure	• How does this text differ from one that gives information about ___________? • What is the genre of the text? Why is it important for a reader to understand the genre? • Why does the author choose to delay introduction of the major conflict? • Is this a piece of literature or informational text? How does this text differ from a text that provides facts or a story about ___________ (the topic)? Give specific examples from the text. • Consider how the author introduces readers to the setting and characters. Why does the author choose this text structure? Provide evidence from the text. • How does the author use dialog in the text? What effect does it have? Give examples. • How does the way the author begins the text affect the middle and the ending? Does this structure contribute to your understanding or enjoyment of the text? • Who is narrating the text? What would change if someone else were narrator? • How does the author manipulate time in the text? How does this affect the reader?
Setting	• What is the setting of the text? Cite textual evidence to support your answer. • What role does the setting play in the text? Support your answer with the text. • What impact does the setting have on ___________ (character's/person's) life? • How does the setting affect the overall tone of the text? Support your answer with the text. • What is the historical significance of the setting of the text? • What impact does the time period have on the text? Support your answer with the text. • How would the story change if it took place in a different setting?

Table 2.7 Common Question Stems for Text-Dependent Questions by Grade Level *(cont.)*

5th Grade Text-Dependent Questions *(cont.)*	
How Does the Text Work? *(cont.)*	
Plot	• How does ___________ (event) bring about a turning point? Explain using words from the text. • How does ___________ (event 1) relate to ___________ (event 2)? • How does ___________ (event) affect the development of ___________ (character/characters)? • Why does the author emphasize the events of ____ (chapter/paragraph #)? • Describe how the events in the text build on each other. • Why does the author use flashbacks/foreshadowing/flash-forward/multiple narrators? How does this affect the plot? Use evidence from the text. • What is the significance of ___________ (event)? Provide evidence from the text. • What is the climax of the text? Support your answer with specifics from the text.
Characters/ Individuals	• What do ___________ (character/person)'s actions reveal in the ___________ (paragraph/page)? What can you infer about ___________ (character/person) from these actions? • How does the author show ___________ (character/person)'s growth/change over the course of the text? • Why does the author choose to include ___________ (character that is not a main character)? • What does the author want readers to understand about ___________ (character/person)? • What is ___________ (character 1)'s relationship to ___________ (character 2)? Use the text to explain. • What is ___________ (character/person's) motivation in ____ (paragraph #/ sentence #)? • What does the dialog between ___________ (character/person) and ___________ (character/person) reveal about these characters/people? How does it relate to their personalities? Provide examples from the text.

Table 2.7 Common Question Stems for Text-Dependent Questions by Grade Level *(cont.)*

5th Grade Text-Dependent Questions *(cont.)*

How Does the Text Work? *(cont.)*	
Point of View	• Why did the author choose this character/these characters to narrate the text? • How do the characters' points of view contribute to the conflict and its resolution? • How does the author show ___________'s point of view developing over time? • How does the author use different points of view to develop the theme/main idea/characters? Cite evidence from the text. • How is ___________ (character's) viewpoint expressed through dialog in the text? • How does the author's point of view affect the way the text is presented? • Why does the author choose to have multiple narrators? • Why does the author use first/third person perspective in this text? • What culture does this text/story come from? How does that affect the way the text is presented? • What conflicting viewpoints are presented in this text? • How does the author respond to evidence that conflicts with his or her viewpoint?
What Does the Text Mean?	
Tone	• What emotions do you experience while reading this text? What words does the author use to create these emotions? • What language does the author use to create the tone? Cite specific textual examples. • How does the tone affect your perception of the text? • Does the author use a formal or casual tone? State specific words or phrases that help achieve this tone. • What is the author's opinion of ___________ (subject/character)? What specific words in the text support this idea? • How do the characters' dialog and actions contribute to the tone of the text?
Author's Purpose	• What is the author's main purpose in writing this text? • What question is the author trying to answer in the text? • What specific language does the author use to persuade the reader? • Does the author achieve his or her purpose in the text? Explain using evidence from the text. • Why does the author ___________? • What does the author want the reader to understand? • How, specifically, does the author try to achieve his or her purpose? Cite textual examples. • How does the style and content of the text contribute to the author's purpose?

Table 2.7 Common Question Stems for Text-Dependent Questions by Grade Level *(cont.)*

5th Grade Text-Dependent Questions *(cont.)*

What Does the Text Mean? *(cont.)*	
Language Usage	• What is the meaning of the word ____________ as it is used in paragraph # ____? What other words could the author have used here? • What is implied by the words/phrases used in paragraph #____? • What emotions do the characters experience in paragraph/chapter #____? What words convey these emotions in the text? • Which words in the text/story show ____________? How can you tell? • Why did the author choose the word/phrase ____________ to describe ____________? How does this word help a reader understand more about ____________? • What if the author used ____________ instead of ____________? How would this change the text? • Reread paragraph #____. Which words carry the most impact? Why are they important?
Figurative Language	• How does the author's use of ____________ (personification/metaphor/hyperbole/similie/idiom/adage/proverb/synonym/antonym/homograph) enhance the reader's understanding of ____________? • Which words does the author use to appeal to your senses in the #____ paragraph/sentence? • Describe the figurative language the author uses in the text. How does this language add to a reader's understanding of the ____________ (theme/characters/setting/plot)? • What is the purpose of the comparison between ____________ and ____________? How does this help the reader better understand the text? • Which examples of figurative language help you imagine ____________? • What is the reader expected to infer from the figurative language in sentence/paragraph # _____?
Making Inferences	• Why does ____________ (character) feel ____________? Include specific words and phrases from the text in your answer. • Reread sentence/paragraph #____. What is stated explicitly, and what is implied? • What can you infer by the end of the _____ paragraph? • Reread sentence #____. How does it help you predict what will happen next? • What can you infer from the dialog on page #____? Use evidence from the text to support your ideas. • What does the author want us to infer from ____________? • How does the narrator think/feel about ____________? • In the #____ sentence, the author uses the word ____________. To what does this word refer?

Ordering Text-Dependent Questions

The final step to preplanning your lesson is to put the text-dependent questions into logical order. The questions should move students from general to specific and lower-level analysis to higher-level analysis. The order should roughly mirror the skills described as one progresses through Anderson and Krathwohl's adaptation of Bloom's Taxonomy (2001). By the end, students should have a comprehensive relationship with the complexities of the text, be able to tackle the performance task, take an argumentative position concerning the stated learning goals, and craft an "I Can" statement that provides an assessment of their performance.

For example, begin your text-dependent questions by targeting the gist of the text, such as, "What is the text about?" and "What is the author trying to share?" These questions apply beginning-level thinking involving knowledge and comprehension. Then, move to questions that begin to press the students for specifics. In this way, you move toward applying and analyzing the content of the text. For example, if the lesson revolves around explicit and implicit information, ask, "Which sentences give us explicit information about (the topic)?" or "Which sentences implicitly give us information about (the topic)?" Finally, transition into pushing students toward evaluating the deeper structure of the text and the synthesis of concepts woven throughout, such as, "Which sentences help us determine the theme of the text?", "What details help us more deeply understand this theme?", or "How does the author develop the theme over the course of the text?"

The text-dependent questions should ready students for the performance task assessment that concludes the close reading experience. We are not suggesting that the questions need always be asked in this order. We are suggesting that you know what each question requires of students, and you ask questions that advance student learning. Begin with what they know. If they have a basic understanding of the topic, perhaps ask fewer questions about the specifics of what the text says and more questions about how the text works and what the text means.

Try It!

Directions: Analyze the following passage and preplan for a close reading lesson. Use the guidelines and tables in this section along with your knowledge of your students to identify the areas of complexity, plan initial text-dependent questions, and anticipate differentiation needs. Write on the following chart (page 57) or use a digital copy of the chart in the Digital Download (planningclosereading.pdf).

Make sure to tab or mark the pages you find most helpful to your work. These are the pages to which you can return when you plan actual lessons to use with your students.

Forces of the Earth: Undersea Volcanoes (Lexile 760)

Some of the biggest volcanoes on Earth have never been seen by human eyes. That's because they are very deep underwater. One would have to dive down a mile and a half (2.4 km) just to reach the tops of these giants. This string of underwater volcanoes is called the Mid-Ocean Ridge.

The Mid-Ocean Ridge is the biggest mountain range on our planet. It's more than 30,000 miles (48,280 km) long and almost 500 miles (804.7 km) wide. Its hundreds of mountains and volcanoes zigzag under the ocean between the continents. They wind their way around the globe like the seam on a baseball. Nearly every day, at least one underwater volcano erupts. Hot lava pours out of the volcano and onto the ocean floor.

The bottom of the sea is ever changing. After erupting from deep inside Earth, the lava cools, forming new rocks. Layers of rocky lava pile up and, over millions of years, expand the sea floor. The expanding sea floor, in turn, pushes the continents. A million years ago, the earth looked very different than it does today. A million years from now, it will have changed even more.

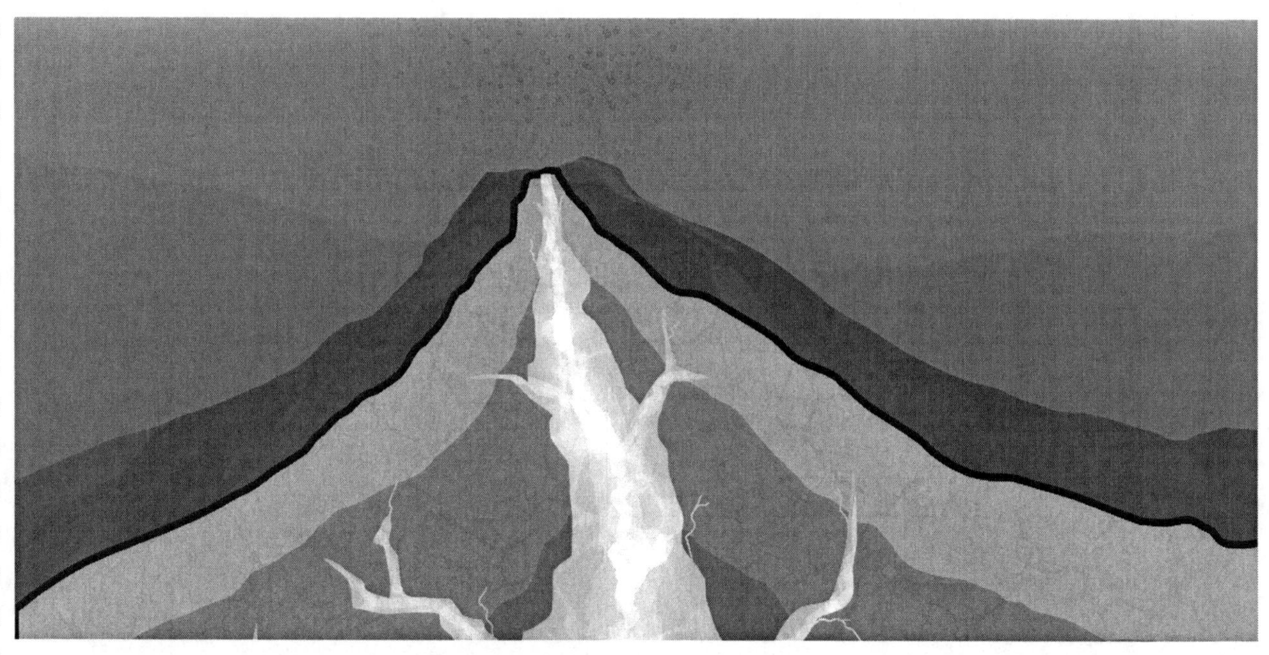

Try It! *(cont.)*

Planning Chart for Close Reading

Planning	Date:________ Grade: ______ Discipline:________ Purpose(s):________ Standard(s):________ Text Selection (literary or informational):________ Performance Assessment: ________ Materials: ________
Text Selection	Title:________ Author:________ Page(s) or section(s):________ How should this text be chunked?________ ________
Areas of Complexity	Lexile Level:________ Meaning or Purpose:________ Structure:________ Language Features:________ Knowledge Demands:________
Text-Dependent Questions	1.________ 2.________ 3.________ 4.________ 5.________
Performance Task	________ ________ ________ ________
Differentiation	Additional Support: ________ ________ Extension:________ ________

Section 3:
Teaching Close Reading

Scaffolding in the Close Reading Approach

As you embark on a close reading experience with your class, it is important to consider how best to support close reading at the level specifically needed by your students to achieve the learning goals you have established. You know your class, so you must make individualized choices that will help to gradually remove scaffolding for the students in your class. Remember, the goal is for *every* student to be able to read and engage with the complex text that you have chosen. Student struggle is only useful inasmuch as it is productive. Proficiency will not be achieved by allowing student struggles to end in failure. Thus, carefully supporting your students throughout a close reading is essential. You must be ready to offer instructional scaffolds in the form of questions, prompts, and cues (like reminding students of previously learned information or cueing them to look at a particular line of the text) throughout the experience. Constantly listen for issues that may arise, and assist students' progress through the process.

You have already identified the areas of challenge in your chosen text through the preplanning work of assessing the quantitative features and applying the appropriate qualitative rubric provided in Section Two. But there are some critical decisions that must be considered as you move forward.

- ➜ Who is doing the reading?
- ➜ How should the text be chunked?
- ➜ What sort of annotations should be used?
- ➜ What types of resources do students need?

We will consider each of these questions individually, plus a few more. However, it is important to remember that it is never possible to anticipate every twist in a dynamic classroom. The areas in which students struggle or make leaps will inform each lesson. The job of educators is to notice these areas and reactively adjust teaching in response. Table 3.1 (page 56) presents the elements of a close reading lesson in a format that highlights planning and decision-making.

Determine How to Scaffold the Close Read

- Who is doing the close reading?
- How many times do students revisit the text?
- Does any (minimal) frontloading need to occur?
- How should the text be chunked?
- What types of annotations should be used?
- What types of student resources are needed?

Table 3.1 Teaching Close Reading

Teaching

Limited Frontloading ❑ yes ❑ no

Describe:

First Read

Who Reads? ❑ teacher ❑ student

Student Resources

❑ graphic organizer ❑ group consensus form

❑ note taking guide ❑ summary form

Second Read

Who Reads? ❑ teacher ❑ student

Student Resources

❑ graphic organizer ❑ group consensus form

❑ note taking guide ❑ summary form

Additional Reads

Who Reads? ❑ teacher ❑ student

Student Resources

❑ graphic organizer ❑ group consensus form

❑ note taking guide ❑ summary form

Extension	Reteaching

Who Is Doing the Close Reading?

The first of the remaining lesson decisions is, perhaps deceptively, the most basic of all—who will be doing the actual reading? With those just beginning their journey as readers, the decision is easy. The teacher, being a fully literate reader, reads the passage aloud, at least for the first read. This provides students with the most information. It allows modeling of not only basic reading skills but also the deeper questions that you are teaching them to generate. For these beginning readers, the close reading approach becomes a *close thinking* approach. These beginning readers may not have the technical skills to decode a complex piece of text, but they certainly have the thinking skills to notice and question challenging aspects of the writing.

More experienced students will tackle the text for the first time on their own. After all, one of the goals for the close reading approach is to create a challenge that forces students to productively struggle through worthy texts. There is, however, a place where the struggle can overcome the productivity. Sometimes a text provides such a strong technical challenge that students can lose sight of the overall meaning of the passage. Or they become so distracted by an intellectual twist that they are unable to accurately focus on the themes or arguments. It may be possible to predict these issues based on your knowledge of your class and the specific text or to uncover them while conducting formative assessments during the lesson. In either case, it may be productive to aid students in taking a step back to refocus on the pertinent parts of the text by choosing to read either a section or the entire text aloud yourself. In these cases, students, relieved of the duty to accurately decode, may consider other areas of interest in a rich piece of writing. Nuance and context that would be otherwise missed may materialize. After the initial read, do not dismiss reading aloud if you believe it might meaningfully further the goals of the lesson.

How Many Times Do Students Revisit the Text?

The number of times students revisit each text is based on the lesson goals and the characteristics of the text. Some texts are sufficiently complex, challenging, and rewarding to merit spending several days with. Others may reveal the bulk of their mysteries after only two iterations of the close reading approach. A text that is not complex enough to spend at least two sessions with is unlikely to be a good candidate for this type of deep and detailed reading. A typical close reading will range from two to four sessions with a short, challenging text. Students must be given sufficient opportunity to engage in a productive struggle. Again, the goal is that every student in the class will gain full comprehension of these complex texts. There must be sufficient opportunity for each student to delve gradually deeper into the chosen reading.

It is critical to remain cognizant of student engagement level and avoid having the experience become rote or boring because of too many readings. Remember, each reread does not have to be of the entire text. A question you ask may involve rereading only a line or a paragraph. Rereadings are targeted as a way to conduct an analysis of the word, sentence, paragraph, or text level. This is why text selection is an essential part of the close reading process. A properly chosen piece of text will not only be worthy of the scrutiny afforded during a close reading experience but will also allow for the type of structured scaffolding that will draw in students of every level.

Does Any Frontloading Need to Occur?

After selecting the text, think about the knowledge demands needed for the piece. It is best, of course, if students can use context clues in the text to illuminate unfamiliar concepts and terms. For example, *The Great Kapok Tree* by Lynne Cherry is a richly complex text about the interconnectedness of life. Given the illustrations and context within the text, little or no front-loading is necessary to achieve deep comprehension. Unfamiliar animals and words can be determined through close reading and careful observation. However, sometimes it can be appropriate to front-load information that will provide necessary background knowledge for interpreting the text. For example, *The Diary of Anne Frank* is much more meaningful to a student who has some general information about the Nazis and WWII. After students have read the text once, you may decide that students need more background information to appreciate the text. At this point, you may elect to provide some background information on Nazi Germany by showing a short video, for example. Afterward, students may be better prepared to tackle the second reading. In addition, you may consider pairing the close reading approach with texts that may have higher knowledge demands or with, or subsequent to, other classroom activities surrounding that topic. If this is not possible, or if you choose to tackle a text with high knowledge demands that you are not confident are possessed by all your students, insert the background information after students have interacted with the text during the first reading. Don't assume they do not know or cannot do until they have been given an opportunity to try.

How Should the Text Be Chunked?

Chunking is a technique for breaking larger pieces of text into smaller, more manageable pieces. A paragraph may be chunked into sentences and phrases, with a longer text chunked into paragraphs and sections. Sometimes, a teacher may wish to pre-chunk the text for students. This has the advantage of saving class time and ensuring that everyone has an identical starting place. Other times, teachers may choose to have the class chunk the text. This has the advantage of involving students with the text from the onset.

By virtue of their necessarily short nature, close reading texts should not prove too daunting to chunk in any way you find preferable. In a truly short, single paragraph text, it would seem obvious to number each sentence or line. However, if the text is particularly challenging in its vocabulary and word choice, it may be more useful to chunk it by phrases so that individual words are easier to find. In a text with many short paragraphs, perhaps a lot of dialog, paragraph chunking generally makes sense.

The main consideration is convenience. Balance the usefulness of easily identifying individual sentences or words with the amount of work it takes to number them and the amount of clutter the numbering might create on the page. At the heart of chunking are the text-dependent questions and their corresponding answers.

Chunking is meant to enable efficient references. Consider these two examples.

- "In paragraph 4, the author begins calling Katherine, Katy, indicating that they are on a more familiar footing now." Efficient—paragraph chunking works well.
- "In paragraph two in the—one, two, three, four, five—fifth sentence, the author uses the word *rotation*." Inefficient—chunking by line or sentence would be better.

Figure 3.1 shows two examples of chunked texts. "Legless Fearless" has been chunked into numbered paragraphs. In the poem "Did You See?", each line is numbered. Model close reading lessons for each text can be found on pages 235 and 141, respectively.

Figure 3.1 Examples of "Chunked" Texts

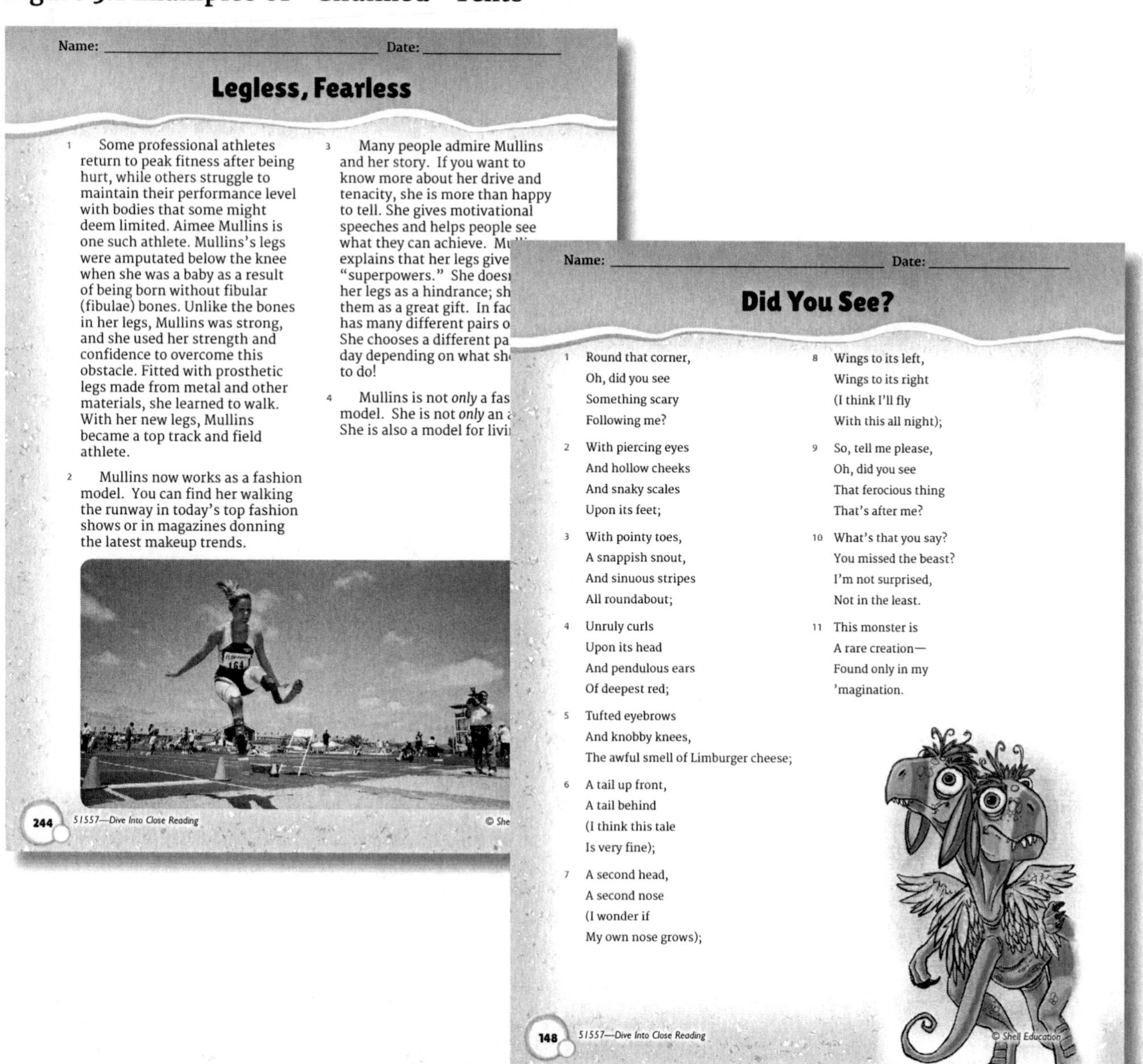

Name: ________________ Date: ________

Legless, Fearless

1 Some professional athletes return to peak fitness after being hurt, while others struggle to maintain their performance level with bodies that some might deem limited. Aimee Mullins is one such athlete. Mullins's legs were amputated below the knee when she was a baby as a result of being born without fibular (fibulae) bones. Unlike the bones in her legs, Mullins was strong, and she used her strength and confidence to overcome this obstacle. Fitted with prosthetic legs made from metal and other materials, she learned to walk. With her new legs, Mullins became a top track and field athlete.

2 Mullins now works as a fashion model. You can find her walking the runway in today's top fashion shows or in magazines donning the latest makeup trends.

3 Many people admire Mullins and her story. If you want to know more about her drive and tenacity, she is more than happy to tell. She gives motivational speeches and helps people see what they can achieve. Mu... explains that her legs give... "superpowers." She does... her legs as a hindrance; sh... them as a great gift. In fac... has many different pairs o... She chooses a different pa... day depending on what sh... to do!

4 Mullins is not *only* a fas... model. She is not *only* an a... She is also a model for livi...

244 51557—Dive Into Close Reading © She...

Name: ________________ Date: ________

Did You See?

1 Round that corner,
Oh, did you see
Something scary
Following me?

2 With piercing eyes
And hollow cheeks
And snaky scales
Upon its feet;

3 With pointy toes,
A snappish snout,
And sinuous stripes
All roundabout;

4 Unruly curls
Upon its head
And pendulous ears
Of deepest red;

5 Tufted eyebrows
And knobby knees,
The awful smell of Limburger cheese;

6 A tail up front,
A tail behind
(I think this tale
Is very fine);

7 A second head,
A second nose
(I wonder if
My own nose grows);

8 Wings to its left,
Wings to its right
(I think I'll fly
With this all night);

9 So, tell me please,
Oh, did you see
That ferocious thing
That's after me?

10 What's that you say?
You missed the beast?
I'm not surprised,
Not in the least.

11 This monster is
A rare creation—
Found only in my
'magination.

148 51557—Dive Into Close Reading © Shell Education

What Types of Annotations Should Be Used?

The ability for a reader to meaningfully interact with a text is enhanced and supported through text annotation. Text annotation enables students to engage with a text in a physical way, preventing them from skimming or discounting areas of challenge. However, random—though aesthetically pleasing—multi-colored highlights on a page do not add to the construction of meaning. In order for annotations to be useful, they must be consistent, and they must apply to the skills and standards being targeted. The way you approach annotation will depend on the age and skill level of your students and your own preferences. As long as the annotations are consistent and focused on the skills appropriate to your students, the variations are limitless.

Whatever the annotation, it is imperative to initially teach students the process of annotating. Once they are comfortable with this skill and the way to use it in your classroom, it will become an integral part of every close reading experience. Begin by introducing the standard marks students will use. See Table 3.2 for annotation ideas. A copy of Table 3.2 is also included in the Digital Download. You may want to create and display a poster, defining these marks for easy reference. Also, provide students with a copy of the annotations chart to keep with their reading materials.

Table 3.2 Annotation Ideas

Grade 3

	Annotation	When Do I Use It?
Author's Message	main idea	This is the main idea.
Author's Craft	√	I found it! (e.g., title page, table of contents, or graph)
Questions	?	What does this mean? or I have a question.
	*	I should research this.
Opinions	!	Wow! I am surprised! or I think this is important!
	author's opinion	This is the author's opinion.
Language	unknown word	I don't know this word.
	figurative language	Examples: metaphor, simile, idiom, multiple meaning word, nonliteral word, personification, alliteration, hyperbole, or onomatopoeia
Connections	1 ⟷ 2	This goes with this. or This leads to this. or These are connected somehow.
Reflections and Predictions	Margin Notes	These are thoughts I had while reading. and I think this will happen next.
Arguments	What the author says is true	The author is making an argument or important statement.
	goes against the author's argument	This goes against the author's argument or main idea.

Grades 4–5

	Annotation	When Do I Use It?
Author's Message	main idea	This is the theme or main idea.
Author's Craft	√	I found a text feature! (e.g., index, glossary, or headings)
Questions	?	This is unclear. or I have a question.
	*	I should research this.
Opinions	!	Wow! I am surprised! or I think this is important!
	author's opinion	This is the author's opinion.
Language	(unknown word)	I don't know this word.
	figurative language	Examples: metaphor, simile, idiom, adage, proverb, personification, alliteration, synonym, antonym, homograph, hyperbole, or onomatopoeia
Connections	1◄~~~~~~~~►2	These ideas, characters, or events are connected.
Reflections and Prediction	Margin Notes ↔ Text Evidence AC	These are my thoughts and predictions about the text. or The arrow points to evidence in the text.
Arguments	(What the author says is true) CC	This is the author's claim.
	(goes against the author's argument) E	This is the counter claim.
	(This is evidence.) AC	This is evidence of the claim or counter claim.

Next, model your thinking for students as you read a piece of text aloud. Explain that the annotations help you return to a text to clarify questions, research confusing words, focus on important features, and make connections across the text. Have students practice annotating the same text you read aloud. Then, invite them to try it on their own with a new piece of text. Once they have had time to annotate, encourage peer discussion of the annotations. Finally, reconvene the class to make sure that everyone is consistently using the same symbols. As the class becomes more adept with using annotation tools, experiment by adding more symbols.

Before beginning each close reading experience, determine the types of annotations to use. For example, if it is a lesson centering on challenging language, students will focus on annotating unfamiliar words or words used in unfamiliar ways. For lessons about key ideas and details, students might focus on underlining phrases that indicate the key ideas and circling those that provide supporting details. Not every type of annotation must be used in each lesson. Annotations are only useful inasmuch as they support students' learning goals and needs. Pencils are the preferred annotation tool. They eliminate the distraction of color.

Teacher Tip
Annotations may be done by writing directly on the text, employing the use of sticky notes, or using clear page-protectors over book pages and using dry erase markers to annotate.

What Types of Student Resources Are Needed?

Each close reading experience requires that students have a text to read and tools to annotate their reading. However, as you plan, consider what other types of materials will maximize the close reading experience for students, such as graphic organizers. There may be times when additional support is needed, such as partnered texts, appropriate realia, maps, illustrations, or even partnered multi-media presentations. These scaffolds should, however, not be introduced until students have an initial read of the text.

Bear in mind that formative assessments may reveal areas where certain students may benefit from scaffolded support. One cannot always anticipate what supports will be needed, but it is helpful to have options in mind when lesson planning. Get them ready, just in case. For example, inviting struggling students into a smaller group to review challenging vocabulary is one form of scaffolding. Having in mind the types of scaffolds you will use with a group to support vocabulary or conceptual development eases any worries caused by having to think of scaffolds on the spot.

Finally, provide a summative performance task to assess mastery of skills taught for this lesson. The task should prompt students to use writing, speaking, or creating to demonstrate their new understanding. Sample performance tasks are provided in Section Four, plus lesson-specific organizers are offered with each sample lesson in Section Five. While the larger group starts this task, you can work with the smaller group to ready them to eventually also complete the extension task. Remember that working with a small group does not mean they are excluded from the reading of the complex text or the extension task. The goal is to ensure they have an additional opportunity to gain the language and concepts needed to also move forward.

Putting It All Together

Let's return to Mrs. Marquand's fourth grade class for a model of how a close reading lesson might play out. Before the lesson, Mrs. Marquand has completed the preplanning chart, considered the text complexity of the passage for her lesson, and identified possible scaffolds. She has carefully created text-dependent questions designed to help her students dig deeper into the text with each reading.

Lesson Resource Checklist

- ❑ Pre-chunked/numbered text or text ready to be chunked
- ❑ Student-friendly lesson purpose posted where students can see and refer to it
- ❑ "I Can" statement that matches the lesson purpose
- ❑ Annotation tools (e.g., pencils, sticky notes, page protector, or dry erase markers)
- ❑ Text-dependent questions
- ❑ Graphic organizers
- ❑ Scaffolding tools (e.g., partner text, realia, maps, or illustrations)
- ❑ Formative performance task

During the close reading lesson, Mrs. Marquand briefly introduces the purpose and sets expectations. She guides students to "chunk" the text by numbering each paragraph. She reviews a few relevant annotation marks and presents a broad text-dependent question before sending students into the text.

As students read and annotate on their own, Mrs. Marquand is an active observer, taking notes, offering words of encouragement and additional leading questions where needed. She lets students struggle and records their challenges. After students have grappled with the text on their own, they partner with peers to compare their thinking and work together to analyze the complex text. Mrs. Marquand continues to listen, watch, and respond. She adds to partner conversations and pulls the whole class together for discussion and continued leading questions as needed.

The class completes several phases of reading and annotating with a text-dependent question in mind, discussing with a partner, discussing with the whole class, and considering new questions and prompts. Not all returns to the text are to read it in its entirety. Sometimes students are reading a few sentences, looking at phrasing, and contrasting a couple of chunks. With each phase, students discover deeper meaning, and the teacher crafts specific responses to observed needs. These phases may take place in one session or across two to three sessions spread over a couple days.

Multiply this experience across a school year and across content areas, and students will build a foundation that will help them develop the skills needed to independently confront complex texts.

Try It!

Directions: Return to the passage you analyzed on page 55. Use the guidelines and tables in this section along with your knowledge of your students to prepare to teach a close reading lesson. Write on the following chart (page 68), or use a digital copy of the chart in the Digital Download (teachingclosereading.pdf).

Make sure to tab or mark the pages you find most helpful to your work. These are the pages to which you can return when you plan actual lessons to use with your students.

Forces of the Earth: Undersea Volcanoes (Lexile 760)

Some of the biggest volcanoes on Earth have never been seen by human eyes. That's because they are very deep underwater. One would have to dive down a mile and a half (2.4 km) just to reach the tops of these giants. This string of underwater volcanoes is called the Mid-Ocean Ridge.

The Mid-Ocean Ridge is the biggest mountain range on our planet. It's more than 30,000 miles (48,280 km) long and almost 500 miles (804.7 km) wide. Its hundreds of mountains and volcanoes zigzag under the ocean between the continents. They wind their way around the globe like the seam on a baseball. Nearly every day, at least one underwater volcano erupts. Hot lava pours out of the volcano and onto the ocean floor.

The bottom of the sea is ever changing. After erupting from deep inside Earth, the lava cools, forming new rocks. Layers of rocky lava pile up and, over millions of years, expand the sea floor. The expanding sea floor, in turn, pushes the continents. A million years ago, the earth looked very different than it does today. A million years from now, it will have changed even more.

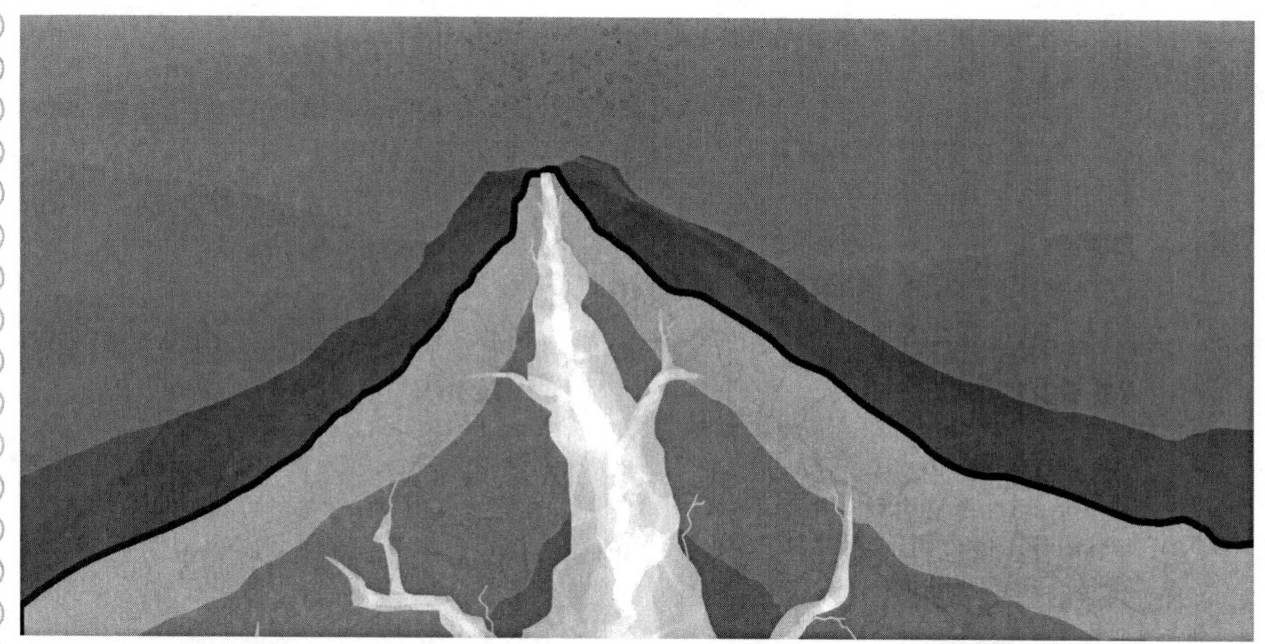

Try It! *(cont.)*

Teaching Close Reading

Teaching

Limited Frontloading ❑ yes ❑ no

Describe:

First Read

Who Reads? ❑ teacher ❑ student

Student Materials

❑ graphic organizer ❑ group consensus form

❑ note taking guide ❑ summary form

Second Read

Who Reads? ❑ teacher ❑ students

Student Resources

❑ graphic organizer ❑ group consensus form

❑ note taking guide ❑ summary form

Additional Reads

Who Reads? ❑ teacher ❑ students

Student Resources

❑ graphic organizer ❑ group consensus form

❑ note taking guide ❑ summary form

Extension	**Reteaching**

Section 4:
Assessing and Extending Close Reading

One cannot be certain what students have learned or are learning until there is an assessment given. Formative assessments are used to inform instruction throughout the learning process. A formative assessment is an assessment *for* learning, not *of* learning. It provides a snapshot of where the student's development is at a particular point in time. Assessment is a continual process that occurs throughout close reading. As you engage with your students, you will repeatedly assess their learning and scaffold accordingly. However, it is useful to have built-in checkpoints for formative assessments at specific times during your lesson. "I Can" statements provide an avenue for students to assess their learning. Stating what he or she can do in relation to the learning targets builds student ownership of learning and self-efficacy. It is also encouraged to have a formal performance task at the end of a close reading lesson. These performance tasks serve as summative assessments, which are a good way to gauge the outcomes of your students' close reading. We have included formative and summative assessments with each of the sample lessons included in the Sample Lesson Section (page 79).

Figure 4.1 presents the Planning Chart for Close Reading introduced in Section Two. In this section, we will address the last two elements.

Figure 4.1 Planning for Close Reading

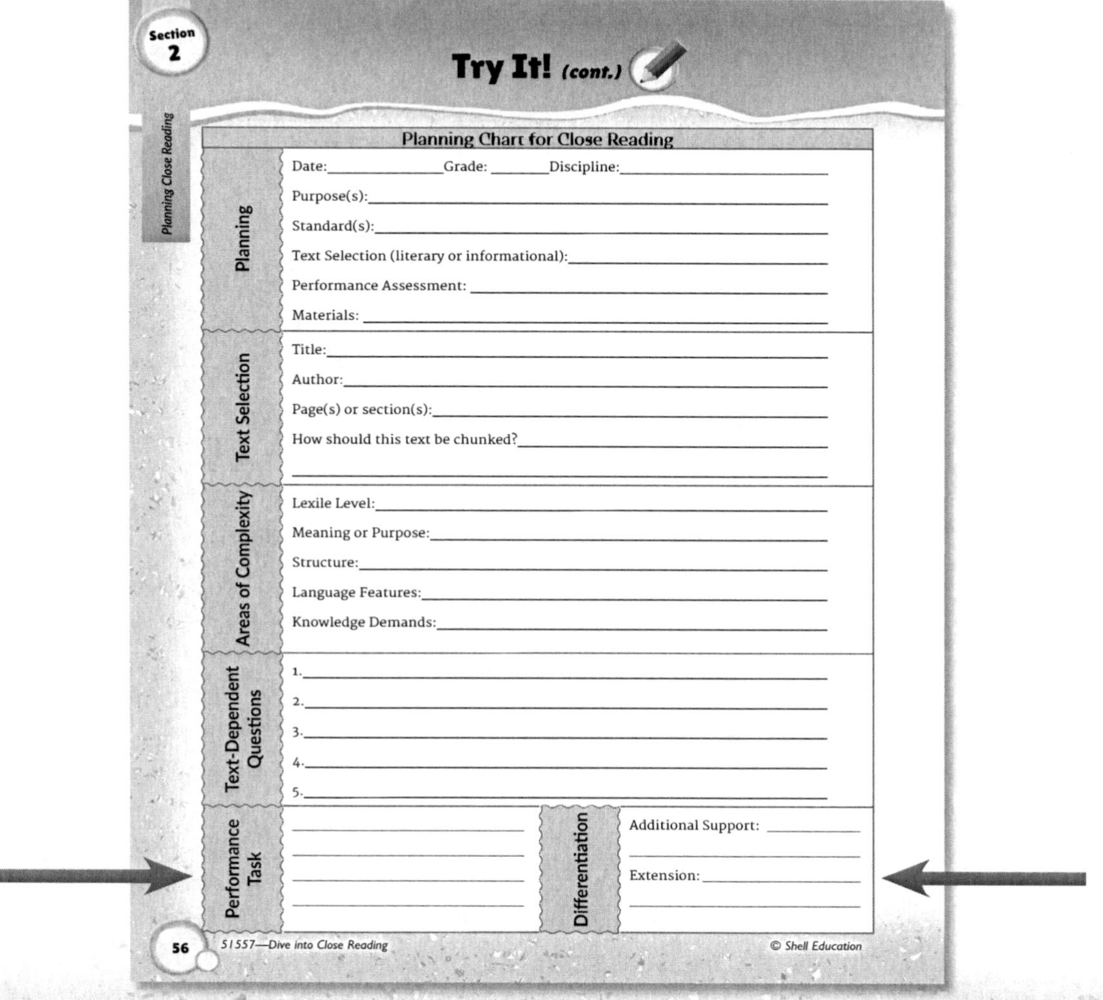
Section 2

Planning Close Reading

Try It! *(cont.)*

Planning Chart for Close Reading

Planning	Date: ____ Grade: ____ Discipline: ____ Purpose(s): ____ Standard(s): ____ Text Selection (literary or informational): ____ Performance Assessment: ____ Materials: ____
Text Selection	Title: ____ Author: ____ Page(s) or section(s): ____ How should this text be chunked? ____
Areas of Complexity	Lexile Level: ____ Meaning or Purpose: ____ Structure: ____ Language Features: ____ Knowledge Demands: ____
Text-Dependent Questions	1. ____ 2. ____ 3. ____ 4. ____ 5. ____
Performance Task	____
Differentiation	Additional Support: ____ Extension: ____

56 51557—Dive into Close Reading © Shell Education

Creating and Using Formative Assessments

As students participate in close reading, there will be numerous opportunities for you to observe, probe, and evaluate student learning. The two biggest keys to making effective use of formative assessments are noticing the areas of challenge and anticipating the flexibility needed in planning to address the next areas of challenge as the lesson progresses.

Assessing What You Hear

Partner talk and table talk during a close reading lesson provides rich data to monitor and assess student learning. As students discuss the text and text-dependent questions, listen carefully for indications of understanding or confusion. Engage with student pairs to support their discussions and ask follow-up questions that spur students to dig deeper. If it is clear that one student is dominating the conversation, pose a question to the other student. If students seem to be struggling unproductively or showing a lack of understanding, make a notation and be ready to scaffold or reteach. It is not necessary to leap to the rescue of struggling students, but it is important to remain aware of problem areas and structure the lessons to offer scaffolds that promote continued learning. When problems persist, students may lose focus or fall behind, so it is important to remember that the goal of the close reading approach is for *every* student to be able to tackle and successfully read increasingly complex, challenging, age-appropriate texts.

Assessing What You See

As students work through annotating their texts and producing written reactions on their graphic organizers, you will have another opportunity to assess their understanding. Once again, it is important to tune in to students' work and evaluate strengths and growth areas. Are the same instances of challenging vocabulary coming up on many students' annotations? Are all students clearly able to identify the main idea and supporting details of the text, recording them accurately on their graphic organizers? Are students' paired discussions focused and on target? Are there instances of figurative language causing unanticipated challenges? Are there repeated questions coming up in students' margin notes? Look carefully at what students are annotating, and carefully consider students' written responses to text-dependent questions.

Text-Dependent Question Observation Guides

Your assessment of what is seen and heard must directly relate to the lesson's goals. Creating pertinent, probing text-dependent questions is essential. Once students are focused on well-considered TDQs and you are engaged in listening and seeing students' progress and struggles, you will need an efficient, organized way to keep track of your observations. Table 4.2 offers two observational guides—one for literature and one for informational text—to assist you in quickly recording what you see and hear in terms of the students' mastery of the meaning, structure, language, and knowledge demands of the text.

Table 4.1 Observation Guides

Observation Guide (Literature)

	Meaning	Structure	Language	Knowledge Demands
1st Reading Notes	❑ main idea ❑ key details ❑ vocabulary word use ❑ development of characters or themes	❑ macro (overall) organization ❑ micro (sentence/ paragraph) organization ❑ visual layout ❑ visual supports ❑ relationship among ideas and vocabulary ❑ relationship among ideas, characters, and setting	❑ vocabulary word meaning ❑ idioms ❑ unconventional jargon, vernacular, or technical terminology ❑ tone ❑ author's purpose ❑ figurative language ❑ point of view ❑ theme	❑ cultural or historic knowledge ❑ literary knowledge ❑ technical knowledge
2nd Reading Notes	❑ main idea ❑ key details ❑ vocabulary word use ❑ development of characters or themes	❑ macro (overall) organization ❑ micro (sentence/ paragraph) organization ❑ visual layout ❑ visual supports ❑ relationship among ideas and vocabulary ❑ relationship among ideas, characters, and setting	❑ vocabulary word meaning ❑ idioms ❑ unconventional jargon, vernacular, or technical terminology ❑ tone ❑ author's purpose ❑ figurative language ❑ point of view ❑ theme	❑ cultural or historic knowledge ❑ literary knowledge ❑ technical knowledge

Table 4.1 Observation Guides *(cont.)*

Observation Guide (Literature) *(cont.)*

	Meaning	Structure	Language	Knowledge Demands
3rd Reading Notes	❑ main idea ❑ key details ❑ vocabulary word use ❑ development of characters or themes	❑ macro (overall) organization ❑ micro (sentence/ paragraph) organization ❑ visual layout ❑ visual supports ❑ relationship among ideas and vocabulary ❑ relationship among ideas, characters, and settings	❑ vocabulary word meaning ❑ idioms ❑ unconventional jargon, vernacular, or technical terminology ❑ tone ❑ author's purpose ❑ figurative language ❑ point of view ❑ theme	❑ cultural or historic knowledge ❑ literary knowledge ❑ technical knowledge
4th Reading Notes	❑ main idea ❑ key details ❑ vocabulary word use ❑ development of characters or themes	❑ macro (overall) organization ❑ micro (sentence/ paragraph) organization ❑ visual layout ❑ visual supports ❑ relationship among ideas and vocabulary ❑ relationship among ideas, characters, and setting	❑ vocabulary word meaning ❑ idioms ❑ unconventional jargon, vernacular, or technical terminology ❑ tone ❑ author's purpose ❑ figurative language ❑ point of view ❑ theme	❑ cultural or historic knowledge ❑ literary knowledge ❑ technical knowledge

Table 4.1 Observation Guides *(cont.)*

Observation Guide (Informational Text)

	Meaning	Structure	Language	Knowledge Demands
1st Reading Notes	❑ main idea ❑ key details ❑ vocabulary word use ❑ development of arguments	❑ macro (overall) organization ❑ micro (sentence/ paragraph) organization ❑ visual layout ❑ visual supports ❑ relationship among ideas and vocabulary	❑ vocabulary word meaning ❑ idioms ❑ unconventional jargon, vernacular, or technical terminology ❑ author's purpose	❑ cultural or historic knowledge ❑ discipline-based knowledge ❑ technical knowledge
2nd Reading Notes	❑ main idea ❑ key details ❑ vocabulary word use ❑ development of arguments	❑ macro (overall) organization ❑ micro (sentence/ paragraph) organization ❑ visual layout ❑ visual supports ❑ relationship among ideas and vocabulary	❑ vocabulary word meaning ❑ idioms ❑ unconventional jargon, vernacular, or technical terminology ❑ author's purpose	❑ cultural or historic knowledge ❑ discipline-based knowledge ❑ technical knowledge
3rd Reading Notes	❑ main idea ❑ key details ❑ vocabulary word use ❑ development of arguments	❑ macro (overall) organization ❑ micro (sentence/ paragraph) organization ❑ visual layout ❑ visual supports ❑ relationship among ideas and vocabulary	❑ vocabulary word meaning ❑ idioms ❑ unconventional jargon, vernacular, or technical terminology ❑ author's purpose	❑ cultural or historic knowledge ❑ discipline-based knowledge ❑ technical knowledge
4th Reading Notes	❑ main idea ❑ key details ❑ vocabulary word use ❑ development of arguments	❑ macro (overall) organization ❑ micro (sentence/ paragraph) organization ❑ visual layout ❑ visual supports ❑ relationship among ideas and vocabulary	❑ vocabulary word meaning ❑ idioms ❑ unconventional jargon, vernacular, or technical terminology ❑ author's purpose	❑ cultural or historic knowledge ❑ discipline-based knowledge ❑ technical knowledge

To use an observational guide, attach it to a clipboard or carry it in a convenient place while walking around the room during annotation times, partner talks, or class discussions. Record students' names or initials to the right of the topics with which they are struggling. Add additional notes and plans in the first column. After the first reading, you may not wish to take any action, unless there are glaring problems that students seem unable or unwilling to work through. However, if, after observing the second or third readings, it is obvious that the same students are continuing to wrestle with the same issues, or if a growing number of students are grappling with the same issue, it may be time to intervene. Figure 4.1 provides a sample of a completed guide from Mrs. Xuan's classroom.

Figure 4.2 Completed Sample Observation Guide

Observation Guide (Literature)				
	Meaning	**Structure**	**Language**	**Knowledge Demands**
1st Reading Notes Whole class discussion on language and details	☑ main idea ❑ key details ❑ vocabulary word use ❑ development of characters or themes groups 3+5	❑ macro (overall) organization ❑ micro (sentence/paragraph) organization ❑ visual layout ❑ visual supports ❑ relationship among ideas and vocabulary ❑ relationship among ideas, characters, and setting	☑ vocabulary word meaning Izzy, Jose, Dan, TC, Ronnie ☑ idioms ❑ unconventional jargon, vernacular, or technical terminology ❑ tone ☑ author's purpose Jessie, Leslie, Latisha, Phil ☑ figurative language ❑ point of view ❑ theme	☑ cultural or historic knowledge ❑ literary knowledge ❑ technical knowledge
2nd Reading Notes To Do: Small group focus on vocab @ idioms Group 3 work on details	❑ main idea ❑ key details group 3 ❑ vocabulary word use ❑ development of characters or themes W/7	❑ macro (overall) organization ❑ micro (sentence/paragraph) organization ❑ visual layout ❑ visual supports ❑ relationship among ideas and vocabulary ❑ relationship among ideas, characters, and setting	☑ vocabulary word meaning ☑ idioms ❑ unconventional jargon, vernacular, or technical terminology ❑ tone ☑ author's purpose Dan, Izzy, Jose, Jessie, Leslie ❑ figurative language ❑ point of view ❑ theme	☑ cultural or historic knowledge Johan? ❑ literary knowledge ❑ technical knowledge
3rd Reading Notes one-on-one with Izzy	☑ main idea ❑ key details ❑ vocabulary word use ❑ development of characters or themes Izzy	❑ macro (overall) organization ❑ micro (sentence/paragraph) organization ❑ visual layout ❑ visual supports ❑ relationship among ideas and vocabulary ❑ relationship among ideas, characters, and setting	☑ vocabulary word meaning Izzy ❑ idioms ❑ unconventional jargon, vernacular, or technical terminology ❑ tone ❑ author's purpose ❑ figurative language ❑ point of view ❑ theme	❑ cultural or historic knowledge ❑ literary knowledge ❑ technical knowledge
4th Reading Notes Great!	❑ main idea ❑ key details ❑ vocabulary word use ❑ development of characters or themes	❑ macro (overall) organization ❑ micro (sentence/paragraph) organization ❑ visual layout ❑ visual supports ❑ relationship among ideas and vocabulary ❑ relationship among ideas, characters, and setting	❑ vocabulary word meaning ❑ idioms ❑ unconventional jargon, vernacular, or technical terminology ❑ tone ❑ author's purpose ❑ figurative language ❑ point of view ❑ theme	❑ cultural or historic knowledge ❑ literary knowledge ❑ technical knowledge

The completed sample observation guide (Figure 4.1) is taken from Mrs. Xuan's fifth grade classroom that engaged in a literary text close reading, focusing on key ideas and details. The students sit in heterogeneous rotating table groups for discussion and collaborative work. As she moved around the room during partner discussions, she realized that several students were not clear on some of the language in the complex text. She noted specific students and/or table groups and the exact problematic language. Additionally, two groups focused on unimportant details in the text. Mrs. Xuan attempted to refocus the groups by asking them which details were important for understanding the main idea of the text. After listening to the groups for a few minutes longer, she determined that it was a good time to have a whole class discussion about the specific language used in the text and how the details relate to the main idea. She noted that decision on her observation guide.

Once again, during the second reading, Mrs. Xuan circled the room observing the partner discussions. It was clear that significantly more students were understanding the text. There were still a few students who were new to English and who were wrestling with the more complex vocabulary and figurative language. Additionally, Johan, who seemed clear before, asked a question that made Mrs. Xuan wonder if he had become confused. She put a question mark (?) next to his name to remind her to check in with him later. Table Group 5 was now progressing without issue. But Table Group 3 was still discussing on insignificant details. Mrs. Xuan decided to schedule a small group session with the students who needed extra support at the end of the lesson. Additionally, she decided to invite Table Group 3 to work with Table Group 7 to clear up their confusion about the details.

After the third reading, Mrs. Xuan was happy to see that almost all the students had understood the text. However, Izzy was still unable to identify the key details and language. Mrs. Xuan made a note to work with Izzy one-on-one.

Because of the individual and small group scaffolds Mrs. Xuan offered as she circulated and the collaborative conversations among students, after the final reading, everyone was showing a clear understanding of the text and the tasks they were assigned. Mrs. Xuan was ready to move students on to their summative assessments.

Creating and Using Summative Assessments—The Performance Task

Summative assessments are used at the end of a series of lessons to determine what learning has taken place. They let the teacher and students know what was learned as the result of the close reading experiences. It gives students the opportunity to demonstrate their learning and teachers the chance to evaluate whether any additional instruction is needed. For the purposes of the close reading approach, performance tasks that are based on learning goals are the summative assessments used. These tasks reflect the knowledge gained through students' experiences with the text-dependent questions. There are endless numbers of performance tasks that can be chosen for students. Certain tasks, however, lend themselves better to certain age levels and goals. Please see Table 4.3 (page 74) for some suggested performance tasks at various grade levels.

Table 4.2 Sample Performance Tasks

Grade Level	Sample Tasks
3rd	• Students produce maps of the locations described in the text. • Students rewrite the story from the point of view of one of the secondary characters. • Students compare and contrast the text content and content from another medium shared in class. • Students rewrite the story/text using a different text structure. • Students judge the effectiveness of a literary text and an informational text on the same topic. • Students role-play a debate between two characters, highlighting their different motivations and points of view.
4th	• Students create memes demonstrating the author's point of view and purpose in writing this text. • Students write essays describing the changes undergone by the protagonist of the story. • Students create posters showing the cause and effect of key events in the text. • Including key details from the text, students create short films based on the story/text. • Students write critiques of an author's argument. • Students organize the data from the text into charts.
5th	• Students create mock social media pages for each of the main characters of the story/text. • Students write persuasive essays regarding the central theme of the text, supporting their positions with relevant quotes and details from the text. • Citing specific textual evidence, students create slide shows comparing and contrasting the tones from different parts of the text. • Students create story maps, tracing the effects of the key events of the text on each of the main characters. • Students make audio or video podcasts that critically examine a topic in a text. • Students compile evidence from the text supporting and refuting the main arguments in the text and present the data in visual formats (e.g., chart, graph, or Venn diagram).

What Should I Do for Students Who Comprehend at the End of Close Reading?

If the summative assessment indicates that students have completely comprehended the material used in the close reading approach, outstanding! Your students were able to accomplish the intended purpose. For them, it is time to move forward. Bear in mind that they now have a bit more experience and a bit more success upon which to draw as you plan future lessons. They are in a better position to push just a little further with the next close reading experience. The process should never be stagnant. Each time this approach is utilized, it's like shooting for the sweet spot where students are engaged, challenged, and capable of growth. If the challenges are too few, students will not have an opportunity to stretch and learn. They may even become bored. Think back to the formative evaluations. If students sailed through without any struggle, it may be necessary to rethink your challenge level for the next close reading lesson. Return to the description of text complexity in Section Two, and choose an element to amp up.

What Makes for a Good Performance Task?

- It aligns with the standards being taught.
- It utilizes a format that enables students with various language and reading proficiencies to demonstrate knowledge.
- It targets a high level of Bloom's Taxonomy/Depth of Knowledge.
- Optional: It incorporates STEM features to broaden appeal and experience.

How Do I Extend Learning for Students Who Did Not Understand?

If there are students who are still struggling and not showing mastery of the lesson purpose through their performance tasks, it is time to plan how to move them forward by considering what and how to reteach. Remember, the goal of every close reading experience is for *each* student, including those who read below grade level and English language learners, to show deep comprehension of challenging grade-level texts. When this goal is not reached, it is necessary to identify problem areas and scaffold their learning until they reach the targeted goals.

There are many ways to support students who struggle. Table 4.4 (page 76) offers specific options for reteaching. In response to your observations, you may incorporate scaffolds for individual students during a close reading lesson. Alternatively, you may record the need for reteaching, then plan to use the reteach option during the next close reading lesson. See the Glossary of Reteaching Ideas (pages 270–272) for explanations of each reteaching idea.

Table 4.4 Reteaching Ideas (See pages 270–272 for full descriptions.)

Identified Area for Growth	Reteaching Ideas	
Vocabulary	• Frayer cards • word maps • graphic organizers • word sorts • T-chart	• words in context • vocabulary matrices • personal dictionaries • connect two
Key Details	• Gimme 5 • graphic organizers	• concept maps
Main Idea	• concept maps • tweet the main idea	• newspaper headlines and story titles
Plot Structure	• storyboards • Freytag's Pyramid • plot skeleton	• Somebody Wanted But So Then (SWBST) • story summary graphic organizers
Text Structure	• graphic organizers • character web • story maps	• task cards • signal terms
Character Analysis	• graphic organizers • character web	• Venn diagrams • character profiles
Text Features	• text feature BINGO • text feature checklist	• graphic organizers
Theme	• graphic organizers • essential questions	• hash tags • task cards
Figurative Language	• graphic organizers • song lyrics	• task cards
Tone & Mood	• graphic organizers • essential questions • task cards	• flip-flop • inquiry charts
Opinion/Argument Development	• graphic organizers • task cards	• Toulmin Model of Arguments • claim/evidence/analysis
Reading Visuals	• Somebody Wanted But So Then (SWBST) • graphic organizers	• task cards • Visual Thinking Strategies (VTS)

Try It!

Directions: Return to the close reading plans you created on page 66. Use the guidelines and tables in this section along with your knowledge of your students to create a performance task and prepare for observation and reteaching. Write on the following chart (page 79), or use a digital copy of the chart in the Digital Download (planningclosereading.pdf).

Make sure to tab or mark the pages you find most helpful to your work. These are the pages to which you can return when you plan actual lessons to use with your students.

Forces of the Earth: Undersea Volcanoes (Lexile 760)

Some of the biggest volcanoes on Earth have never been seen by human eyes. That's because they are very deep underwater. One would have to dive down a mile and a half (2.4 km) just to reach the tops of these giants. This string of underwater volcanoes is called the Mid-Ocean Ridge.

The Mid-Ocean Ridge is the biggest mountain range on our planet. It's more than 30,000 miles (48,280 km) long and almost 500 miles (804.7 km) wide. Its hundreds of mountains and volcanoes zigzag under the ocean between the continents. They wind their way around the globe like the seam on a baseball. Nearly every day, at least one underwater volcano erupts. Hot lava pours out of the volcano and onto the ocean floor.

The bottom of the sea is ever changing. After erupting from deep inside Earth, the lava cools, forming new rocks. Layers of rocky lava pile up and, over millions of years, expand the sea floor. The expanding sea floor, in turn, pushes the continents. A million years ago, the earth looked very different than it does today. A million years from now, it will have changed even more.

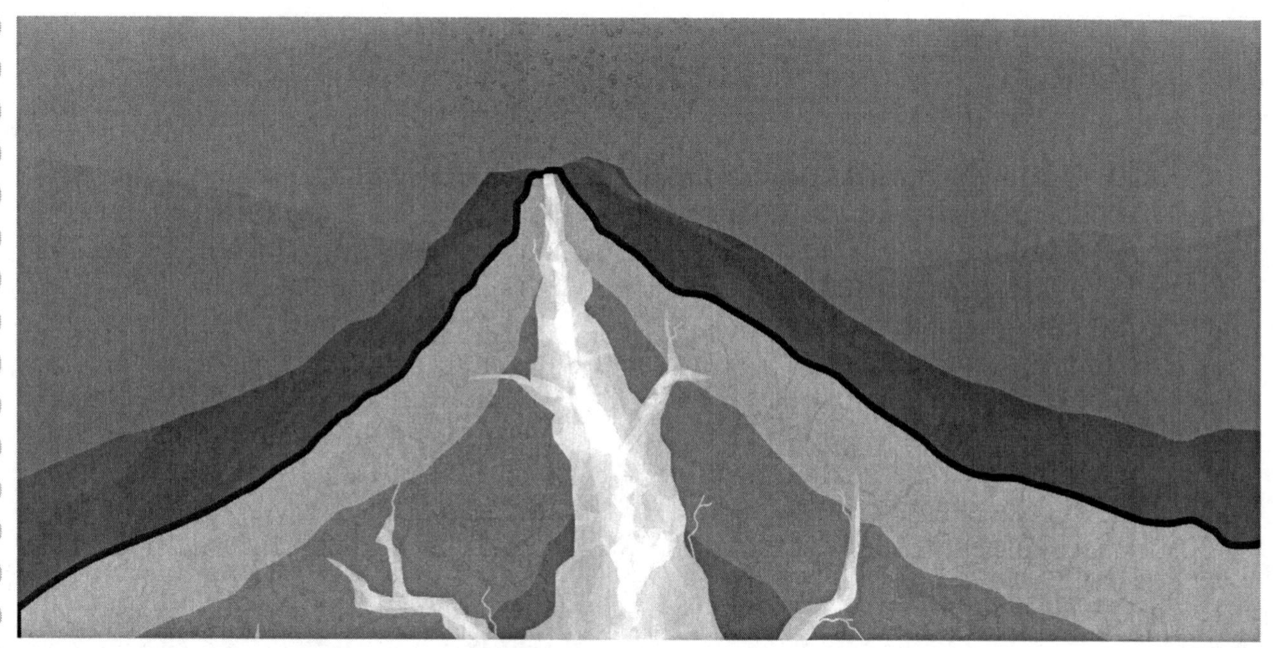

Try It! *(cont.)*

Planning Chart for Close Reading

Planning	Date:________ Grade: _____ Discipline:________ Purpose(s):________ Standard(s):________ Text Selection (literary or informational):________ Performance Assessment: ________ Materials: ________
Text Selection	Title:________ Author:________ Page(s) or section(s):________ How should this text be chunked?________ ________
Areas of Complexity	Lexile Level:________ Meaning or Purpose:________ Structure:________ Language Features:________ Knowledge Demands:________
Text-Dependent Questions	1.________ 2.________ 3.________ 4.________ 5.________

Performance Task	________ ________ ________ ________	**Differentiation**	Additional Support: ________ ________ Extension: ________ ________

Section 5:
Literary Text Close Reading Lessons

If you have completed the Try It! activities at the end of each of the previous sections, you now have a planned close reading lesson that you may choose to use with your students. You also have a set of tabbed pages to refer to as you plan additional lessons. In this section, you will find a bank of sample close reading lessons. You may choose to use the actual lesson (all of the passages and resources are provided) or use them as models as you create lessons.

You will find nine close reading lessons built around literary texts. A tenth text is provided along with planning resources to allow you to plan a close reading lesson.

The Fox and the Crow

Purpose

WHAT: Analyze the development of the moral of a fable.

HOW: Recreate the development of a moral in a new fable.

I CAN: I can use key details to analyze and identify the moral of a fable.

Standards

- **Reading:** Recount stories, including fables, folktales, and myths from diverse cultures; determine the central message, lesson, or moral, and explain how it is conveyed through key details in the text.
- **Writing:** Provide a sense of closure.
- **Language:** Distinguish shades of meaning among related words that describe states of mind or degrees of certainty.

Performance Assessment

- Student will write fables, focusing on events that lead to a moral that brings the story to a satisfying close.

Text Selection

- "The Fox and the Crow—A Retelling of Aesop's Fable"
- Text is divided into paragraphs.

Materials

- *The Fox and the Crow* passage, one copy per student (page 88; foxandcrow.pdf)
- *Check Your Understanding* activity (page 89)
- *Can You See It?* activity (page 90)
- *The Moral of the Fable* activity (page 91)
- *The Moral of the Fable Scoring Rubric* (page 92)

Text-Dependent Questions (See pages 40–43 for more information.)

- What is the main idea of the story?
- Identify phrases in the text that describe what Crow thinks of himself at the beginning, middle, and end of the text.
- What did Fox notice about Crow? What did Fox *say* he noticed about Crow?
- Why did Crow drop the cheese?
- What did Fox want to eat before he spotted the cheese?
- What is the moral (or lesson learned) of the story?

The Fox and the Crow *(cont.)*

Areas of Complexity

	Measure	Explanation
Quantitative	Lexile Level	590L
Qualitative	Meaning or Purpose	The text includes narrated descriptions of Crow's conceited behavior. Fox takes advantage of this, which leads to the moral of the story.
	Structure	The text organization revolves around the dialog between Fox and Crow and concludes with a moral.
	Language Features	Language is accessible and familiar and can be determined through context clues.
Reader/Task	Knowledge Demands	The characters are likely familiar to students, and illustrations show what they are. While words like *conceited* and *flatterer* may be unfamiliar to students, context clues help with understanding. Students must understand the elements of a fable to complete the performance assessment.

Text Synopsis

The fable is about a fox that outsmarts a crow in order to get a piece of cheese. The fox takes advantage of the crow's conceit to trick him into dropping the cheese. This leads to the moral of the story: Never trust a flatterer.

Differentiation

Additional Support—After giving students an initial opportunity to analyze the text, you may need to assist students with unfamiliar words (*flatterer, conceited*) in order to increase comprehension.

Extension—Instruct students to summarize the fable by retelling it in five sentences or fewer.

The Fox and the Crow *(cont.)*

Phase 1—Hitting the Surface

Who Reads	Annotations (See page 63.)		
❑ teacher	☑ highlight main points	☑ underline key details	☑ write questions
☑ students	❑ circle key vocabulary	❑ arrows for connections	❑ other: ____________

Procedure

1. Before students read, explain the purposes (from page 83).
2. Have students read the text independently. As they read, students will annotate their copies of the text to answer the question *What is the story about?* Students should also note any questions they have about the text.
3. Throughout each phase, as students read, circulate to observe their work, and provide scaffolds as guides for those who need assistance. These might be additional layered questions, prompts to encourage them to reflect on a certain part of the passage, or cues to remember related information. Insights you gain through this formative assessment can also influence the next questions to be asked of the whole group.
4. **Partners**—After students have read and annotated the text once, pairs can share their thinking related to the initial question.
5. **Whole Class**—Regroup as a class, and display the text for all students. Ask students to share their responses to the question regarding what the text is about. Have them support their responses with their annotations. If possible, record student annotations on a displayed copy of the text.
6. As a class, discuss the question *What is the moral (or lesson learned) of the fable?* Encourage students to reference specific events from the story as they respond.

Phase 2—Digging Deeper

Who Reads	Annotations (See page 63.)		
❑ teacher	❑ highlight main points	☑ underline key details	❑ write questions
☑ students	☑ circle key vocabulary	❑ arrows for connections	❑ other: ____________

Procedure

1. Say, "The author of this fable uses many descriptive words. Words are used to describe the cheese, Crow's actions, the way Crow sang, and the personality of Fox. Annotate the story by circling descriptive words and phrases."

The Fox and the Crow *(cont.)*

Phase 2—Digging Deeper *(cont.)*

Procedure *(cont.)*

2. Ask students to circle words or phrases that describe important details in the fable. (For example, *bellow* describes how Crow began to sing.)
3. Have each student think of one word to describe Crow and one word to describe Fox. Have them write these words above each character's picture.
4. **Partners**—After students have read and annotated the text once, have pairs share the words they have circled and explain how those words help them understand the fable.
5. **Whole Class**—Regroup as a class, and display the text for all students. Ask students to share their descriptive words and phrases. If possible, record student annotations on a displayed copy of the text.

Phase 3—Digging Even Deeper

Who Reads	Annotations (See page 63.)		
☐ teacher	☐ highlight main points	☑ underline key details	☐ write questions
☑ students	☐ circle key vocabulary	☑ arrows for connections	☑ other: notes in the margin

Procedure

1. Ask, "What does Crow think of himself?" Encourage students to refer to the text as they respond.
2. Before students read the text a second time, say, "Now, let's reread to identify phrases in the text that describe what Crow thinks of himself at the beginning, middle, and end of the text. Don't forget to mark the text with underlining and write notes in the margins so you'll remember what you were thinking."
3. If needed, ask additional layered/scaffolded questions, such as:
   - How does the Crow describe himself after finding the cheese?
   - Why did he describe himself in that way?
   - Why didn't Crow notice Fox right away?
   - What did Fox notice about Crow's behavior?
   - Why did Fox begin to compliment Crow?

The Fox and the Crow *(cont.)*

Phase 3—Digging Even Deeper *(cont.)*

Procedure *(cont.)*

4. **Partners**—After students have read and annotated the text, have pairs share their thinking related to Crow's self-image.
5. Have students return to the text to connect Crow's behavior to Fox's plan.
6. If needed, ask additional layered/scaffolded questions, such as:
    - What did Fox want to eat before he spotted the cheese?
    - What did Fox notice about Crow?
    - What did Fox *say* he noticed about Crow?
    - Why did Crow drop the cheese?
    - What made Fox think he could get Crow to open his mouth and drop the cheese?
7. **Partners**—After students have read and annotated the text, have pairs share their thinking related to Crow's behavior and Fox's plan.
8. **Whole Class**—Regroup as a class, and display the text for students to see. Ask students to share their responses to the question regarding Crow's behavior and Fox's plan. Have them support their responses with their annotations. If possible, record student annotations on a displayed copy of the text.
9. Prior to the performance task, have students think about the passage individually by completing the *Check Your Understanding* activity (page 89).

Performance Assessment

1. Provide students with the performance task *The Moral of the Fable* (page 91).
2. Explain that students' assignments will be graded based on *The Moral of the Fable Scoring Rubric* (page 92). The scoring rubric is for both students and teachers to guide and score work.

Name: ______________________ Date: ______________

The Fox and the Crow: A Retelling of Aesop's Fable

1 In a clearing in the forest, an old picnic table stood empty—or nearly so. A hunk of yellow cheese was there, alone and forgotten by some earlier picnickers.

2 "Caw! Caw!" Overhead, a sleek black crow swooped down to the table. He teetered on his skinny legs and hopped over to the cheese.

3 "What have we here?" The crow pecked at the cheese. "It's a tasty morsel! Aren't I clever to find this cheese? Caw!" With that, the crow grabbed the cheese in his beak and flittered to an overhanging branch. He puffed out his chest and strutted conceitedly, pleased with himself.

4 About that time, a cunning fox wandered by. "I'm hungry," said the fox. "Time to eat!" Just then, he spied the crow and thought, "Crow is tasty . . . but the cheese in his beak looks even tastier."

5 The crow continued to strut and caw, unaware of the hungry fox.

6 *That crow certainly likes the sound of his own voice,* thought the fox. *I have an idea!*

7 "Oh, Mr. Crow," he said. You are a beautiful bird with a haunting voice!"

8 *It's about time someone noticed my splendor*, thought the crow.

9 "Please, Mr. Crow, will you sing your dulcet tones just for me?" the fox implored.

10 The crow was flattered. He enjoyed having an audience. He decided to sing loud and long for the fox. The crow opened his beak wide to bellow his first note, "Caaaaawwwwwwww!" But he forgot about the cheese! It dropped from his beak and plopped to the ground, where the quick fox gobbled it up.

11 "Thank you, Mr. Crow. That was delicious!"

12 "But . . . but . . . it was mine," wailed the crow.

13 "It was yours," said the fox. "But perhaps next time, you'll remember: Never trust a flatterer."

Name: ______________________________ Date: ______________

Check Your Understanding

Directions: Use the text "The Fox and the Crow" to answer the questions.

1. How does Crow describe himself after finding the cheese, and why?

____

____

____

____

2. What did Fox notice about Crow's behavior?

____

____

____

____

3. What did Fox do to trick Crow?

____

____

____

____

____

____

____

Name: ______________________ Date: ______________

Can You See It?

Directions: The author of "The Fox and the Crow" uses descriptive language to help the reader visualize the characters and their actions. Complete the chart by drawing images to match the descriptions from the fable.

Descriptive Language	Visual
In a clearing in the forest, an old picnic table stood empty—or nearly so. A hunk of yellow cheese was there.	
(The crow) teetered on his skinny legs and hopped over to the cheese.	
The crow opened his beak wide to bellow his first note.	

Name:______________________________ Date: ______________

The Moral of the Fable

Directions: Write a fable using animals as characters. Your fable should end with a conclusion that includes a moral or lesson that can be learned from the story. Develop your story around one of the following morals, or create your own.

- Be careful what you wish for.
- The early bird catches the worm.
- It pays to be honest.
- Slow and steady wins the race.
- Show respect for others.

Name: ______________________ Date: ______________

The Moral of the Fable Scoring Rubric

Directions: Complete the self-assessment section of this rubric. Then, turn this in with your completed *The Moral of the Fable* activity. (4 means "I strongly agree." 1 means "I do not agree.")

Self-Assessment

	4	3	2	1
My sequence of events is clear and logical.				
Events in the fable lead to a moral (lesson learned).				
I chose words and phrases that paint a picture in the reader's mind.				
I end my fable with a moral that teaches a lesson.				

Additional comments: ______________________

____

____

Teacher Assessment

	4	3	2	1
The sequence of events is clear and logical.				
Events in the fable lead to a lesson learned.				
The writer chooses words and phrases that paint a picture in the reader's mind.				
The fable ends with a moral that teaches a lesson.				

Additional comments: ______________________

____

____

Rubric based on work by Lapp, D., B. Moss, M. Grant, & K. Johnson (2015)

A Cry for Help

Purpose

WHAT: Determine what the text states and to make logical inferences from it.

HOW: Write a conclusion to the story with solutions to the implied problem.

I CAN: I can understand a story and make logical inferences about the details.

Standards

- **Reading:** Determine central ideas or themes of a text and analyze their development; summarize the key supporting details and ideas.
- **Writing:** Provide a conclusion (in the form of an ending to the story) that follows from the narrated experiences or events.
- **Language:** Choose words and phrases to convey ideas precisely.

Performance Assessment

- Students will write conclusions with solutions to the problem that illustrate their understanding of the author's main message—the environment must be cared for.

Text Selection

- "A Cry for Help"
- Text is chunked into paragraphs.

Materials

- *A Cry for Help* passage, one copy per student (page 98; cryforhelp.pdf)
- *Main Ideas* activity (page 99)
- *Words Hold Meaning* activity (page 100)
- *You Be the Author* activity (page 101)
- *You Be the Author Scoring Rubric* (page 102)

Text-Dependent Questions (See pages 44–48 for more information.)

- What do you think the text is mostly about?
- Who is telling the story? How do you know?
- Where does the story take place?
- How does the author use color words to describe the setting and changes in the environment?
- What are the different tones the author shares in this story, and how do you know?
- Why does the author title this story in this way?

A Cry for Help *(cont.)*

Areas of Complexity

	Measure	Explanation
Quantitative	Lexile Level	710L
Qualitative	Meaning or Purpose	The text includes significant ideas with several levels of inferred meaning.
	Structure	The text organization is somewhat unconventional; may have two or more story lines and some shifts in time and point of view. The author contrasts life in clear vs. polluted oceans. The picture in the text supports it directly, but the image is only fully understood when the underlying message of the text is understood.
	Language Features	Language is accessible and familiar and can be determined through context clues.
Reader/ Task	Knowledge Demands	Experiences portrayed are common life experiences; everyday cultural or literary knowledge is required. Students must comprehend the author's underlying message to complete the performance task.

Text Synopsis

This story is about a girl who determines that the underwater environment is being destroyed and endangering life in the ocean. The author wants readers to know that they have roles in saving the environment. The language and illustrations help readers identify the problem and realize the author's main message.

Differentiation

Additional Support—You may need to cue students to look at the illustration on the bottom left of the text to identify key characters.

As needed, students can transfer their annotations to the *Words Hold Meaning* activity (page 100). This graphic organizer supports students as they reread the text.

Extension—Prompt students to convey the author's ideas more precisely by revising words and phrases from the text. This focuses students on a close study of the language of the text.

A Cry for Help *(cont.)*

Phase 1—Hitting the Surface

Who Reads	Annotations (See page 64.)		
❑ teacher	☑ highlight main points	☑ underline key details	☑ write questions
☑ students	❑ circle key vocabulary	❑ arrows for connections	❑ other: ______________

Procedure

1. Before students read, explain the purposes (from page 93).
2. Have students read the text independently. As they read, students will annotate their copies of the text to answer the question *What do you think the text is mostly about?*
3. Throughout each phase, as students read, circulate to observe their work, and provide scaffolds as guides for those who need assistance. These might be additional layered questions, prompts to encourage them to reflect on a certain part of the passage, or cues to remember related information. Insights you gain through this formative assessment can also influence the next questions to be asked of the whole group.
4. **Partners**—After students have read and annotated the text once, pairs can share their thinking as related to the initial question.
5. **Whole Class**—Regroup as a class, and display the text for all students. Ask students to share their responses to the question regarding what the text is about. Have them support their responses with their annotations. If possible, record student annotations on a displayed copy of the text.

Phase 2—Digging Deeper

Who Reads	Annotations (See page 64.)		
❑ teacher	❑ highlight main points	☑ underline key details	☑ write questions
☑ students	❑ circle key vocabulary	❑ arrows for connections	❑ other: ______________

Procedure

1. Before students read the text a second time, say, "Now, let's reread to answer the questions *Who is telling the story?* and *Where does the story take place?* Don't forget to mark the text with underlining, notes, and questions in the margins so you'll remember what you were thinking."

A Cry for Help *(cont.)*

Phase 2—Digging Deeper *(cont.)*

Procedure *(cont.)*

2. **Partners**—After reading, have student pairs share their annotations and think about the two text-dependent questions.
3. Next, students will dig deeper by returning to the text to contrast paragraphs 1 and 4. Have students annotate in response to the following question:
    - How does the author use color words to describe the setting and changes in the environment? (*cool colors in paragraph 1 and red as alarm/alert/stop/emergency in paragraph 4*)
4. **Whole Class**—Have students share with the whole group. Make sure to ask them to support their responses with their annotations. If possible, record student annotations on a displayed copy of the text.
5. If needed, ask additional layered/scaffolded questions, such as:
    - What words does the author use to describe the setting?
    - Is the setting described in a positive or negative way? What evidence tells you this?
6. Direct students to return to the text to compare the first half of the text (paragraphs 1–3) to the second half (paragraphs 4–5).
7. Ask, "How and where does the author's tone shift in this story?" If students need more layered/scaffolded questions, ask the following:
    - How are the two halves of the text different?
    - What language does the author use to let us know how Pena is feeling in paragraphs 1 through 3 compared to paragraphs 4 through 5?
8. **Partners**—Allow time for students to share their annotations and think with their partners.
9. **Whole Class**—Lead a whole class discussion where students support their responses with their annotations. If possible, record student annotations on a displayed copy of the text.

A Cry for Help *(cont.)*

Phase 3—Digging Even Deeper

Who Reads

- ☐ teacher
- ☑ students

Annotations (See page 64.)

- ☑ highlight main points
- ☐ underline key details
- ☑ write questions
- ☑ circle key vocabulary
- ☑ arrows for connections
- ☐ other: ____________

Procedure

1. Direct students to read the title again. Ask, "Why does the author title this story in this way?"
2. If students don't understand the title, ask the following questions:
   - Looking at the title and mermaid's quote in paragraph 4, what is the lesson the author is teaching us in this story? What is the problem the author is helping us to identify?
3. **Partners**—Ask students to share their annotations and thoughts with their partners.
4. **Whole Class**—Have students share their responses, supported by annotations, with the whole class. If possible, record student annotations on a displayed copy of the text.
5. Prior to the performance task, have students think about the passage individually by completing the *Main Ideas* activity (page 99).

Performance Assessment

1. Provide students with the performance task *You Be the Author* (page 101). Students can refer to their annotated "A Cry for Help" passages as they write endings that illustrate their understandings of the author's main message.
2. Explain that students' assignments will be graded based on the *You Be the Author Scoring Rubric* (page 102). The scoring rubric is for both students and teachers to guide and score work.

Name: ______________________ Date: ______________

A Cry for Help

1 Pena had been to this cove hundreds of times. But this time was different. The air was still, and when she ducked her head under the water, she saw a strange light she had never seen before. It was hard to tell what color it was. First it was pink, then blue, then green, but sometimes it seemed pure white. Off in the distance, she thought she heard someone singing, but that was impossible. *People can't sing underwater*, she thought.

2 Pena swam toward the light, making her way to the ledge where she often liked to rest.

3 Far away, she saw something move. It looked like a long tail. She had seen some small fish and luscious sea anemones in these waters, but never anything larger. And she knew it was crazy, but she almost felt as if whatever it was had been trying to lead her forward. Pena thrust her arms back into the clear waters and dove in after it. She swam deeper and farther than ever before.

4 Pena rounded the rocky bend and froze. As she looked around, she tried to remember to keep breathing. In front of her lay the entrance to an underground city. Garlands of mussel shells glittered around her. She could make out an intricate system of underwater caves in the distance. A girl dressed in a seaweed gown swam toward her. As she floated closer, Pena could see a dark green tail peeking out from under the seaweed. The girl stopped in front of Pena and held a strange red shell out to her. "Will you help us?" she asked.

5 Pena looked around to see a circle of mermaids gazing desperately at her. Pena didn't know it yet, but she was their only chance for survival.

Name:_____________________________ Date: ________________

Main Ideas

Directions: Using "A Cry for Help," answer the following questions.

1. What is the lesson the author is teaching us?

____

____

____

____

2. What color words are used by the author to help us know the environment has changed? What do the words signify?

____

____

____

____

3. How does the main character, Pena, feel at the end of the story? What will she most likely do now?

____

____

____

____

Name: ______________________ Date: ______________

Words Hold Meaning

Directions: Complete this chart as you read "A Cry for Help." Identify key word choices by the author and their significance to the story and your understanding of the story.

Author's Words	Meaning

Name: ______________________ Date: ____________

You Be the Author

Directions: Write an ending to "A Cry for Help" that illustrates your understanding of the author's main message. Make sure to consider the tone and events from the story.

Name: ______________________ Date: ______________

You Be the Author Scoring Rubric

Directions: Complete the self-assessment section of this rubric. Then, turn this in with your completed *You Be the Author* activity. (4 means "I strongly agree." 1 means "I do not agree.")

Self-Assessment

	4	3	2	1
I identified the problem in the story.				
My conclusion matches the author's writing style.				
The sequence of my conclusion is clear and logical.				
I chose words and phrases that clearly explain the author's message.				
My conclusion offers a solution for the problem.				

Additional comments: ______________________

____

____

Teacher Assessment

	4	3	2	1
The problem in the story is identified.				
The conclusion matches the author's writing style.				
The sequence of the conclusion is clear and logical.				
Words and phrases are used that clearly explain the author's message.				
The conclusion offers a solution for the problem.				

Additional comments: ______________________

____

____

Rubric based on work by Lapp, D., B. Moss, M. Grant, & K. Johnson (2015)

Slimy

Purpose

WHAT: Determine what the text states, and make logical inferences from it.

HOW: Write a speech that demonstrates understanding of the story's moral.

I CAN: I can make logical inferences to determine the moral of a story.

Standards

- **Reading:** Determine central ideas or themes of a text, and analyze their development; summarize key supporting details and ideas.
- **Writing:** Draw evidence from a literary or informational text.
- **Language:** Choose words and phrases to convey ideas precisely.

Performance Assessment

- Students will write speeches that demonstrate understanding of the story's moral.

Text Selection

- "Slimy"
- Text is chunked into paragraphs.

Materials

- *Slimy* passage, one copy per student (page 108; slimy.pdf)
- *Add 'Em Up* activity (page 109)
- *Clear as a Bell* activity (page 110)
- *The Award Goes to...* activity (page 111)
- *The Award Goes to... Scoring Rubric* (page 112)

Text-Dependent Questions (See pages 49–53 for more information.)

- What happens in the story?
- What details help us understand the moral?
- How does the moral develop throughout the story?
- What do the idioms in paragraph 10 tell the reader?
- Why did the author include the idioms in paragraph 10?
- How does the author guide the reader to understand Maria's personality?

Slimy *(cont.)*

Areas of Complexity

	Measure	Explanation
Quantitative	Lexile Level	790L
Qualitative	Meaning or Purpose	The story moral is explicitly stated; however, it invites deeper questioning.
	Structure	The structure of the passage is conventional and chronological.
	Language Features	The language is descriptive and sometimes idiomatic.
Reader/Task	Knowledge Demands	The text requires understanding of the roles of mascots and sports players. It also requires students to have background knowledge about idioms before completing this lesson. Students must analyze the main character to complete the performance task.

Text Synopsis

Maria tries out for the football team, but instead of landing a position on the field, she is chosen to be team mascot. With her mother's help, she decides to make the best of it and become a star mascot.

Differentiation

Additional Support—The *Clear as a Bell* (page 108) graphic organizer can help students organize and share their thinking as they define the similes used to describe how Maria feels.

Extension—Students make inferences about Coach based on his actions in the story.

Slimy *(cont.)*

Phase 1—Hitting the Surface

Who Reads

- ❑ teacher
- ☑ students

Annotations (See page 64.)

- ☑ highlight main points
- ☑ underline key details
- ❑ write questions
- ❑ circle key vocabulary
- ❑ arrows for connections
- ❑ other: ______________

Procedure

1. Before students read, explain the purposes (from page 103).
2. Have students read the text independently. As they read, have students annotate their copies of the text to answer the question *What happens in this story?*
3. Throughout each phase, as students read, circulate to observe their work, and provide scaffolds as guides for those who need assistance. These might be additional layered questions, prompts to encourage them to reflect on a certain part of the passage, or cues to remember related information. Insights you gain through this formative assessment can also influence the next questions to be asked of the whole group.
4. **Partners**—After students have read and annotated the text once, pairs can share their thinking as related to the initial question.
5. **Whole Class**—Regroup as a class, and display the text for all students. Ask students to share their responses to the question regarding what the text is about. Have them support their responses with their annotations. If possible, record student annotations on a displayed copy of the text.

Slimy *(cont.)*

Phase 2—Digging Deeper

Who Reads

- ☐ teacher
- ☑ students

Annotations (See page 64.)

- ☑ highlight main points
- ☑ underline key details
- ☐ write questions
- ☐ circle key vocabulary
- ☑ arrows for connections
- ☐ other: ______________

Procedure

1. Before students read the text a second time, say, "Now, let's reread to find out the following: *What details help us understand the moral? How does the moral develop throughout the story?* Don't forget to mark the text with underlining, notes, and questions in the margins so you'll remember what you were thinking."
2. **Partners**—After reading, have student pairs share their annotations and thoughts about the two text-dependent questions.
3. If needed, ask additional layered/scaffolded questions, such as:
   - Look at the first sentence of the ninth paragraph. Does that sentence give us a clue to the moral of the story? (*Yes, it tells us that Maria is disappointed but hints that good things might happen anyway.*)
   - Look at the second sentence of the ninth paragraph. Does that sentence give us a clue to the moral of the story? (*No, it just talks about making the costume.*)
   - Look at the third sentence of the ninth paragraph. Does that sentence give us a clue to the moral of the story? (*Yes, it shows that Maria can overcome her disappointment and do something exciting.*)
4. **Whole Class**—Have students share with the whole group. Make sure to ask them to support their responses with their annotations. If possible, record student annotations on a displayed copy of the text.
5. **Partners**—Allow time for students to share their annotations and thoughts with their partners. Direct partners to work together to complete the *Add 'Em Up* activity (page 109).
6. **Whole Class**—Use students' responses on the *Add 'Em Up* activity to lead a whole class discussion of the moral of the story.

Slimy *(cont.)*

Phase 3—Digging Even Deeper

Who Reads

☐ teacher

☑ students

Annotations (See page 64.)

☐ highlight main points ☑ underline key details ☑ write questions

☑ circle key vocabulary ☐ arrows for connections ☐ other: ____________

Procedure

1. Direct students to read paragraph 10. Ask students, "What does it mean to be as brave as a lion, as smart as a fox, and as happy as a lark?"
2. **Partners**—Ask students to share their annotations and thoughts with their partners.
3. If needed, ask additional layered/scaffolded questions, such as:
   - What are lions associated with?
   - What are foxes associated with?
   - What are larks associated with?
4. **Whole Class**—As a class, discuss the text-dependent question *Why did the author include the series of similes in paragraph 10?*
5. You may choose to have students record their understanding of similes with the *Clear as a Bell* activity (page 110).
6. Prior to the performance task, have students read the text again to mark text that describes the main character, Maria. *How does the author guide the reader to understand Maria's personality?*

Performance Assessment

1. Assign the performance task *The Award Goes to...* (page 111).
2. Explain that students' assignments will be graded based on the *The Award Goes to... Scoring Rubric* (page 112). The scoring rubric is for both students and teachers to guide and score work.

Name: ______________________ Date: ______________

Slimy

1 It was time for tryouts, and Maria knew just what team she wanted to be on.

2 "You're trying out for the football team? But, honey, you play soccer," her mom said.

3 "The best part about soccer is kicking, so I want to be the kicker on the football team," Maria answered.

4 Following tryouts, the coach posted the team roster. Maria was ecstatic when she saw her name, but her heart sank when she saw the word Slimy next to it. Maria was confused.

5 "What position does a slimy play?" Maria asked a player standing nearby.

6 "Slimy's not a position," he answered with a laugh. "Slimy the Snail is our mascot. Slimy is just some kid in a snail costume who runs around waving at the crowd."

7 All Maria could think to say was, "Our mascot is a snail?" She turned before he could see her tears.

8 Later, she told her mother the news.

9 "I know you're disappointed, but sometimes watching the mascot can be more fun than watching the players," her mom said. "Why don't we make a new snail costume? You'll be the best middle school mascot of all time!"

10 At the first game, when Maria walked onto the field in her colorful new costume, the crowd erupted with chants of "Slimy! Slimy!" She danced, led cheers, and ran through the bleachers. At halftime, Maria grabbed a football and asked a cheerleader to hold the ball upright on the field. She ran up and kicked the ball as hard as she could, sending it sailing between the goalposts. The crowd cheered wildly, and Maria felt like a superstar. She might have been dressed like a snail, but she felt as brave as a lion, as smart as a fox, and as happy as a lark. After the game, Coach said, "Maria, I saw your great kick. I think you should be on the team after all!"

11 "Thanks, Coach," she said. "But I think I'll just work on being the best middle school mascot of all time!"

Name:_______________________________________ Date: ___________________

Add 'Em Up

Directions: Choose a moral from the box. "Add" together details from "Slimy" to support the moral.

detail ____

detail ____

detail ____

+ detail ____

---

moral ____

Possible Morals
Disappointments can become triumphs.
Even small roles can be exciting.
There are different ways to be successful.
Your attitude can make a negative situation positive.
Talent always shines through.

Name: ______________________________ Date: ________________

Clear as a Bell

Directions: Define the three similes from paragraph 10 of "Slimy." Explain what the simile means, then explain what it tells you about Maria.

Simile	Meaning	Maria

Simile	Meaning	Maria

Simile	Meaning	Maria

Name:______________________________ Date: ______________

The Award Goes to...

Directions: Create a team award to give Maria at the end of the season. The award should match the moral of the story. Give the award a name. Then, write a speech for Coach that describes the award and why Maria deserves it.

____

Eastern Middle School

Snails Football Team

______________________ Award

Coach's Speech

____

____

____

____

____

____

____

Name: ______________________________ Date: ________________

The Award Goes to... Scoring Rubric

Directions: Complete the self-assessment section of this rubric. Then, turn this in with your completed *The Award Goes to...* activity. (4 means "I strongly agree." 1 means "I do not agree.")

Self-Assessment

	4	3	2	1
The name of my award matches the moral of the story.				
My description of the award matches the moral of the story.				
I explained why Maria deserves the award.				
I described Maria accurately.				

Additional comments: ______________________________

____

____

____

Teacher Assessment

	4	3	2	1
The name of the award matches the moral of the story.				
The description of the award matches the moral the story.				
The writer explains why Maria deserves the award.				
The writer describes Maria accurately.				

Additional comments: ______________________________

____

____

____

Rubric based on work by Lapp, D., B. Moss, M. Grant, & K. Johnson (2015)

My Life: The Fruit Fly's Story

Purpose

WHAT: Comprehend content presented in diverse formats.

HOW: Use the unusual format of the text to write a new story.

I CAN: I can comprehend and use an unusual story format.

Standards

- **Reading:** Describe the logical connection between particular sentences and paragraphs in a text.
- **Writing:** Introduce a topic and group related information together.
- **Language:** Choose words and phrases for effect.
- **Science:** Describe that organisms have unique and diverse life cycles but that all have in common birth, growth, reproduction, and death.

Performance Assessment

- Students will use fictional time line formats to present information about a bat's life in entertaining ways.

Text Selection

- "My Life: The Fruit Fly's Story"
- Text is divided by days of the fruit fly's life.

Materials

- *My Life: The Fruit Fly's Story* passage, one copy per student (page 118; fruitflysstory.pdf)
- *What Do You Know?* activity (page 119)
- *No Nonsense* activity (page 120)
- *My Life: The Bat's Story* activity (page 121)
- *My Life: The Bat's Story Scoring Rubric* (page 122)

Text-Dependent Questions (See pages 40–43 for more information.)

- What is the story about?
- How does the time line of the story communicate factual information about fruit flies?
- How does the fruit fly describe the inside of the egg?
- How is the larva stage described?
- What can be concluded from days 15 through 39?
- What was the cause of the fruit fly's death?
- What text features help the reader organize the facts in the story?
- Why does the fruit fly ask if we "get it" at the end of Day 11?
- How is the text both literary and informative.

My Life: The Fruit Fly's Story *(cont.)*

Areas of Complexity

	Measure	Explanation
Quantitative	Lexile Level	130L
Qualitative	Meaning or Purpose	The text uses an entertaining story to detail the life of a fruit fly.
	Structure	The text is organized by the days of the fruit fly's life, from Day 1 when the fruit fly is an egg to Day 40 when the fruit fly dies. The text combines fiction elements with nonfiction facts.
	Language Features	Scientific vocabulary is presented, and supportive context clues are provided.
Reader/Task	Knowledge Demands	While words such as *larvae* and *pupae* may be unfamiliar to students, context clues help with understanding. Students must blend fiction elements and nonfiction facts to complete the performance assessment.

Text Synopsis

The story is about a fruit fly that tells about the stages of her life from Day 1 in the egg to Day 40 when she dies of old age.

Differentiation

Additional Support—You may need to assist students in understanding the nature of a fictional story versus a fictional story that conveys factual information.

Extension—Instruct students to present information about a fruit fly's life as if broadcasting it on a scientific television show.

My Life: The Fruit Fly's Story *(cont.)*

Phase 1—Hitting the Surface

Who Reads	Annotations (See page 63.)		
☐ teacher	☑ highlight main points	☐ underline key details	☑ write questions
☑ students	☑ circle key vocabulary	☐ arrows for connections	☑ other: draw visualization

Procedure

1. Before students read, explain the purposes (from page 113).
2. Have students read the text independently. As they read, have students annotate their copies of the text to answer the question *What is the story about?*
3. Throughout each phase, as students read, circulate to observe their work, and provide scaffolds as guides for those who need assistance. These might be additional layered questions, prompts to encourage them to reflect on a certain part of the passage, or cues to remember related information. Insights you gain through this formative assessment can also influence the next questions to be asked of the whole group.
4. **Partners**—After students have read and annotated the text once, pairs can share their thinking related to the initial question.
5. **Whole Class**—Regroup as a class, and display the text for all students. Ask students to share their responses to the question regarding what the story is about. Have them support their responses with their annotations. If possible, record student annotations on a displayed copy of the text.

Phase 2—Digging Deeper

Who Reads	Annotations (See page 63.)		
☐ teacher	☑ highlight main points	☑ underline key details	☐ write questions
☑ students	☐ circle key vocabulary	☑ arrows for connections	☑ other: notes in the margin

Procedure

1. Before students read the text a second time, ask, "What does the author tell us about the fruit fly?" Encourage students to refer to the text in their responses.
2. Then say, "Now, let's reread to answer the question *How does the author describe the fruit fly's life?* Don't forget to mark the text with underlining and write notes in the margins so you'll remember what you were thinking."

My Life: The Fruit Fly's Story *(cont.)*

Phase 2—Digging Deeper *(cont.)*

Procedure *(cont.)*

3. If needed, ask additional layered/scaffolded questions, such as:
    - How does the fruit fly describe the inside of the egg?
    - How is the larva stage described?
    - What can be concluded from days 15 through 39?
    - What was the cause of the fruit fly's death?
4. **Partners**—After students have read and annotated the text, pairs can share their thinking about the stages of the fly's life.
5. Ask students to return to the text and use the illustration to answer the same question.
6. If needed, ask additional layered/scaffolded questions, such as:
    - How is the illustration helpful?
    - How are the illustration and the text connected?
    - What can be learned from the illustration that is not included in the text?
7. **Whole Class**—Regroup as a class, and display the text for all students. Ask students to share their responses to the question regarding the life stages of a fruit fly. Have them support their responses with their annotations. If possible, record student annotations on a displayed copy of the text.
8. You may choose to have students complete the *What Do You Know?* activity (page 119) to record their understanding of the passage.

My Life: The Fruit Fly's Story *(cont.)*

Phase 3—Digging Even Deeper

Who Reads	Annotations (See page 63.)		
☑ teacher	☐ highlight main points	☐ underline key details	☐ write questions
☑ students	☐ circle key vocabulary	☐ arrows for connections	☑ other: mark fact and fiction

Procedure

1. Read Day 11 aloud. Lead students to appreciate the joke by asking:
   - Why does the fruit fly ask if we "get it" at the end of Day 11?
   - What words in "time sure flies" have double meanings?
   - Why is it funny for a fruit fly to use the word *fly*?
2. Ask students to review their annotations and discuss the text-dependent question *How is the text both literary and informative?* Students will mark the facts and the fictional elements as they reread the passage.
3. If needed, ask additional layered/scaffolded questions, such as:
   - What facts are included in the story?
   - What about the story makes it obviously fictional?
4. **Whole Class**—Regroup as a class, and display the text for all students. Ask students to share the literary and informational elements of the story. If possible, record student annotations on a displayed copy of the text.
5. Discuss the effects of the fiction elements on the reader. If needed, ask additional layered/scaffolded questions, such as:
   - How do the fiction elements interrupt or enhance the flow of facts?
   - What text features help the reader organize the facts in the story?
6. **Partners**—Ask partners to mark the organizational features of the text to answer the text-dependent question *What text features help the reader organize the facts in the story?*
7. Prior to the performance task, have students think about the passage individually by completing the *No Nonsense* activity (page 120).

Performance Assessment

1. Assign the performance task *My Life: The Bat's Story* (page 121).
2. Explain that students' assignments will be graded based on the *My Life: The Bat's Story Scoring Rubric* (page 122). The scoring rubric is for both students and teachers to guide and score work.

Name: ______________________ Date: ______________

My Life: The Fruit Fly's Story

1 Day 1: Hello? Hello? Is anyone there? Something strange is happening. This sounds crazy, I know, but I think I'm an egg. Yes, yes, that's right—an egg. It's very soft and squishy in here, and it smells like rotten fruit.

2 Day 2: I was right! I was an egg! And now I'm kind of wormy. There are a lot of other kids around me, too. One kid said we are larvae. I'm pretty hungry, and this rotten fruit tastes really good.

3 Day 3: Still wormy. Still eating.

4 Day 4: Yep, still eating.

5 Day 5: All I can say is this rotten fruit is delicious!

6 Day 6: Hey, something has come over me. The kid next to me says we're pupae now. We're starting to grow legs and wings. Cool!

7 Day 7: Still growing.

8 Day 8: Still growing.

9 Day 9: Still growing.

10 Day 10: Ha! I've got six legs and two wings. And guess what? I hatched. That's right. I'm all grown up!

11 Day 11: Good news! I got married today! Now, I'm a newlywed. Time sure flies! (Get it?!)

12 Day 12: You know what? I love to fly! I crash into walls, but still, flying is fun! Zip, zoom, crash. Zip, zoom, crash. Look at me go!

13 Day 13: I laid some eggs today. I'm going to be a mom!

14 Day 14: I'd better get ready. The kids are coming soon.

15 Day 15: The kids have arrived! Now, I'm a mom!

16 Day 21: Now, I'm a grandma!

17 Day 27: Now, I'm a great-grandma!

18 Day 33: Now, I'm a great-great-grandma!

19 Day 39: Now, I'm a great-great-great grandma!

20 Day 40: Now, I'm . . .

21 Editor's Note: Our beloved Grandma Fruit Fly died today of very old age. She was 40 days old. May she rest in peace.

Name:______________________ Date: ______________

What Do You Know?

Directions: Use the text "My Life: The Fruit Fly's Story" to answer the questions.

1. How is the larvae stage different from the pupae stage?

2. Is the fruit fly male or female? Identify four pieces of evidence from the text.

3. How does the fruit fly feel about its growing family? Identify evidence from the text.

Name: ______________________ Date: ______________

No Nonsense

Directions: Take the fun fictional elements out of "My Life: The Fruit Fly's Story" to create a simple list of fruit fly facts. Use information from the text and the illustration to describe each stage of a fruit fly's life.

Egg Stage

____

____

Larvae Stage

____

____

Pupae Stage

____

____

Adult Stage

____

____

Name: ______________________ Date: ______________

My Life: The Bat's Story

Directions: Use the facts about bats to create a first person story similar to "My Life: The Fruit Fly's Story." Use a fictional time line format. Choose words and phrases that will help your reader learn the facts and be entertained by the fictional ideas.

Facts about Bats

- Bats are active at night.
- Bats sleep during the day.
- Bats live in large groups called *colonies*.
- Bats use sonar to "see" in the dark.

Name: ______________________ Date: ______________

My Life: The Bat's Story Scoring Rubric

Directions: Complete the self-assessment section of this rubric. Then, turn this in with your completed *My Life: The Bat's Story* activity. (4 means "I strongly agree." 1 means "I do not agree.")

Self-Assessment

	4	3	2	1
I wrote my story in a fictional time line format.				
I included the facts about bats.				
I included fictional elements.				
I chose words and phrases that helped my reader learn the facts.				
I chose words and phrases that helped my reader be entertained.				

Additional comments: ______________________

____

____

Teacher Assessment

	4	3	2	1
The story is written in a fictional time line format.				
The writer included facts about bats.				
The writer included fictional elements.				
The writer chose words and phrases that helped the reader learn the facts.				
The writer chose words and phrases that helped the reader be entertained.				

Additional comments: ______________________

____

____

Rubric based on work by Lapp, D., B. Moss, M. Grant, & K. Johnson (2015)

From 613 King Street to Room 4F

Purposes

WHAT: Identify the narrator's point of view.

WHAT: Determine the meaning of figurative language in the text.

HOW: Use the same narrator's point of view and figurative language to write a narrative.

I CAN: I can interpret and use point of view and figurative language.

Standards

- **Reading:** Compare and contrast the point of view from which different stories are narrated, including the difference between first and third person narrations.
- **Writing:** Introduce a topic or text clearly, state an opinion, and create an organizational structure in which related ideas are grouped to support the writer's purpose.
- **Language:** Choose words and phrases to convey ideas precisely.

Performance Assessment

- Students will use first person point of view to express personal opinions in narrative writing.

Text Selection

- "From 613 King Street to Room 4F"
- Text is chunked by paragraph.

Materials

- *From 613 King Street to Room 4F* passage, one copy per student (page 128; kingstreet.pdf)
- *Who's Talking?* activity (page 129)
- *In My Head* activity (page 130)
- *Another Point of View* activity (page 131)
- *Another Point of View Scoring Rubric* (page 132)

Text-Dependent Questions (See pages 44–48 for more information.)

- What happens in the story?
- What words does the narrator use to describe how she feels at different points in her story?
- What happened in the past? What happens in the present?
- What is the difference between the narrator's living situation before and now?
- What can we infer about the other characters based on the information from the narrator?
- What do we know about the narrator that we would not know if it were written from another point of view?

From 613 King Street to Room 4F *(cont.)*

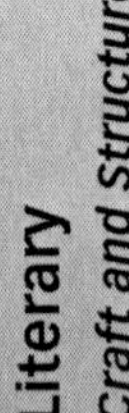

Areas of Complexity

	Measure	Explanation
Quantitative	Lexile Level	680L
Qualitative	Meaning or Purpose	The purpose of the text is to communicate that money and "stuff" are not the most important things in life.
	Structure	The narrator begins by telling how her life used to be and how it is now. Then, she explains more about her current life and focuses on the positive.
	Language Features	Language is accessible and easy to understand.
Reader/Task	Knowledge Demands	The text assumes understanding of family life and different kinds of living environments. Students must understand first person point of view to complete the performance task.

Text Synopsis

The story is told by a young narrator who describes her life before and after her father loses his job. Though the life change was difficult, she looks for the positive aspects of her life now.

Differentiation

Additional Support—To help students make connections to the text, allow them to share their life and home situations. Be sure to remind students to return to the text when they seek response to text-dependent questions.

Students can transfer their annotations to the *Who's Talking?* activity (page 129) as needed. This chart supports students' understanding of figurative language used in the text.

Extension—Instruct students to generate their own questions about the text and ask their partners these questions. Guide students to include higher level questions.

From 613 King Street to Room 4F *(cont.)*

Phase 1—Hitting the Surface

Who Reads	Annotations (See page 64.)		
☐ teacher	☑ highlight main points	☑ underline key details	☑ write questions
☑ students	☐ circle key vocabulary	☐ arrows for connections	☐ other: ________

Procedure

1. Before students read, explain the purposes (from page 123).
2. Have students read the text independently. As they read, have students annotate their copies of the text to answer the question *What is the story about?*
3. Throughout each phase, as students read, circulate to observe their work, and provide scaffolds as guides for those who need assistance. These might be additional layered questions, prompts to encourage them to reflect on a certain part of the passage, or cues to remember related information. Insights you gain through this formative assessment can also influence the next questions to be asked of the whole group.
4. **Partners**—After students have read and annotated the text once, pairs can share their thinking related to the initial question.
5. **Whole Class**—Regroup as a class, and display the text for all students. Ask students to share their responses to the question regarding what the story is about. Have them support their responses with their annotations. If possible, record student annotations on a displayed copy of the text.

From 613 King Street to Room 4F *(cont.)*

Phase 2—Digging Deeper

Who Reads

☐ teacher

☑ students

Annotations (See page 64.)

☐ highlight main points ☐ underline key details ☑ write questions

☑ circle key vocabulary ☐ arrows for connections ☐ other: ______

Procedure

1. Before students read the text a second time, say, "Now, let's reread and focus on the sequence of events. What happened in the past? What happens in the present? Annotate the text with *then* and *now* to clarify whether events happened in the past or present."
2. **Partners**—After marking the text with *then* and *now*, direct partners to read the text together to learn more about the narrator. Say, "Who is telling the story? What words does the narrator use to describe how she feels at different points in the story?"
3. If needed, ask additional layered/scaffolded questions, such as:
   - What does the narrator tell you about her life?
   - What is the difference between the narrator's living situation before and now?
   - What can be learned from the photo that is not communicated in the text?
4. **Whole Class**—Regroup as a class, and discuss the details that the author only hints at. What can you infer about the narrator from the following:
   - *Maybe it will help you.* (paragraph one)
   - *I know I don't really have anything to complain about.* (paragraph five)
5. Direct students to complete the *In My Head* activity (page 130) to sum up the positive and negative elements in the narrator's life.

From 613 King Street to Room 4F *(cont.)*

Phase 3—Digging Even Deeper

Who Reads	Annotations (See page 64.)		
❑ teacher	❑ highlight main points	❑ underline key details	☑ write questions
☑ students	☑ circle key vocabulary	❑ arrows for connections	❑ other: ____________

Procedure

1. Prompt students to review previous discussions by asking, "Who tells the story? Who is the narrator? From what point of view is the story told?"
2. Ask students to return to the text to note other characters in the story. What can we infer about the other characters based on the information from the narrator?
3. **Partners**—After students have read and annotated the text, pairs can share their inferences about the minor characters.
4. **Whole Class**—Regroup as a class, and display the text for all students. Ask students to share their thoughts. If possible, record student annotations on a displayed copy of the text.
5. Discuss the text-dependent question *What do we know about the narrator that we would not know if it were written from another point of view?* You may choose to have partners explore this question further.

Performance Assessment

1. Assign the performance task *Another Point of View* (page 131).
2. Explain that students' assignments will be graded based on the *Another Point of View Scoring Rubric* (page 132). The scoring rubric is for both students and teachers to guide and score work.

Name: ______________________ Date: ____________

From 613 King Street to Room 4F

1 "I'm going to sound really shallow when I say this, but I'll just say it anyway. Maybe it will help you," I whisper. "Because I get it—this is hard." I wrapped my arm around my friend Taylor and continued.

2 "My family used to be wealthy, but not anymore, and I can't stand it. At the beginning of the year, my dad lost his job. He got paid unemployment for a while, but there's no more money left now."

3 "I know he's working hard, and it's not like he's not taking steps to make things better, but all he can find are part-time jobs, so we don't have money to do anything besides just survive. We can afford our food, but that's it. We used to have a house. I used to have my own room with toys, games, a TV, and a computer. Now, I live in a dirty motel."

4 "My mom took a job at my school to help pay the bills. There was a time when I didn't even know we had bills. I just played and went to school."

5 "My parents say this will pass. We just have to sacrifice for a little while. I know I don't really have anything to complain about. We may not live in a nice house anymore, but we have a place to live, and we have one another. We have dinner together every day. Mom and I come home and meet Dad before he goes to work. I know kids at school who have all kinds of money, but they never have dinner with their parents."

6 "It's hard not having all the stuff other kids do, but I love my parents. I love them with or without stuff, and I love them wherever we live. No amount of money can change that."

Name:______________________________ Date: ______________

Who's Talking?

Directions: List words that signal whether the story is told in first person point of view (I, me, my), second person point of view (you, your), or third person point of view (she, her).

This story is told in ____________________ point of view.

These words signal the point of view.

______________________ ______________________

______________________ ______________________

______________________ ______________________

Name: ______________________________ Date: ____________________

In My Head

Directions: This story is told from the narrator's point of view. We get to know her thoughts and feelings, not just the events. Inside the character silhouette, write things that happen in the narrator's mind. Outside of the character's silhouette, write the events that happen outside of the narrator's mind.

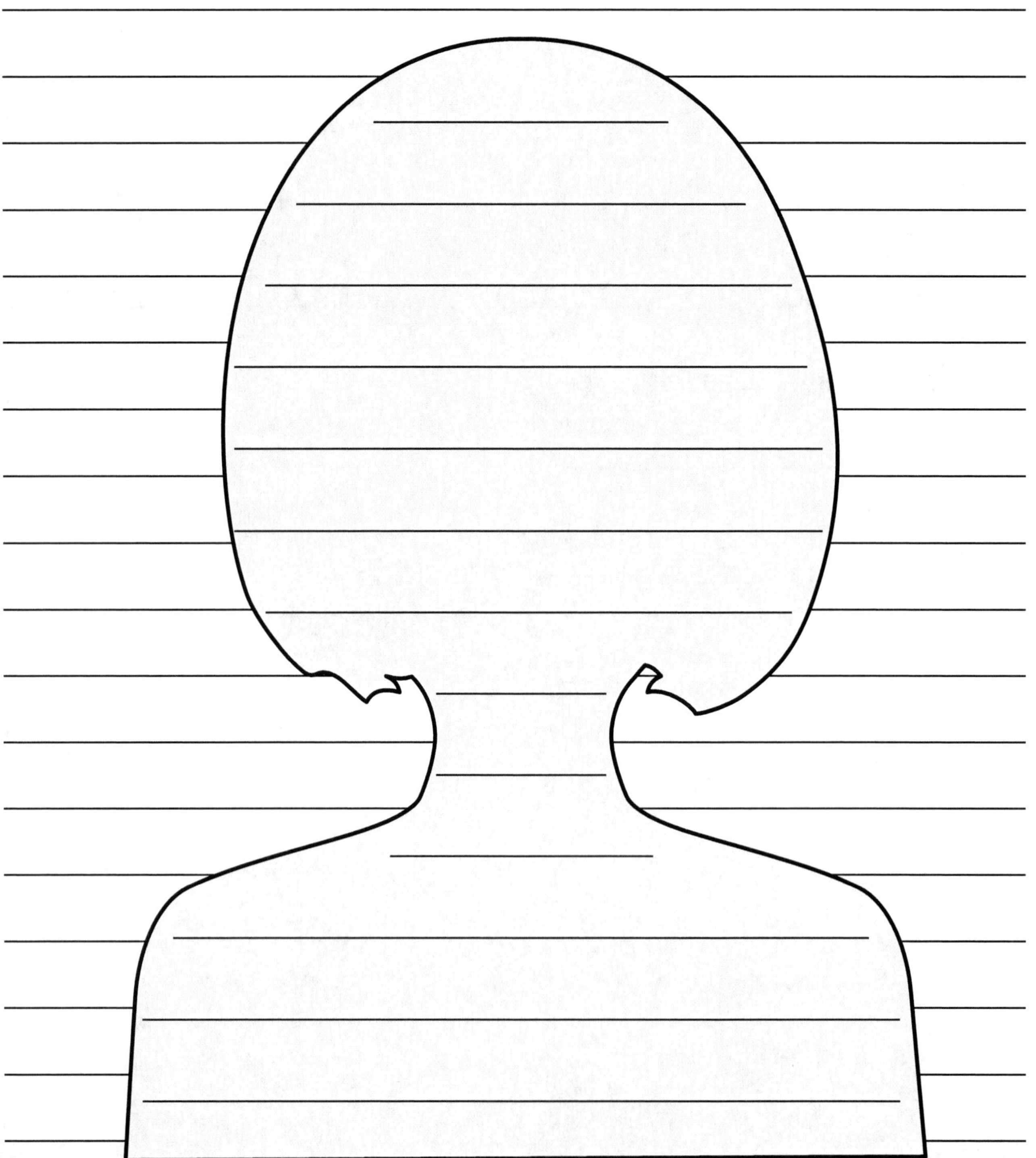

Name:______________________________ Date: ______________

Another Point of View

Directions: Decide whether the author's choice to tell the story from the narrator's point of view was a good choice. Write a paragraph to support your decision with examples from the text. Explain what details could be added or lost if the story were told from the point of view of another character.

Name: ______________________ Date: ______________

Another Point of View Scoring Rubric

Directions: Complete the self-assessment section of this rubric. Then, turn this in with your completed *Another Point of View* activity. (4 means "I strongly agree." 1 means "I do not agree.")

Self-Assessment

	4	3	2	1
I stated my opinion clearly.				
I explained the details that could be added or that would be lost if the point of view were changed.				
I chose strong examples from the text to support my opinion about the point of view.				

Additional comments: ______________________

____

____

Teacher Assessment

	4	3	2	1
The writer stated an opinion clearly.				
The writer explained the details that could be added or that would be lost if the point of view were changed.				
The writer chose strong examples from the text to support the opinion about the point of view.				

Additional comments: ______________________

____

____

Rubric based on work by Lapp, D., B. Moss, M. Grant, & K. Johnson (2015)

The Pup

Purpose

WHAT: Analyze how dialog and writer's craft shape meaning or tone in a story.

HOW: Extend the story with additional dialog.

I CAN: I can analyze dialog and writer's craft.

Standards

- **Reading:** Describe the overall structure of a text.
- **Writing:** Use narrative techniques such as dialog, description, and pacing.
- **Language:** Choose punctuation for effect.

Performance Assessment

- Students will write dialogs between two characters using word choice and punctuation to get reactions from readers.

Text Selection

- "The Pup"
- Text is chunked by paragraph.

Materials

- *The Pup* passage, one copy per student (page 138; thepup.pdf)
- *Reading Reactions* activity (page 139)
- *Author's Toolbox* activity (page 140)
- *May I Speak to the Manager?* activity (page 141)
- *May I Speak to the Manager? Scoring Rubric* (page 142)

Text-Dependent Questions (See pages 49–53 for more information.)

- What is this story about?
- What reactions does the author seem to want from the reader?
- What words indicate whether the dad was truly confused or just pretending to be confused?
- How does the author use description to help the reader understand the sequence of events?
- What elements of writer's craft did the author choose for this passage?

The Pup *(cont.)*

Areas of Complexity

	Measure	Explanation
Quantitative	Lexile Level	810L
Qualitative	Meaning or Purpose	The story relies on word confusion for its humor, which increases complexity.
	Structure	The narrative structure is chronological and includes repetition to increase humor.
	Language Features	Most language is conventional, but there are several pieces of word play based on the word *pup*.
Reader/ Task	Knowledge Demands	Information necessary for understanding the text is largely present in the text. However, for the associated activities, familiarity with story genres is essential. Students must use elements of dialog to complete the performance assessment.

Text Synopsis

When a boy asks for a pup, his dad does not quite understand. Instead of a cute, young dog, the dad brings his son a variety of baby animals (a bat, a hedgehog, and even a shark) that are also called pups.

Differentiation

Additional Support—You may need to review or help students remember and list text structures and elements of writer's craft like repetition and word choice.

Extension—Encourage students to experiment with repetition, word choice, dialog, and dynamic punctuation in the own writing.

The Pup *(cont.)*

Phase 1—Hitting the Surface

Who Reads

- ☐ teacher
- ☑ students

Annotations (See page 64.)

- ☑ highlight main points
- ☑ underline key details
- ☑ write questions
- ☐ circle key vocabulary
- ☐ arrows for connections
- ☐ other: ____________

Procedure

1. Before students read, explain the purposes (from page 133).
2. Have students read the text independently. As they read, have students annotate their copies of the text to answer the question *What is this story about?*
3. Throughout each phase, as students read, circulate to observe their work, and provide scaffolds as guides for those who need assistance. These might be additional layered questions, prompts to encourage them to reflect on a certain part of the passage, or cues to remember related information. Insights you gain through this formative assessment can also influence the next questions to be asked of the whole group.
4. **Partners**—After students have read and annotated the text once, pairs can share their thinking related to the initial question.
5. **Whole Class**—Regroup as a class, and display the text for all students. Ask students to summarize the story. Have them support their responses with their annotations. If possible, record student annotations on a displayed copy of the text.

Phase 2—Digging Deeper

Who Reads

- ☑ teacher
- ☐ students

Annotations (See page 64.)

- ☐ highlight main points
- ☐ underline key details
- ☑ write questions
- ☐ circle key vocabulary
- ☑ arrows for connections
- ☑ other: draw reaction faces in the margin (surprise, worry, humor)

Procedure

1. Ask students to describe the type of sentences used in the story. If they do not do so on their own, guide them to notice the large amount of dialog.

The Pup *(cont.)*

Phase 2—Digging Deeper *(cont.)*

Procedure *(cont.)*

2. Explain to students that a passage with this much dialog would benefit from being read aloud. Direct students to make doodles of faces in the margin to record their own reactions as they listen to you read the text aloud. You may need to model drawing a surprised face, a worried face, and/or a laughing face. Students can add precise words to label their doodle faces.
3. As you read, use your voice to emphasize the surprise, the tension, and the silliness in the passage.
4. **Partners**—Direct partners to share their annotations and discuss the tone or feel created by the author's word choice.
5. If needed, ask additional layered/scaffolded questions, such as:
   - How did you feel when the boy opened the first box? Which words helped create that feeling?
   - How did you feel when the dad said he thought the boy wanted a baby bat? Which words helped create that feeling?
   - How did you feel when the dad brought home a bigger box? Which words helped create that feeling?
   - How did you feel when the dad said other baby animals are called pups? Which words helped create that feeling?
   - How did you feel when the truck with the water tank pulled up to the house? Which words helped create that feeling?
6. **Whole Class**—Regroup as a class, and discuss reactions to the text. Ask the question *What reactions does the author seem to want from the reader?*
7. Ask the text-dependent question *What words indicate whether the dad was truly confused or just pretending to be confused?* If needed, guide students to:
   - "...my dad instructed with a grin." (paragraph 4)
   - "Isn't that what you wanted?" (paragraph 6)
   - "A dog? Why didn't you say so?" (paragraph 11)
   - "I honestly didn't know which kind you wanted." (paragraph 11)
8. To further the discussion, you may choose to have students read the dad's dialog earnestly and sarcastically.
9. Direct students to complete the *Reading Reactions* activity (page 139) to record their strongest reactions to the passage.

The Pup *(cont.)*

Phase 3—Digging Even Deeper

Who Reads

- ❑ teacher
- ☑ students

Annotations (See page 64.)

- ❑ highlight main points
- ❑ underline key details
- ☑ write questions
- ☑ circle key vocabulary
- ❑ arrows for connections
- ❑ other: ____________

Procedure

1. Review the previous discussions by asking, "What is the author's purpose with this story?" Encourage students to reference specific examples from the text in their responses. Then say, "Let's take a look at the text structures and writer's crafts she uses to accomplish this."
2. Ask students to identify the text structures and writer's craft they notice in the text. If needed, ask additional layered/scaffolded questions, such as:
   - What text structures did the author choose for this passage?
   - How did the author use the writer's crafts of repetition and word choice for this passage?
   - Other than periods, what punctuation do you notice?
   - How many times is the word *pup* (or *puppy*) used?
   - What words hold a lot of drama and emotion?
3. **Partners**—Have partners choose one of the text structures or the writer's crafts of repetition and word choice listed by the whole class. Partners will reread the text and focus on their chosen element. They will mark all the examples of their chosen element in the passage and prepare to share which example was most effective in getting a reaction from the reader.
4. **Whole Class**—Regroup as a class, and display the text for all students. Ask partners to share their examples of effective structure or craft. Students may also choose to discuss elements that were not as effective.
5. Have students complete the *Author's Toolbox* activity (page 140) to record their understanding of the text structure and writer's craft.

Performance Assessment

1. Assign the performance task *May I Speak to the Manager?* (page 141).
2. Explain that students' assignments will be graded based on the *May I Speak to the Manager? Scoring Rubric* (page 142). The scoring rubric is for both students and teachers to guide and score work.

Name: ______________________ Date: ______________

The Pup

1 "Dad, can I have a pup? I promise I'll feed it, and walk it, and take 100 percent excellent care of it," I said.

2 "Pups are a lot of responsibility," my dad replied.

3 "I can be responsible," I said, giving him my best puppy dog eyes and hoping he would be impressed.

4 Days later, my dad walked in with a box, and I wondered if he had changed his mind. "Open it," my dad instructed with a grin. Excited, I pried the top off, but when I opened it, some kind of rat with wings flew out! It swooped around the room and then tried to land in my hair!

5 "Get that thing away from me!" I screamed as my father chased it and returned it to the box. "What is that?" I panted.

6 "It's a baby bat," my dad answered. "Isn't that what you wanted?"

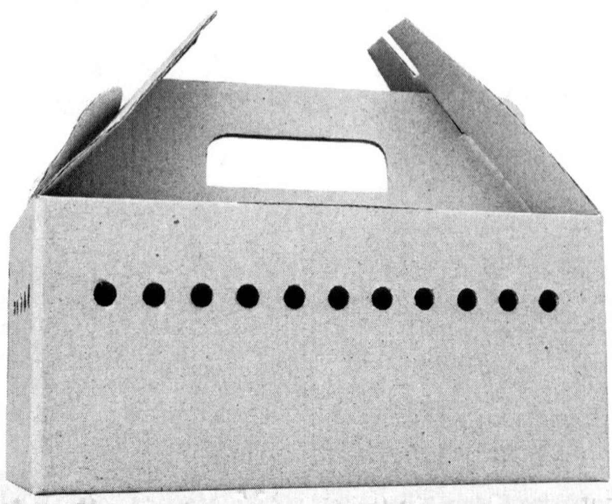

7 I looked at him incredulously and wailed, "I want a pup!"

8 A week later, my dad came home with an even bigger box, but this time, I cautiously peeked inside before opening it. Two beady black eyes peered back at me, and I heard a horrible hissing sound.

9 "It's an adorable baby hedgehog!" exclaimed my dad.

10 I blinked at him in disbelief. "Why are you bringing home bats and hedgehogs when all I want is a little puppy dog," I asked, frustrated and confused.

11 "A dog? Why didn't you say so?" my dad exclaimed. "Baby bats, hedgehogs—even baby seals, dolphins, and rats—are also called pups. I honestly didn't know which kind you wanted."

12 My dad suddenly looked down at his watch nervously and said, "Um, I just remembered there's another pup coming any minute."

13 He ran outside just as an eighteen-wheel truck was barreling up our street with a jumbo tank of water strapped to the back. The brakes squealed, and the tank fell off the back, landed in the street, and smashed into a million pieces.

14 "Run!" my dad yelled. "A pup is also a baby shark!"

Name:______________________________ Date: ________________

Reading Reactions

Directions: Describe your biggest reactions to "The Pup." For each reaction, describe what happened in the story, write a quote from the story, and describe your reaction.

Event	Quote	Your Reaction

Name: ______________________ Date: ______________

Author's Toolbox

Directions: Authors can use many tools to get strong reactions from their readers. Use the chart to record the text structures used in "The Pup." List examples from the passage for each text structure.

Text Structure	Evidence
dialog	
dynamic punctuation	

Directions: Use the chart to record the elements of writer's craft used in "The Pup." List examples from the passage for each element.

Writer's Craft	Evidence
repeated use of *pup/puppy*	
dynamic word choice	

Name:______________________________ Date: ______________

May I Speak to the Manager?

Directions: Write an addition to "The Pup." Pretend the dad wants to return the baby animals he purchased for his son. Write a dialog in which the dad calls the manager to explain why he needs to return the animals. Include the manager's response. Use punctuation and dialog to create a tone and make your reader react to the dad.

Name: ______________________________ Date: ________________

May I Speak to the Manager? Scoring Rubric

Directions: Complete the self-assessment section of this rubric. Then, turn this in with your completed *May I Speak to the Manager?* activity. (4 means "I strongly agree." 1 means "I do not agree.")

Self-Assessment

	4	3	2	1
My dialog includes an explanation of why the dad wants to return the animals.				
My dialog includes the manager's response.				
I used punctuation and word choice to create a tone and make the reader react.				

Additional comments: ______________________________

____

____

____

Teacher Assessment

	4	3	2	1
The dialog includes an explanation of why the dad wants to return the animals.				
The dialog includes the manager's response.				
The writer uses punctuation and word choice to create a tone to make the reader react.				

Additional comments: ______________________________

____

____

____

Rubric based on work by Lapp, D., B. Moss, M. Grant, & K. Johnson (2015)

Did You See?

Purpose

WHAT: Analyze how specific word choices shape key details.

HOW: Write a poem with descriptive words that shape key details.

I CAN: I can interpret and use descriptive words.

Standards

- **Reading:** Determine the meaning of words and phrases as they are used in a text.
- **Writing:** Write narratives to develop real or imagined experiences.
- **Language:** Choose words and phrases for effect.

Performance Assessment

- Students will write poems using descriptive words.

Text Selection

- "Did You See?"
- Text is a rhyming poem divided into two columns.

Materials

- *Did You See?* passage, one copy per student (page 148; didyousee.pdf)
- *Reflecting on Poetry* activity (page 149)
- *Tell Me What It Means* activity (page 150)
- *A Monster of a Poem* activity (page 151)
- *A Monster of a Poem Scoring Rubric* (page 152)
- drawing paper, one per student

Text-Dependent Questions (See pages 40–43 for more information.)

- Does the beast sound scary to you or not? What words does the author use to make you feel that way?
- How does the author help you imagine what the beast looks like?
- How does the author help you imagine what the beast smells like?
- How does the author help you imagine what the beast sounds like?
- How does the author help you imagine what the beast feels like?
- Where does the monster live?

Did You See? *(cont.)*

Areas of Complexity

	Measure	Explanation
Quantitative	Lexile Level	(non-prose)
Qualitative	Meaning or Purpose	The text includes rich, descriptive language that helps the reader visualize.
	Structure	The text is organized as a rhyming poem.
	Language Features	Language is accessible and familiar and can be determined through context clues.
Reader/Task	Knowledge Demands	Potentially unfamiliar words are used in the poem, requiring the use of context clues for understanding. Students must use elements of a poem to complete the performance task.

Text Synopsis

The poem describes a monster that is after the author. The author uses rich, descriptive language to provide readers with visual images. The poem ends with the author revealing that the monster is found in his/her imagination.

Differentiation

Additional Support—After the first read, you may need to explain that this poem does not have a plot like a traditional story. Students should focus on visualizing and not worry about "what happens."

As needed, students can transfer their annotations to the *Tell Me What It Means* activity (page 150). This chart supports students as they reread the text.

Extension—Have student pairs identify the overall tone of the poem. Is it creepy? Scary? Playful? Shocking? Angry?

Did You See? *(cont.)*

Phase 1—Hitting the Surface

Who Reads	Annotations (See page 63.)		
☐ teacher	☐ highlight main points	☐ underline key details	☐ write questions
☑ students	☑ circle key vocabulary	☐ arrows for connections	☑ other: draw visualization

Procedure

1. To begin, explain the purposes (from page 143). Let students know that they will first read the poem to answer the question *What is the poem about?*
2. Distribute copies of the poem with the illustration covered. Direct students to draw what they think the author is describing. Students can read the poem multiple times and add to their drawings.
3. Throughout each phase, as students read, circulate to observe their work, and provide scaffolds as guides for those who need assistance. These might be additional layered questions, prompts to encourage them to reflect on a certain part of the passage, or cues to remember related information. Insights you gain through this formative assessment can also influence the next questions to be asked of the whole group.
4. Reveal the illustration, and have students compare it to their drawings.
5. **Partners**—Student pairs can share their drawings and circle words in the text that match the creatures they visualized.
6. **Whole Class**—Regroup as a class, and display the text for all students. Ask students to share their drawings. Have them support the details in their drawings with words or phrases from the text. If possible, record student annotations on a displayed copy of the text.

Did You See? *(cont.)*

Phase 2—Digging Deeper

Who Reads

- ❑ teacher
- ☑ students

Annotations (See page 63.)

- ❑ highlight main points
- ❑ underline key details
- ☑ write questions
- ☑ circle key vocabulary
- ☑ arrows for connections
- ❑ other: ______________

Procedure

1. Before students return to the text a second time, say, "How does the author let you know what the monster looks like, smells like, sounds like, and feels like? Let's pay close attention to unfamiliar words and the clues that might reveal the meanings of those words so that we understand the author's description. Don't forget to mark the text by circling unfamiliar words and writing possible definitions in the margins."
2. Have students dig deeper by explaining their thinking about a word's meaning. (Example: *The author describes the ears as pendulous. The word sounds like* pendulum. *The illustration shows long ears that hang down. If they are like a pendulum, then they probably swing back and forth.*) Have students write these ideas in the margins.
3. If needed, ask additional layered/scaffolded questions, such as:
   - How does the picture help you know more about the unfamiliar word? Draw arrows to show the connections.
   - Does a part of the unfamiliar word give you a clue about what the whole word means?
   - How do other words in the phrase help you know more about the unfamiliar word? Draw arrows to show the connections.
4. Say, "The author uses the following sentence: *I think I'll fly with this all night*. What clue is the author giving?"
5. **Partners**—After students have read and annotated the text, pairs can share their thinking about the meanings of the unfamiliar words.
6. **Whole Class**—Regroup as a class, and display the text for all students. Ask students to share their responses about word meanings. Have them support their responses with their annotations. If possible, record student annotations on a displayed copy of the text.

Did You See? *(cont.)*

Phase 3—Digging Even Deeper

Who Reads

☐ teacher

☑ students

Annotations (See page 63.)

☑ highlight main points ☑ underline key details ☐ write questions

☐ circle key vocabulary ☐ arrows for connections ☐ other: ______________

Procedure

1. Ask, "What is the author's purpose in writing this poem?" Help students to understand that the poem was likely written for the purpose of entertaining the reader by using playful, descriptive language.
2. Ask students to think of the creature in terms of their senses. The illustration and your drawings are based on what the author wrote about how the beast looks.
3. Ask students to mark the text to answer the following questions:
   - How does the author describe the beast?
   - How does the author help you imagine what the beast smells like?
   - How does the author help you imagine what the beast sounds like?
   - How does the author help you imagine what the beast feels like?
4. **Partners**—Have student pairs share their responses to the questions and annotations.
5. **Whole Class**—Regroup as a class, and display the text for all students. Ask students to share their responses to the questions about the beast. Have them support their responses with their annotations. If possible, record student annotations on a displayed copy of the text.
6. Prior to the performance task, have students think about the passage individually by completing the *Reflecting on Poetry* activity (page 149), or confirm their understanding of unfamiliar words by completing the *Tell Me What It Means* activity (page 150).

Performance Assessment

1. Assign the performance task *A Monster of a Poem* (page 151).
2. Explain that students' assignments will be graded based on the *A Monster of a Poem Scoring Rubric* (page 152). The scoring rubric is for both students and teachers to guide and score work.

Name: ______________________ Date: ______________

Did You See?

1 Round that corner,
Oh, did you see
Something scary
Following me?

2 With piercing eyes
And hollow cheeks
And snaky scales
Upon its feet;

3 With pointy toes,
A snappish snout,
And sinuous stripes
All roundabout;

4 Unruly curls
Upon its head
And pendulous ears
Of deepest red;

5 Tufted eyebrows
And knobby knees,
The awful smell of Limburger cheese;

6 A tail up front,
A tail behind
(I think this tale
Is very fine);

7 A second head,
A second nose
(I wonder if
My own nose grows);

8 Wings to its left,
Wings to its right
(I think I'll fly
With this all night);

9 So, tell me please,
Oh, did you see
That ferocious thing
That's after me?

10 What's that you say?
You missed the beast?
I'm not surprised,
Not in the least.

11 This monster is
A rare creation—
Found only in my
'magination.

Name: ______________________ Date: ______________

Reflecting on Poetry

Directions: Use the text "Did You See?" to answer the following.

1. Write four words that give you an unpleasant feeling about the beast.

2. The author refers to the creature as a monster and a beast. What else does the author call the creature?

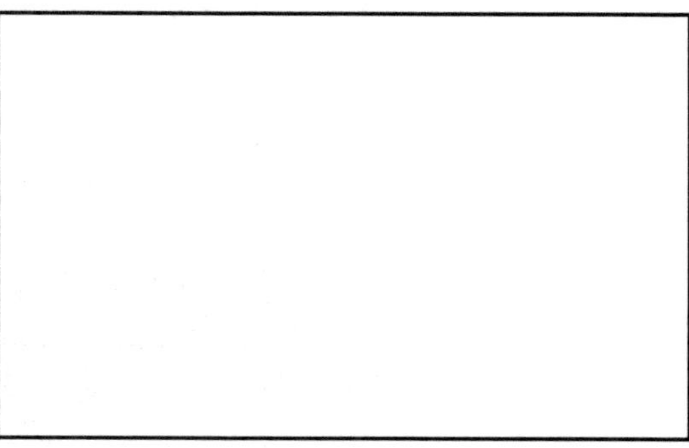

Name: ______________________ Date: ______________

Tell Me What It Means

Directions: The author of "Did You See?" uses descriptive language to help us visualize the monster. Complete the chart by writing a word from the poem that matches each definition.

Descriptive Word or Phrase	Definition
sunken	
not straight	
mean	
beast	
not common	
looking at deeply	
fingers or toes that are connected	
a cluster of hairs	

Name:______________________________ Date: ______________

A Monster of a Poem

Directions: Write a poem about a monster in your imagination. Begin by writing words that describe a magical creature. Decide how you would like your reader to feel about the creature, then choose words that will create that feeling.

Name: ______________________________ Date: ______________

A Monster of a Poem Scoring Rubric

Directions: Complete the self-assessment section of this rubric. Then, turn this in with your completed *A Monster of a Poem* activity. (4 means "I strongly agree." 1 means "I do not agree.")

Self-Assessment

	4	3	2	1
I chose words to describe the details of the magical creature.				
I described the creature's look, sound, smell, and feel.				
I chose words and phrases that created a feeling.				

Additional comments: ______________________________

____

____

____

Teacher Assessment

	4	3	2	1
The writer chose words to describe the details of the magical creature.				
The writer described the creature's look, sound, smell, and feel.				
The writer chose words and phrases that created a feeling.				

Additional comments: ______________________________

____

____

____

Rubric based on work by Lapp, D., B. Moss, M. Grant, & K. Johnson (2015)

Plastic Panic

Purposes

WHAT: Explain what the text states and make inferences.

WHAT: Make connections between different parts of a story.

HOW: Write a narrative of inferred events that precede the story.

I CAN: I can connect different parts of a story to make inferences.

Standards

- **Reading:** Compare different parts of a story.
- **Writing:** Write narratives to develop imagined experiences using descriptive details.
- **Language:** Choose words and phrases to convey ideas precisely.

Performance Assessment

- Students will make inferences about events that precede a story, then write narratives, conveying those events using descriptive details.

Text Selection

- "Plastic Panic"
- Text is divided by paragraphs.

Materials

- *Plastic Panic* passage, one copy per student (page 158; plasticpanic.pdf)
- *What Happened?* activity (page 159)
- *Picture It!* activity (page 160)
- *Pablo's Story* activity (page 161)
- *Pablo's Story Scoring Rubric* (page 162)

Text-Dependent Questions (See pages 44–48 for more information.)

- What is the story about?
- What are the differences between the character and setting described in the first half of the story and the character and setting described in the second half of the story?
- What do you know about the main character in the first half of the story?
- What do you know about the main character in the second half of the story?
- What words and phrases reveal Juan's unusual trait?
- What descriptive language is used to describe the setting?
- How are italics used in this passage?

Plastic Panic *(cont.)*

Areas of Complexity

	Measure	Explanation
Quantitative	Lexile Level	610L
Qualitative	Meaning or Purpose	The purpose of the text is to entertain with a descriptive story.
	Structure	The story fools the reader into thinking one thing about who the main character is and then reveals his real identity at the end of the story. The text moves from the limited perspective of one character to a broad, omnipresent perspective, all through a third person narrative voice.
	Language Features	The story is descriptive and assumes some understanding of words related to the experiences of soldiers.
Reader/ Task	Knowledge Demands	While words such as *mission* and *caravan* may be unfamiliar to students, context clues help with understanding. Students must make inferences about preceding events to complete the performance assessment.

Text Synopsis

The story is about a soldier lost in the desert. He searches for his fellow soldiers, but can't find them. As he is looking for water and shade, he hears the voice of his buddy. As it turns out, the soldier is a toy soldier, and his buddy is a boy who was playing with his plastic toys in a sandbox.

Differentiation

Additional Support—You may need to assist students in using context clues to make meaning of unfamiliar words (*caravan, mission, loomed*) in order to increase comprehension.

As needed, students can transfer their annotations to the *What Happened?* activity (page 159). This chart supports students as they reread the text.

Extension—Instruct students to retell the story from the boy's point of view.

Plastic Panic *(cont.)*

Phase 1—Hitting the Surface

Who Reads	Annotations (See page 64.)		
☐ teacher	☑ highlight main points	☐ underline key details	☑ write questions
☑ students	☑ circle key vocabulary	☐ arrows for connections	☑ other: notes in the margin

Procedure

1. Before students read, explain the purposes (from page 153).
2. Have students read the text independently. As they read, students will annotate their copies of the text to answer the question *What is the story about?*
3. Throughout each phase, as students read, circulate to observe their work, and provide scaffolds as guides for those who need assistance. These might be additional layered questions, prompts to encourage them to reflect on a certain part of the passage, or cues to remember related information. Insights you gain through this formative assessment can also influence the next questions to be asked of the whole group.
4. **Partners**—After students have annotated the text, pairs can share their thinking related to the initial question.
5. Have partners identify and discuss challenging vocabulary that, when clarified, will help them better comprehend the story. If needed, ask additional layered/scaffolded questions such as:
    - What nearby words tell you more about the word *mission*?
    - What nearby words tell you more about the word *caravan*?
    - What nearby words tell you more about the word *loomed*?
6. **Whole Class**—Regroup as a class, and display the text for all students. Ask students to share their initial understanding of the story. Have them support their responses with their annotations. If possible, record student annotations on a displayed copy of the text.

Plastic Panic *(cont.)*

Phase 2—Digging Deeper

Who Reads

- ❑ teacher
- ☑ students

Annotations (See page 64.)

- ❑ highlight main points
- ❑ underline key details
- ❑ write questions
- ☑ circle key vocabulary
- ❑ arrows for connections
- ❑ other: __________

Procedure

1. Say, "The author of this story uses lots of descriptive language. For example, the author does not only say the sun shined on Juan's face. The author said the *burning* sun *beat down* on Juan's face. This precise, descriptive language helps us to better understand the predicament Juan is in."
2. Ask students to annotate the story by circling descriptive words and phrases to answer the text-dependent question *What descriptive language is used to explain the setting?*
3. **Partners**—After students have read and annotated the text once, pairs can share the words and phrases they have circled.
4. **Whole Class**—Regroup as a class, and display the text for all students. Ask students to share the most powerful descriptions they found in the text. If possible, record student annotations on a displayed copy of the text. Discuss how the descriptions affect the reader.
5. Ask students, "If I were to chop this story into two parts, where should I draw the line?" Encourage students to justify their responses by explaining the differences between the two parts of the story.
6. Ask students to read the text to answer the text-dependent questions. Say, "What are the differences between the character and setting described in the first half of the story and the character and setting described in the second half of the story? Write notes in the margin to record your thinking."
7. If needed, ask additional layered/scaffolded questions, such as:
   - What do you know about the main character in the first half of the story?
   - What do you know about the setting in the first half of the story?
   - What do you know about the main character in the second half of the story?
   - What do you know about the setting in the second half of the story?
8. **Partners**—After students have read and annotated the text, pairs can share their thinking about the two parts of the story.
9. **Whole Class**—Regroup as a class, and display the text for all students. Ask students to share their responses to the questions. Have them support their responses with their annotations. If possible, record student annotations on a displayed copy of the text.

Plastic Panic *(cont.)*

Phase 3—Digging Even Deeper

Who Reads	Annotations (See page 64.)		
❑ teacher	❑ highlight main points	❑ underline key details	❑ write questions
☑ students	☑ circle key vocabulary	❑ arrows for connections	❑ other: ______

Procedure

1. Discuss how the author leads the reader into making an inference in the first half of the story. If needed, ask additional layered/scaffolded questions, such as:
    - Who calls the setting a desert? Who calls the setting a sandbox?
    - Who tries to walk? Who picks up Juan?
    - Who uses the words *fellow soldiers* and *caravan*? What lets you know that they were all actually toys?
    - Who is the woman who picks Juan up?
    - What does it mean when the woman says, "You must have forgotten this one in the sandbox."?
2. Have students complete the *What Happened?* activity (page 159) to record the two perspectives that create the twist in the story.
3. Ask students to skim the passage to find italicized phrases and answer the text-dependent question *How are italics used in this passage?* (You may need to point out what italics look like.)
4. Discuss why there are no italicized phrases in the second half of the story. If needed, ask additional layered/scaffolded questions, such as:
    - Why is it important that the reader only see the setting through Juan's thoughts at the beginning of the story?
    - Why is it important that the reader see the setting without Juan's perspective at the end of the story?
5. Prior to the performance task, have students think about the descriptive language of the passage individually by completing the *Picture It!* activity (page 160).

Performance Assessment

1. Assign the performance task *Pablo's Story* (page 161).
2. Explain that students' assignments will be graded based on the *Pablo's Story Scoring Rubric* (page 162). The scoring rubric is for both students and teachers to guide and score work.

Name: ______________________ Date: ______________

Plastic Panic

1 *The first rule of survival is "Don't panic,"* Juan reminded himself. The burning sun beat down on his face. He looked out across the desert, but there was nothing around except an endless sea of sand. Where had everyone gone? Juan remembered marching through the desert with his buddies, heading to their next mission, but suddenly, he was all alone. His fellow soldiers were nowhere to be found—even their usual caravan of jeeps and horses was gone. Nothing about the situation made sense. Juan was starting to panic.

2 The sun was high overhead. *I need to find water, or at least some shade*, he thought. He tried to walk, but his legs wouldn't move in the heavy sand. *Is this what melting feels like?* he wondered. After some long moments had passed, Juan heard a faraway voice calling his name. It sounded like his friend Pablo, and it gave Juan hope.

3 He waited and waited, but Pablo never appeared. Instead, the sound of Pablo's voice faded off into the distance. Juan began to feel like he might never leave this lonely desert, until suddenly, a huge shadow appeared above him. It loomed over him, blocking out the midday sun.

4 "Here he is, Pablo," said a woman's voice. "You must have forgotten this one in the sandbox." Juan felt himself being scooped up gently in a large hand.

5 "Thanks, Mom! He's my favorite!" Pablo answered excitedly.

6 Juan tumbled into a yellow plastic pail and saw the jeeps, the horses, and a pile of his army buddies grinning at him. Juan smiled, too. It had been an exciting adventure, but he was grateful to be home.

Name:______________________________ Date: ________________

What Happened?

Directions: Record the descriptions of events in "Plastic Panic" from Juan's perspective and from Pablo's point of view.

Juan's Experience

____

____

____

____

____

____

____

Pablo's Experience

____

____

____

____

____

____

____

Name: ______________________ Date: ______________

Picture It!

Directions: The author of "Plastic Panic" uses descriptive words and phrases. Complete the graphic organizer by writing descriptive words from the text to describe each object.

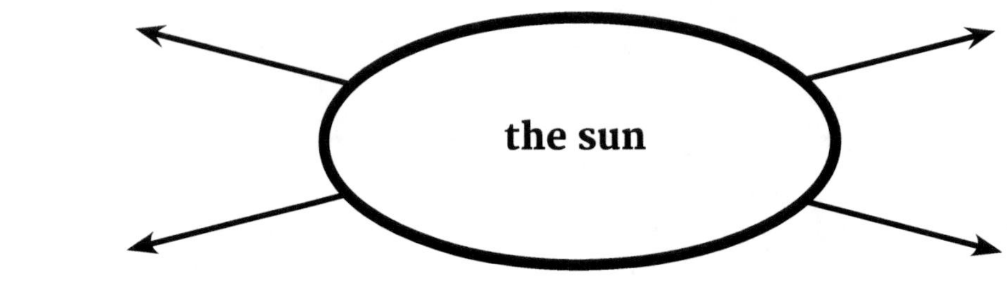

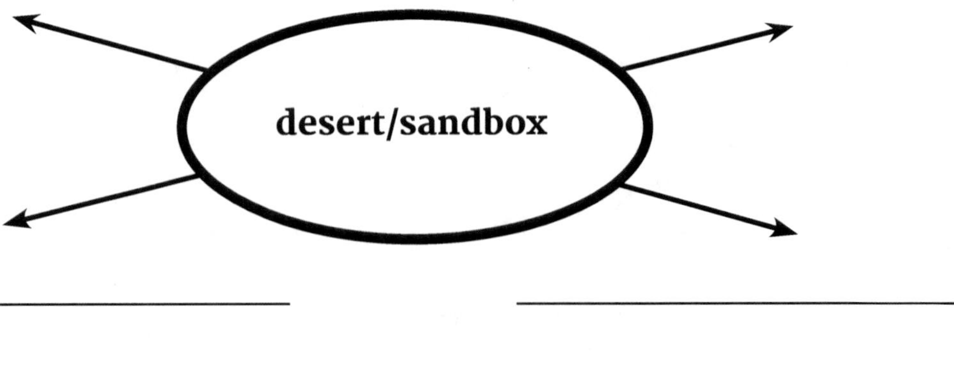

Name:________________________________ Date: ________________

Pablo's Story

Directions: Rewrite "Plastic Panic" to tell the story from Pablo's point of view. Assume Pablo does not know his toy has the thoughts of a real soldier. Use details from the passage to make inferences about the events at the sandbox as Pablo experienced them. Make sure to use descriptive language to describe the setting.

Name: ______________________ Date: ______________

Pablo's Story Scoring Rubric

Directions: Complete the self-assessment section of this rubric. Then, turn this in with your completed *Pablo's Story* activity. (4 means "I strongly agree." 1 means "I do not agree.")

Self-Assessment

	4	3	2	1
I described how Pablo played in the sandbox.				
I described how Juan got separated from the other toys.				
I described how Pablo's mom found his lost toy.				
I used at least three examples of descriptive language.				

Additional comments: ______________________

____

____

____

Teacher Assessment

	4	3	2	1
The writer described how Pablo played in the sandbox.				
The writer described how Juan got separated from the other toys.				
The writer described how Pablo's mom found his lost toy.				
The writer used at least three examples of descriptive language.				

Additional comments: ______________________

____

____

____

Rubric based on work by Lapp, D., B. Moss, M. Grant, & K. Johnson (2015)

A Royal Prisoner

Purpose

WHAT: Integrate ideas from different parts of the text.

HOW: Describe the main character's experiences in a letter.

I CAN: I can integrate different parts of the text to understand a character's experience.

Standards

- **Reading:** Interpret information in the text.
- **Writing:** Use concrete words, phrases, and sensory details to convey experiences and events precisely.
- **Language:** Vary the style and length of sentences to enhance meaning, reader/listener interest, and style.

Performance Assessment

- Students will write letters describing the main character's experiences.

Text Selection

- "A Royal Prisoner"
- Text is divided into paragraphs.

Materials

- *A Royal Prisoner* passage, one copy per student (page 168; royalprisoner.pdf)
- *A Very Somber Game* activity (page 169)
- *Then and Now* activity (page 170)
- *Dear Family* activity (page 171)
- *Dear Family Scoring Rubric* (page 172)

Text-Dependent Questions (See pages 49–53 for more information.)

- What is the story about?
- Who is telling the story?
- What was the narrator's life like in the past?
- What is the narrator's life like in the present?
- Beyond using adjectives, how does the author describe the narrator's life?
- What is *the game*?
- How might the game save the character's life?
- What is the reason the character is in prison?
- How does the structure of the story help you better understand it?

A Royal Prisoner *(cont.)*

Areas of Complexity

	Measure	Explanation
Quantitative	Lexile Level	840L
Qualitative	Meaning or Purpose	The purpose of the text is to explain the plight of a character using descriptive details.
	Structure	The text is an excerpt from a larger narrative. It details the character's current and previous situations. Many details are not explicitly stated.
	Language Features	Vocabulary can be deciphered from context.
Reader/ Task	Knowledge Demands	While the word *courtier* may be unfamiliar to students, context clues help with understanding. Students must use the elements of setting to complete the performance assessment.

Text Synopsis

The text depicts a person of royalty (the narrator) who has been in prison due to a betrayal. He is hungry and thirsty. The only way he can keep himself going until he is rescued is to play *the game* where he ponders a memory from a happier time.

Differentiation

Additional Support—You may need to guide students to notice the clues that lead to the identification of the main character.

As needed, students can transfer their annotations to the *Then and Now* activity (page 170). This graphic organizer supports students as they reread the text.

Extension—Instruct students to discuss their thoughts about what came earlier in the story and what will come after.

A Royal Prisoner *(cont.)*

Phase 1—Hitting the Surface

Who Reads	Annotations (See page 64.)		
❑ teacher	☑ highlight main points	❑ underline key details	☑ write questions
☑ students	❑ circle key vocabulary	❑ arrows for connections	❑ other: ____________

Procedure

1. Explain the purposes (from page 163) before reading the text.
2. Explain that the text is an excerpt from a longer story.
3. Have students read the text independently. As they read, students will annotate their copies of the text to answer the question *What is the story about?*
4. Throughout each phase, as students read, circulate to observe their work, and provide scaffolds as guides for those who need assistance. These might be additional layered questions, prompts to encourage them to reflect on a certain part of the passage, or cues to remember related information. Insights you gain through this formative assessment can also influence the next questions to be asked of the whole group.
5. **Partners**—After students have read and annotated the text once, pairs can share their thinking related to the initial question.
6. If needed, ask additional layered/scaffolded questions, such as:
   - Who is telling the story?
   - What words describe the narrator?
   - What activities were part of the narrator's past life?
   - What people were part of the narrator's past life?
7. **Whole Class**—Regroup as a class, and display the text for all students. Ask students to share their responses to the question about what the story is about. Have them support their responses with their annotations. If possible, record student annotations on a displayed copy of the text.

A Royal Prisoner *(cont.)*

Phase 2—Digging Deeper

Who Reads

☑ teacher
☐ students

Annotations (See page 64.)

☐ highlight main points
☑ underline key details
☐ write questions
☐ circle key vocabulary
☑ arrows for connections
☐ other: ________________

Procedure

1. Before students read the text a second time, say, "This time, I will read the text aloud. As I do, listen for details that will help you understand the game. Annotate the text to answer the text-dependent question *What is the game?*
2. If needed, ask additional layered/scaffolded questions, such as:
   - What does the author tell us about the game?
   - How often does the narrator play the game?
   - What does the narrator hope the game will do for him?
   - How are the marks on the wall related to the game?
   - How are days and years related in the game?
   - What is important about the Yubari melon?
   - Why does the author describe the game in this way?
3. **Partners**—After students have read and annotated the text, have pairs share their thinking about the game. Partners work together to complete the *A Very Somber Game* activity (page 167).
4. **Whole Class**—Regroup as a class, and display the text for all students. Ask students to share their understandings of the game. Have them support their responses with their annotations. If possible, record student annotations on a displayed copy of the text.

Phase 3—Digging Even Deeper

Who Reads

☐ teacher
☑ students

Annotations (See page 64.)

☐ highlight main points
☐ underline key details
☑ write questions
☑ circle key vocabulary
☐ arrows for connections
☑ other: highlight sentences of different lengths

A Royal Prisoner *(cont.)*

Phase 3—Digging Even Deeper *(cont.)*

Procedure *(cont.)*

1. Ask students to consider the story's structure. Ask, "How does the structure of the story help you better understand it?"
2. If needed, ask additional layered/scaffolded questions, such as:
   - What do you notice about the sentences?
   - What do you notice about their length?
   - How do the author's sentences affect the story?
3. If needed, have students highlight the simple sentences in one color and the longer sentences in another color.
4. **Partners**—After students have read and annotated the passage, pairs can share the number of shorter and longer sentences they found.
5. **Whole Class**—Regroup as a class, and display the text for all students. Ask students to share simple and compound/complex sentences. If possible, record student annotations on a displayed copy of the text.
6. Discuss the impact of the variation in sentence length. You may choose to have students read sections of the text aloud to note the flow.
7. Ask students to read the passage again to answer the text-dependent questions *What was the narrator's life like in the past?* and *What is the narrator's life like in the present?*
8. If needed, ask additional layered/scaffold questions, such as:
   - Beyond using adjectives, how does the author describe the narrator's life?
   - What words and phrases help you visualize the narrator's prison life?
   - What words and phrases help you visualize the narrator's royal life?
9. If needed, ask additional layered/scaffolded questions, such as:
   - How are the five senses addressed?
   - How are the seasons addressed?
10. Prior to the performance task, have students think about the passage individually by completing the *Then and Now* activity (page 170).

Performance Assessment

1. Assign the performance task *Dear Family* (page 171).
2. Explain that students' assignments will be graded based on the *Dear Family Scoring Rubric* (page 172). The scoring rubric is for both students and teachers to guide and score work.

Name: ______________________ Date: ______________

A Royal Prisoner

1 When the sun rose, it was time to play the game again. This was the game that would save my life—at least I hoped it would. My body was failing without water or food, but maybe I could save my mind long enough to be rescued.

2 The marks on the wall showed it had been nine days—nine days since I had seen the world outside my cell, nine days since I had seen my family, nine days since I had learned the mapmaker had deceived me. So today, I would try to remember what my life had been like nine years ago. Yesterday, I had spent an hour painting in the details of my life eight years ago. Today, I would live deeper inside my memories.

3 It was a different time then. Nine years ago, the villagers still bowed to me, and I was surrounded by courtiers. In the summer, they washed me in the cool water of the glaciers of Sannomado. In the autumn, they danced for me, their figures casting long shadows in the candlelight. In the winter, they brought me hot stones to warm the pads of my feet. And in the spring, they gave me the first bite of the Yubari melon.

4 Oh, melon! Yes, that is the memory I would live inside today.

Name:______________________ Date: ______________

A Very Somber Game

Directions: Use the graphic organizer to record details about the game described in "A Royal Prisoner."

The Royal Prisoner Game

Number of Players:______________

Goal:______________________________

____

How to Play

1. ______________________________

____

____

2. ______________________________

____

____

3. ______________________________

____

____

4. ______________________________

____

____

Name: ______________________________ Date: ____________________

Then and Now

Directions: Complete the graphic organizer with descriptions about the past and present life of the narrator from "A Royal Prisoner."

	In the Past	In the Present
Food		
People		
Entertainment		

Name:________________________ Date: ______________

Dear Family

Directions: Write a letter from the royal prisoner to his family, describing his time in prison. Mimic the author's style by using the five senses to describe the setting and by varying your sentence length.

Dear Family,

____

____

____

____

____

____

____

____

____

____

____

____

____

____

____

____

Name: ______________________ Date: ______________

Dear Family Scoring Rubric

Directions: Complete the self-assessment section of this rubric. Then, turn this in with your completed *Dear Family* activity. (4 means "I strongly agree." 1 means "I do not agree.")

Self-Assessment

	4	3	2	1
I included key details from the text.				
My writing style includes details that use the senses to describe the setting.				
My writing style includes varied sentence length.				

Additional comments: ______________________

____

____

____

Teacher Assessment

	4	3	2	1
The writer included key details from the text.				
The writer's style included details that use the senses to describe the setting.				
The writer's style included varied sentence length.				

Additional comments: ______________________

____

____

____

Rubric based on work by Lapp, D., B. Moss, M. Grant, & K. Johnson (2015)

Try It!

Directions: Use the following passage and the planning forms that follow (pages 174–175) to plan a close reading lesson.

Finding a Fairy

I could go on and make this into a most interesting story about all the ordinary things that the children did. However, when I told about the children being tiresome, as you are sometimes, your aunts would perhaps write in the margin of the story with a pencil, "How true!" or "How likelife!" Then, you would see it and would very likely be annoyed. So I will only tell you the really astonishing things that happened. And you may leave the book out quite safely, for no aunts and uncles are likely to write "How true!" on the edge of the story. Grown-ups find it very difficult to believe really wonderful things. That is, unless they have what they call proof. But children will believe almost anything, and grown-ups know this. That is why they tell you Earth is round like an orange. But you can see perfectly well that it is flat and lumpy. That is why they say the Earth goes round the sun. But you can see for yourself that the sun gets up in the morning and goes to bed at night. It is easy to see that Earth knows its place and lies as still as a mouse. Yet I daresay you believe all that about Earth and the sun. And if so, you will find it quite easy to believe that before Anthea and Cyril and the others had been in the country a week, they had found a fairy. At least they called it that. That was what it called itself. And of course, it knew best. But it was not at all like any fairy you have ever seen or heard of or read about.

Try It! *(cont.)*

Planning Chart for Close Reading

Planning	Date:_______________Grade: _______Discipline:___________________________ Purpose(s):___________________________ Standard(s):___________________________ Text Selection (literary or informational):___________________________ Performance Assessment: ___________________________ Materials: ___________________________
Text Selection	Title:___________________________ Author:___________________________ Page(s) or section(s):___________________________ How should this text be chunked?___________________________ ___________________________
Areas of Complexity	Lexile Level:___________________________ Meaning or Purpose:___________________________ Structure:___________________________ Language Features:___________________________ Knowledge Demands:___________________________
Text-Dependent Questions	1.___________________________ 2.___________________________ 3.___________________________ 4.___________________________ 5.___________________________
Performance Task	___________________________ ___________________________ ___________________________ ___________________________
Differentiation	Additional Support: _______________ ___________________________ Extension: ___________________________ ___________________________

Try It! *(cont.)*

Teaching Close Reading

Teaching

Limited Frontloading ❑ yes ❑ no

Describe:

First Read

Who Reads? ❑ teacher ❑ student

Student Materials	
❑ graphic organizer	❑ group consensus form
❑ note taking guide	❑ summary form

Second Read

Who Reads? ❑ teacher ❑ student

Student Resources	
❑ graphic organizer	❑ group consensus form
❑ note taking guide	❑ summary form

Additional Reads

Who Reads? ❑ teacher ❑ student

Student Resources	
❑ graphic organizer	❑ group consensus form
❑ note taking guide	❑ summary form

Extension	**Reteaching**

Section 6: Informational Text Close Reading Lessons

In the following pages, you will find nine close reading lessons built around informational texts. A tenth text is provided along with planning resources to allow you to plan an additional close reading lesson.

Lincoln's Hat

Purpose

WHAT: Understand how authors connect ideas within a text.

HOW: Write diary entries that summarize key details from a text.

I CAN: I can connect and summarize key ideas from a text.

Standards

- **Reading:** Determine the main idea of the text; recount the key details and explain how they support the main idea.
- **Writing:** Write narratives to develop real or imagined experiences or events using effective technique, descriptive details, and clear event sequence.
- **Language:** Choose words and phrases for effect.
- **Social Studies:** Generate questions about individuals and groups who have shaped significant historical changes and continuities.

Performance Assessment

- Students will write fictional diary entries from the perspective of Lincoln's Hat.

Text Selection

- "Lincoln's Hat"
- Text is chunked into paragraphs.

Materials

- *Lincoln's Hat* passage, one copy per student (page 184; lincoln.pdf)
- *Museum Ad* activity (page 185)
- *Lincoln's Hat: Key Idea and Details* activity (page 186)
- *Dear Diary* activity (page 187)
- *Dear Diary Scoring Rubric* (page 188)

Text-Dependent Questions (See pages 40–43 for more information.)

- What is this text about? What does the author want readers to know?
- What are the author's main points about Lincoln?
- Identify details about Lincoln's Hat.
- How does the text show the connection between President Lincoln and his hat?

Lincoln's Hat *(cont.)*

Areas of Complexity

	Measure	Explanation
Quantitative	Lexile Level	720L
Qualitative	Meaning or Purpose	Even though this is an informational text, the hat is presented as a parallel, or extended metaphor, for Lincoln himself.
	Structure	The structure of the text is unconventional, not introducing the narrator until the second paragraph.
	Language Features	New vocabulary is introduced explicitly. The main language is conventional.
Reader/Task	Knowledge Demands	The article assumes familiarity with the life and death of Abraham Lincoln and the context in which he lived and died. Students must understand elements of a diary to complete the performance assessment.

Text Synopsis

This unusual nonfiction text informs the reader about Abraham Lincoln through details about the hat he wore. The stovepipe hat made the very tall man seem even taller. It gave him a place to hold papers and made him have to duck through doorways. This is a unique look at the life of a well-known American figure.

Differentiation

Additional Support—If students are not familiar with Abraham Lincoln, present a time line of his life, death, and accomplishments.

Extension—Have students compare this text to more traditional biographies of Lincoln. Have students brainstorm other iconic items that could be used to tell the story of a famous life.

Lincoln's Hat *(cont.)*

Phase 1—Hitting the Surface

Who Reads

❑ teacher

☑ students

Annotations (See page 63.)

☑ highlight main points ❑ underline key details ❑ write questions

☑ circle key vocabulary ❑ arrows for connections ❑ other: draw visualization

Procedure

1. Before students read, explain the purposes (from page 179).
2. Have students read the text independently. As they read, have students annotate their copies of the text to answer the questions *What is this text about? What does the author want readers to know?*
3. Throughout each phase, as students read, circulate to observe their work, and provide scaffolds as guides for those who need assistance. These might be additional layered questions, prompts to encourage them to reflect on a certain part of the passage, or cues to remember related information. Insights you gain through this formative assessment can also influence the next questions to be asked of the whole group.
4. **Partners**—After students have read and annotated the text once, pairs can share their thinking as related to the initial questions.
5. **Whole Class**—Regroup as a class, and display the text for all students. Ask students to share their responses to the question regarding what the text is about. Have them support their responses with their annotations. If possible, record student annotations on a displayed copy of the text.

Lincoln's Hat *(cont.)*

Phase 2—Digging Deeper

Who Reads

☐ teacher

☑ students

Annotations (See page 63.)

☑ highlight main points ☑ underline key details ☑ write questions

☐ circle key vocabulary ☐ arrows for connections ☐ other: ____________

Procedure

1. Before students read the text a second time, say, "Now, let's reread to find answers to the question *What are the author's main points about Lincoln?* Mark the text with your thinking by highlighting the biggest ideas in the text and writing questions in the margins."
2. **Partners**—After reading, have student pairs share their annotations and thoughts about the text-dependent question.
3. Next, guide students to dig deeper by returning to the text and focusing on paragraphs 2 and 3. Say, "What details do we learn in these paragraphs?"
4. If needed, ask additional layered/scaffolded questions, such as:
   - In the second paragraph, which sentences explain how Lincoln's hat changes him?
   - From the third paragraph, what did you learn about how Lincoln used his hat?
   - How do these details help you understand the connection between Lincoln and his hat?
5. **Partners**—After students have read and annotated the text, pairs can share their annotations and their thinking.
6. **Whole Class**—Regroup as a class, and display the text for all students. Ask students to share their responses to the questions about Lincoln and his hat. Have them support their responses with their annotations. If possible, record student annotations on a displayed copy of the text.
7. You may choose to have students complete the *Museum Ad* activity (page 185) to summarize key details.

Lincoln's Hat *(cont.)*

Phase 3—Digging Even Deeper

Who Reads

❑ teacher

☑ students

Annotations (See page 63.)

☑ highlight main points ☑ underline key details ☑ write questions

❑ circle key vocabulary ❑ arrows for connections ❑ other: ______________

Procedure

1. Before returning to the text, remind students that key ideas in a text are supported by details. If more clarification is needed, say, "Details give more information, examples, and explanations to help the reader understand the key points." Have students review their annotations and share key ideas with the group. List a representative sample of the key ideas on the board.
2. Have students complete the *Lincoln's Hat: Key Idea and Details* activity (page 186). Have students begin with one of the key ideas from the board and return to the text to find phrases to add to the graphic organizer. As you circulate, assess whether pairs are struggling with the relationship between Lincoln and his hat. If they do not seem to be able to hone in on this relationship, gather students together and ask additional layered/scaffolded questions, such as:
    - What do we know from the text about what Lincoln was like physically?
    - What was the hat like physically?
    - What happened to the hat when Lincoln was riding?
    - How did Lincoln die?
    - What sort of pattern do you see in these details?
3. **Partners**—Have student partners compare and revise their graphic organizers.
4. **Whole Class**—Regroup as a class, and display the graphic organizer for all students. Ask students to share their work and their thinking.

Performance Assessment

1. Assign the performance task *Dear Diary* (page 187).
2. Explain that students' assignments will be graded based on the *Dear Diary Scoring Rubric* (page 188). The scoring rubric is for both students and teachers to guide and score work.

Name: ________________________ Date: ______________

Lincoln's Hat

1 Abraham Lincoln was a big man. He was big in character. He was big in heart. And he was even bigger in height!

2 Just how big was Lincoln? He was six feet and four inches tall. That is tall even today. But back then, most men were about a foot shorter. And Lincoln seemed even taller because of the hat he wore. It was called a *stovepipe hat* because it was tall and cylindrical like the fat pipes that came out of stoves at that time. Lincoln's hat made him more than seven feet tall.

3 The hat wasn't just for looks. Lincoln used it like a briefcase. He kept letters, bills, and notes stuffed inside his hat. If he forgot something, he just took off his hat and looked through his papers to help him remember.

4 Imagine when Lincoln came through a door. People were smaller in those days, so doorways were shorter as well. Lincoln often had to duck to keep his hat from falling off—and all his papers from falling out!

5 Lincoln's hat traveled with him nearly everywhere. Once, it even saved his life! Lincoln was riding a horse at night, and a shot rang out. The shooter missed Lincoln but hit his hat instead. Later, on the sad day when Lincoln was shot and killed at Ford's theater, his hat was found in the theater box. That hat can still be seen today at the Smithsonian in Washington, DC.

Name:______________________________ Date: ________________

Museum Ad

Directions: Create a poster to advertise the Lincoln's Hat exhibit at the Smithsonian. Use details from "Lincoln's Hat" to convince people that they should visit the museum and see this important piece of history.

Name: ______________________ Date: ______________

Lincoln's Hat: Key Idea and Details

Directions: Identify phrases from the text that help to establish the key idea. Next, identify details that help to support the key idea.

Key Idea:

Phrases that present the key idea:

Details that support the key idea:

Name:________________________________ Date: ______________

Dear Diary

Directions: Imagine you are Lincoln's hat. Write in your diary about your experiences with Lincoln. Use details from the text.

Name: ______________________ Date: ______________

Dear Diary Scoring Rubric

Directions: Complete the self-assessment section of this rubric. Then, turn this in with your completed *Dear Diary* activity. (4 means "I strongly agree." 1 means "I do not agree.")

Self-Assessment

	4	3	2	1
The experiences show a relationship between Lincoln and the hat.				
The sequence of events is clear and logical.				
I used at least three details from the text.				
I chose words and phrases that paint a picture in the reader's mind.				

Additional comments: ______________________

____

____

____

Teacher Assessment

	4	3	2	1
The experiences show a relationship between Lincoln and the hat.				
The sequence of events is clear and logical.				
The writer used at least three details from the text.				
The writer chose words and phrases that paint a picture in the reader's mind.				

Additional comments: ______________________

____

____

____

Rubric based on work by Lapp, D., B. Moss, M. Grant, & K. Johnson (2015)

Underwater Architect

4th Grade

Informational
Key Ideas and Details

Purpose

WHAT: Summarize key ideas and details in a text.

HOW: Use details to create an advertisement.

I CAN: I can summarize the most important information from a text.

Standards

- **Reading:** Explain events, procedures, ideas, or concepts in a historical, scientific, or technical text, including what happened and why, based on specific information in the text.
- **Writing:** Write informative/explanatory texts to examine a topic and to convey ideas and information clearly.
- **Language:** Acquire and use accurately grade-appropriate general academic and domain-specific words and phrases.
- **Science:** Recognize that plants and animals have internal and external structures that function to support survival, growth, behavior, and reproduction.

Performance Assessment

- Students will use specific quotes and details from the text to summarize ways in which a chambered nautilus's shell protects it.

Text Selection

- "Underwater Architect"
- Text is divided into two paragraphs.

Materials

- *Underwater Architect* passage, one copy per student (page 194; underwater.pdf)
- *Shell Details* activity (page 195)
- *Underwater Metaphor* activity (page 196)
- *Shells for Sale* activity (page 197)
- *Shells for Sale Scoring Rubric* (page 198)

Text-Dependent Questions (See pages 44–48 for more information.)

- What is this text about? What does the author want readers to know?
- How is the nautilus's body designed to help the animal survive?
- How do the survival features of the nautilus and the octopus differ?
- What is unique about the colors on the nautilus's shell?
- What happens to the shell as the nautilus grows?
- What do we learn about the nautilus from the author's comparison in paragraph 2?

Underwater Architect *(cont.)*

Areas of Complexity

	Measure	Explanation
Quantitative	Lexile Level	690L
Qualitative	Meaning or Purpose	Information is presented explicitly, but some analysis is necessary to understand the descriptive details.
	Structure	Structure is conventional; however, the diagrams add interest and content.
	Language Features	Some language is subject-specific, and the passage includes some figurative references. The sentence structure is complex, and key details may be overlooked.
Reader/Task	Knowledge Demands	Some general understanding of ocean life and shelled animals is needed to support visualization of the descriptive text. Students must sort and prioritize the details to complete the performance assessment.

Text Synopsis

This informational text describes the body of the nautilus. Specifically, the author explains how the shell of the nautilus protects it from predators through camouflage and guarding against the teeth of predators. Illustrations and captions provide additional clarification about how the nautilus's color pattern makes the animal difficult to see.

Differentiation

Additional Support—Encourage students to use the illustrations to predict and prepare to read the text. You may also choose to create and display a science word bank based on words from the passage. Guide students to use context clues from the text and illustrations to draft definitions. Students can use the word bank as they complete the assignments and as they read other texts about animals, adaptations, or camouflage.

Extension—Share texts about other animals that use camouflage. Guide students to compare protective adaptations of animals in different environments.

Underwater Architect *(cont.)*

Phase 1—Hitting the Surface

Who Reads

☐ teacher

☑ students

Annotations (See page 64.)

☑ highlight main points ☑ underline key details ☑ write questions

☑ circle key vocabulary ☐ arrows for connections ☐ other: ____________

Procedure

1. Explain the purposes (from page 189) before students read.
2. Have students read the text independently. As they read, have students annotate their copies of the text to answer the questions *What is this text about? What does the author want readers to know?*
3. Throughout each phase, as students read, circulate to observe their work, and provide scaffolds as guides for those who need assistance. These might be additional layered questions, prompts to encourage them to reflect on a certain part of the passage, or cues to remember related information. Insights you gain through this formative assessment can also influence the next questions to be asked of the whole group.
4. **Partners**—After students have read and annotated the text once, pairs can share their thinking related to the initial questions. If needed, ask additional layered/scaffolded questions, such as:
   - How is the nautilus's body designed to help the animal survive?
   - What survival feature does the nautilus have that the octopus and squid do not?
   - What information do the illustrations present?
5. **Whole Class**—Regroup as a class, and display the text for all students. Ask students to share their responses to the question regarding what the text is about. Have them support their responses with their annotations. If possible, record student annotations on a displayed copy of the text.

Underwater Architect *(cont.)*

Phase 2—Digging Deeper

Who Reads	Annotations (See page 64.)		
☐ teacher	☑ highlight main points	☑ underline key details	☑ write questions
☑ students	☑ circle key vocabulary	☑ arrows for connections	☐ other: ______________

Procedure

1. Before students read the text a second time, say, "Now, let's reread to find details about the shell. Reread the first paragraph to find the answer to the question *What is unique about the color on the nautilus's shell?* Don't forget to mark the text with underlining and notes in the margin so you'll remember what you were thinking."
2. If needed, ask additional layered/scaffolded questions, such as:
   - How are the colors described in paragraph one?
   - How are the colors described in the illustration?
   - How does the color pattern help the nautilus survive?
   - What phrases clarify the meaning of *camouflage*? Use arrows to connect *camouflage* to the words that clarify it.
3. **Partners**—After reading, have student pairs share their annotations and thoughts about the text-dependent question.
4. **Whole Class**—Regroup as a class, and display the text for all students. Ask students to share their responses to the question regarding what the text is about. Have them support their responses with their annotations. If possible, record student annotations on a displayed copy of the text.
5. Direct students to reread the second paragraph and mark details about the shell. Remind students of the text-dependent question *How is the nautilus's body designed to help the animal survive?*
6. **Partners**—After reading, partners can work together and use their annotations to complete the *Shell Details* activity (page 195).

Underwater Architect *(cont.)*

Phase 3—Digging Even Deeper

Who Reads	Annotations (See page 64.)		
☐ teacher	☐ highlight main points	☑ underline key details	☐ write questions
☑ students	☑ circle key vocabulary	☐ arrows for connections	☐ other: ____________

Procedure

1. Before returning to the text, explain that a metaphor is a comparison that authors use to describe something. Have students find the metaphor in "Underwater Architects" and reread to understand the author's description.
2. **Partners**—After reading and annotating the text, pairs can share their thinking about the metaphor and work together to complete the *Underwater Metaphor* activity (page 196).
3. **Whole Class**—Regroup as a class, and display the text for all students. Ask students, "How is a nautilus like a castle wall?" Encourage students to refer to the text as they respond. If possible, record student annotations on a displayed copy of the text.
4. Guide students to return to the images in the passage. What information do the illustrations present?
5. Have students mark the displayed text, on the board or through a document camera, to connect details in the text and the illustrations or captions that expand or explain the details.

Performance Assessment

1. Assign the performance task *Shells for Sale* (page 197).
2. Explain that students' assignments will be graded based on the *Shells for Sale Scoring Rubric* (page 198). The scoring rubric is for both students and teachers to guide and score work.

Name: ______________________ Date: ______________

Underwater Architect

1 The chambered nautilus is related to both the octopus and the squid, and, like its relatives, it has multiple arms (up to 90!). But the nautilus has an effective trait the others don't have. It has a beautiful shell that protects it from predators. The shell offers camouflage through a pattern of light and dark shades of color that mimic the animal's surroundings. The top of the shell is dark. It blends in with the dark sea. Conversely, the shell is light on the bottom. This blends in with the light coming from above the water. Inside, the shell is divided. New chambers develop inside the shell as the animal grows, creating a larger multi-faceted shell.

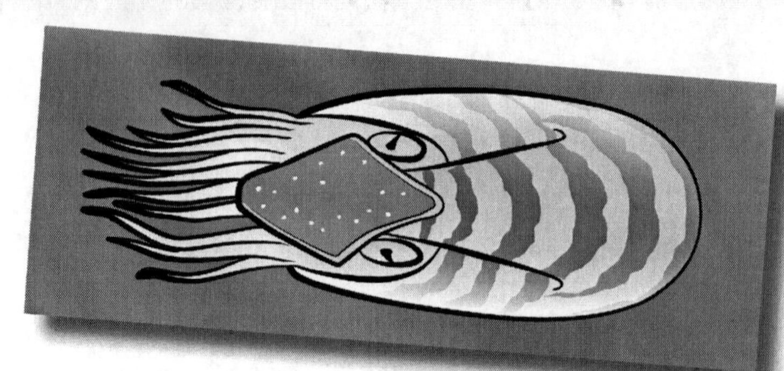

2 The nautilus can pull itself inside the shell if it feels threatened. Its hard shell offers protection from the sharp teeth of predators. Snails and hermit crabs also use shells for protection. In this same way, humans once built walls around castles. These tall rock walls protected the people inside the castle from arrows and cannons.

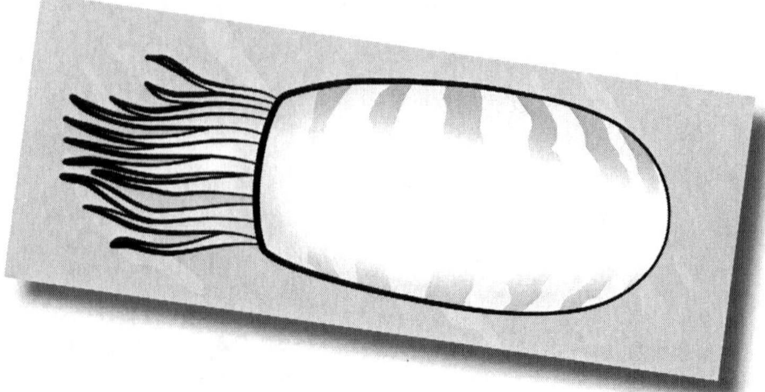

Name: ______________________ Date: ______________

Shell Details

Directions: Use the chart to record different types of details from the text.

Details about How the Shell Looks

Details about How the Shell Is Made

Details about the Shell's Job

Name: ______________________ Date: ______________

Underwater Metaphor

Directions: Copy the metaphor from the text that uses a comparison to describe the nautilus. Then, add details from the text about the two things being compared.

Metaphor (comparison):

____

____

____

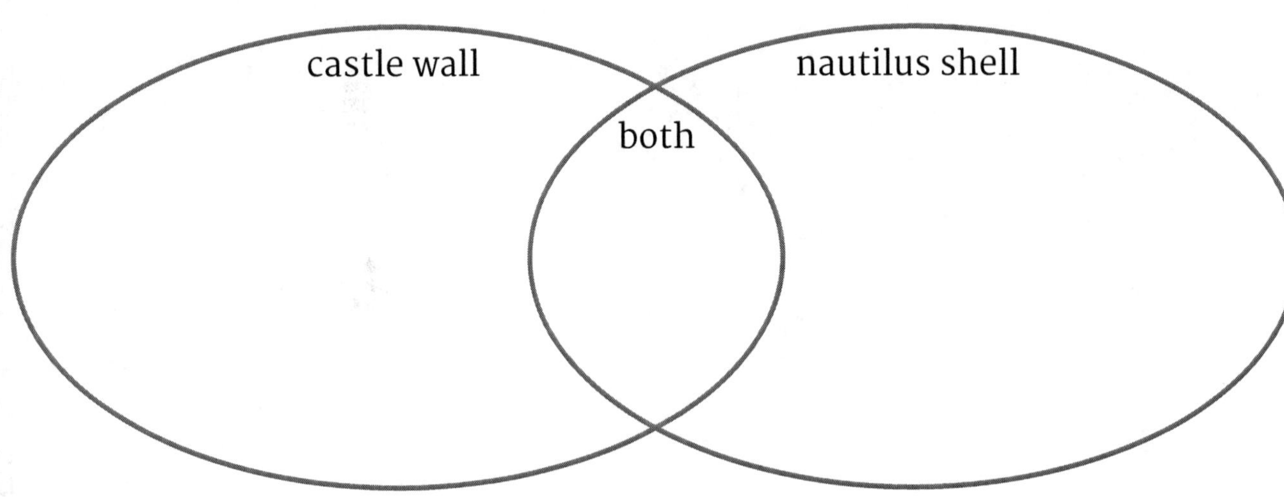

What do we learn about the nautilus from the author's comparison in paragraph two?

____

____

____

____

____

____

Name:______________________________ Date: ________________

Shells for Sale

Directions: Write an advertisement for a company selling nautilus shells to underwater creatures that do not have shells. Make sure to include details that will make animal customers want to buy the shells. Use science words from the text so that your customers know you are an expert. Include a drawing and a caption to highlight an important detail.

Name: ______________________________ Date: ______________

Shells for Sale Scoring Rubric

Directions: Complete the self-assessment section of this rubric. Then, turn this in with your completed *Shells for Sale* activity. (4 means "I strongly agree." 1 means "I do not agree.")

Self-Assessment

	4	3	2	1
I included details about the shell that would make animals want to have one.				
My drawing highlights an important detail.				
My caption describes my drawing.				
I used science words from the text.				

Additional comments: ______________________________

____

____

Teacher Assessment

	4	3	2	1
The writer included details about the shell that would make animals want to have one.				
The drawing highlights an important detail.				
The caption describes the drawing.				
The writer used science words from the text.				

Additional comments: ______________________________

____

____

Rubric based on work by Lapp, D., B. Moss, M. Grant, & K. Johnson (2015)

Blood, Sweat, and Tears

Purposes

WHAT: Determine what the text explicitly says and what can logically be inferred.

HOW: Use explicit and implicit information to write a comparison.

I CAN: I can use explicit and implicit information from a text.

Standards

- **Reading:** Explain events, procedures, ideas, or concepts in a historical, scientific, or technical text, including what happened and why, based on specific information in the text.
- **Writing:** Write informative/explanatory texts to examine a topic and to convey ideas and information clearly.
- **Language:** Acquire and use accurately grade-appropriate, general academic, and domain-specific words and phrases.
- **Science:** Compare information provided by different sources about the past.

Performance Assessment

- Students will write three paragraphs comparing fictional and historical pirates.

Text Selection

- "Blood, Sweat, and Tears"
- Text is organized in paragraphs.

Materials

- *Blood, Sweat, and Tears* passage one copy per student (page 204; bloodsweattears.pdf)
- *Explicit and Implicit Details* activity (page 205)
- *A Jolly Good Time!* activity (page 206)
- *The Pirate Life* activity (page 207)
- *The Pirate Life Scoring Rubric* (page 208)

Text-Dependent Questions (See pages 49–53 for more information.)

- What is this text about? What does the author want readers to know?
- How does the author describe the lives of historical pirates?
- How does the author describe the lives of fictional pirates?
- What did historical and fictional pirates look like?
- What does that sentence say explicitly?
- What do you think the author is trying to say with that sentence?

Blood, Sweat, and Tears *(cont.)*

Areas of Complexity

	Measure	Explanation
Quantitative	Lexile Level	870L
Qualitative	Meaning or Purpose	The passage explicitly states the main ideas, but some details require inference to fully understand
	Structure	The passage is structured as a comparison.
	Language Features	The language is descriptive and sometimes idiomatic. The text assumes familiarity with some terminology associated with sailing and pirates.
Reader/Task	Knowledge Demands	The text requires and assumes familiarity with both the life of historical sailors and literary and pop-culture depictions of pirates. Students must use the elements of comparison writing to complete the performance assessment.

Text Synopsis

This informational passage describes the living and working conditions of historical pirates. The gritty description of true pirate life is contrasted with the romantic fictional portrayals of pirates in popular culture.

Differentiation

Additional Support—Present additional examples of implicit and explicit details in other texts.

Extension—Have students research the real experiences of other romanticized figures (e.g., princesses or knights).

Blood, Sweat, and Tears *(cont.)*

Phase 1—Hitting the Surface

Who Reads

- ❑ teacher
- ☑ students

Annotations (See page 64.)

- ☑ highlight main points
- ☑ underline key details
- ☑ write questions
- ❑ circle key vocabulary
- ❑ arrows for connections
- ❑ other: ____________

Procedure

1. Before students read, explain the purposes (from page 199).
2. Have students read the text independently. As they read, students will annotate their copies of the text to answer the questions *What is this text about? What does the author want readers to know?*
3. Throughout each phase, as students read, circulate to observe their work, and provide scaffolds as guides for those who need assistance. These might be additional layered questions, prompts to encourage them to reflect on a certain part of the passage, or cues to remember related information. Insights you gain through this formative assessment can also influence the next questions to be asked of the whole group.
4. **Partners**—After students have read and annotated the text once, pairs can share their thinking as related to the initial questions.
5. **Whole Class**—Regroup as a class, and display the text for all students. Ask students to share their responses to the question regarding what the text is about. Have them support their responses with their annotations. If possible, record student annotations on a displayed copy of the text.
6. Direct students to return to the text to mark details that answer the questions *How does the author describe the lives of historical pirates? How does the author describe the lives of fictional pirates?*
7. **Partners**—After students have read and annotated the text, have pairs share their thinking related to the questions. If needed, ask additional layered/scaffolded questions, such as:
   - What did historical and fictional pirates look like?
   - What activities did historical pirates do?
   - What words describe a fictional pirate's life?
8. **Whole Class**—Regroup as a class, and display the text for all students. Ask students to share their responses to the questions regarding what the text is about. Have them support their responses with their annotations. If possible, record student annotations on a displayed copy of the text.

Blood, Sweat, and Tears *(cont.)*

Phase 2—Digging Deeper

Who Reads

☐ teacher

☑ students

Annotations (See page 64.)

☐ highlight main points
☑ underline key details
☐ write questions
☑ circle key vocabulary
☑ arrows for connections
☐ other: ____________

Procedure

1. Before students return to the text, review the meanings of *explicit* (said outright, explained) and *implicit* (suggested but not directly stated, implied) so that students can use academic language as they describe their thinking about the text. If needed, use the second paragraph to provide examples of explicit and implicit details.
2. If needed, ask additional layered/scaffolded questions, such as:
   - Look at the first sentence of the paragraph. Does it make you dig to understand the meaning? (*No, it states the meaning outright.*)
   - What about the second sentence in the paragraph? Does that sentence explicitly tell us anything about the life of a pirate? (*Yes, it tells us that a pirate wore the same clothes as any other sailor.*)
   - What do you think the author was trying to say with that sentence? (*It implies that a historical pirate could not be identified by sight on a Caribbean dock.*) The same sentence can give explicit information and also imply that other things are true.
3. Ask students to read the text again and look for explicit and implicit details about the life of pirates. If needed, ask additional layered/scaffolded questions, such as:
   - Look at the last two sentences in the first paragraph, "But say you are standing on a Caribbean dock around 1700. Then no, not so much." What does that statement imply about the life of a historical pirate?
   - Look at the last sentence of the second paragraph, "This was risky business..." What does this imply about the life of a historical pirate?
   - Look at the second sentence on the final paragraph, "Technology such as engines, radios, and GPS didn't exist." What does that statement imply about the life of a historical pirate?
4. **Partners**—After students have read and annotated the text, pairs can share their thinking about the explicit and implicit details they identified. Have partners use their annotations to complete the *Explicit and Implicit Details* activity (page 205).
5. **Whole Class**—Regroup as a class, and display the text for all students. Ask students to share their responses to the question regarding explicit and implicit details. Have them support their responses with their annotations. If possible, record student annotations on a displayed copy of the text.

Blood, Sweat, and Tears *(cont.)*

Phase 3—Digging Even Deeper

Who Reads

- ☐ teacher
- ☑ students

Annotations (See page 64.)

- ☐ highlight main points
- ☐ underline key details
- ☐ write questions
- ☑ circle key vocabulary
- ☑ arrows for connections
- ☐ other: ____________

Procedure

1. Remind students that readers often need to read a text several times. During each reading, they analyze different features to better comprehend its meaning, structure, language, author's purpose, and message.
2. Before students read the text again, say, "As you reread the text, focus in on the specific words the author uses to describe fictional pirates. Guide students to decode the hyphenated adjectives in paragraph three. If needed, encourage students to act out the words *leg-slapping* and *back-patting*.
3. **Partners**—After students have read and annotated the text once, pairs can share their thinking as related to the initial question.
4. Before assigning the performance task, have students complete the *A Jolly Good Time!* activity (page 206).

Performance Assessment

1. Assign the performance task *The Pirate Life* (page 207).
2. Explain that students' assignments will be graded based on *The Pirate Life Scoring Rubric* (page 208). The scoring rubric is for both students and teachers to guide and score work.

Name: ______________________ Date: ______________

Blood, Sweat, and Tears

1 You can easily recognize a pirate by the peg leg, eye patch, and parrot perched on his shoulder—right? If you're watching a movie, sure. Or reading a kid's book? You bet. But say you are standing on a Caribbean dock around 1700. Then, no, not so much.

2 In reality, a pirate was a sailor first. He wore the same clothes that any sailor would wear. The difference was that pirate gangs searched sea and shore to rob whatever they could find of value. Their primary goal was to raid ships or coastal towns. Pirates seized cash and gold but also valuable goods and even the ships themselves! This was risky business, as you can imagine, but came with handsome rewards. As a matter of fact, a pirate could make more money in a single haul than a sailor did in a lifetime.

3 Judging by the movies, a pirate's life was once a leg-slapping, back-patting, rip-roaring, jolly good time! Who wouldn't want to cruise the high seas with Captain Jack Sparrow? A pirate's life looks like a little mischief mixed with fun.

4 The truth is, the life of a pirate was hard and dangerous. During the Golden Age of Piracy, technology such as engines, radios, and GPS didn't exist. If it was cold at sea, pirates couldn't light a fire for warmth—a fire on board a wooden ship was dangerous! Pirates, like all sailors, had to keep their ships clean and well maintained. Every sailor on board had to work constantly to care for the ship. And if they had any illusions, every sailor learned that being a pirate was less about gold and more about blood, sweat, and tears.

Name:________________________________ Date: ________________

Explicit and Implicit Details

Directions: Identify examples of explicit statements found in "Blood, Sweat, and Tears" about historical and fictional pirates. Write the phrases in the chart.

What information about historical and fictional pirates is explicitly stated in the text?	
Historical Pirates	**Fictional Pirates**

Directions: Identify examples of statements found in "Blood, Sweat, and Tears" that hint at implicit information about historical and fictional pirates. Write the phrases and the implicit information in the chart.

What information about historical and fictional pirates is implicitly stated in the text?	
Statement from the Text	**Implicit Information**

Name: ______________________ Date: ______________

A Jolly Good Time!

Directions: Draw a scene with historical pirates and a scene with fictional pirates. Label your drawings with key details from the passage.

Name:________________________ Date: ____________

The Pirate Life

Directions: Write three paragraphs comparing and contrasting historical pirates to those portrayed in popular culture. Use evidence from "Blood, Sweat, and Tears" to support your ideas. Make sure to reference both explicit and implicit ideas from the text.

Name: ______________________ Date: ______________

The Pirate Life Scoring Rubric

Directions: Complete the self-assessment section of this rubric. Then, turn this in with your completed *The Pirate Life* activity. (4 means "I strongly agree." 1 means "I do not agree.")

Self-Assessment

	4	3	2	1
I included three paragraphs.				
My organization is clear and logical.				
I included accurate details of historical and fictional pirates.				
I included at least three accurate quotes from the text that support my statements.				

Additional comments: ______________________

____

____

Teacher Assessment

	4	3	2	1
The writer included three paragraphs.				
The organization is clear and logical.				
The writer included accurate details of historical and fictional pirates.				
The writer included at least three accurate quotes from the text that support their statements.				

Additional comments: ______________________

____

____

____

Rubric based on work by Lapp, D., B. Moss, M. Grant, & K. Johnson (2015)

Going Batty

Purpose

WHAT: Comprehend step-by-step directions and how they teach the reader to complete a task.

HOW: Use step-by-step directions to teach a reader how to create a piece of origami.

I CAN: I can use step-by step directions to teach my reader to complete a task.

Standards

- **Reading:** Assess how point of view or purpose shapes the content and style of the text. Use text features to locate information relevant to a given topic.
- **Writing:** Introduce a topic and group related information together. Include illustrations when useful to aiding comprehension.
- **Language:** Use sentence-level context as a clue to the meaning of a word or phrase.

Performance Assessment

- Students will create a piece of origami and write step-by-step directions with illustrations to teach others to make the art.

Text Selection

- "Going Batty"
- Text is chunked into steps.

Materials

- *Going Batty* passage, one copy per student (page 214; goingbatty.pdf)
- *Poof!* activity (page 215)
- *Write the Instructions* activity (page 216–217)
- *Write the Instructions Scoring Rubric* (page 218)

Text-Dependent Questions (See pages 40–43 for more information.)

- What is this text about? What does the author want readers to know?
- What text features do you notice in this passage? How do they help you understand the information in the passage?
- What structure did the author use when writing this text? How does this structure help you access information?

Going Batty *(cont.)*

Areas of Complexity

	Measure	Explanation
Quantitative	Lexile Level	(non-prose)
Qualitative	Meaning or Purpose	The purpose is stated clearly in the first paragraph. The playfully spooky tone requires understanding of the implication that bats are something fun and not to be afraid of.
	Structure	Information is presented explicitly and in logical order.
	Language Features	Language is accessible, but there are a couple instances of word play based on the word *batty*.
Reader/Task	Knowledge Demands	The reader is expected to compare complex, specific verbal instructions with illustrated examples. It is necessary to understand the cultural role of bats as mildly spooky to fully understand the text. Students must use language to specifically describe a real-world activity to complete the performance assessment.

Text Synopsis

This procedural text teaches the reader to create an origami bat. Eight detailed steps with accompanying illustrations describe the process for turning a square piece of paper into a fun and spooky bat. The author encourages the reader to enjoy the spooky perception of bats in Western culture.

Differentiation

Additional Support—Students may need a mini-lesson on text features. Consider generating a list of common text features (table of contents, headings, numbering, maps, illustrations, tables, glossaries, etc.) by searching through a few unrelated texts in the classroom. If needed, discuss cultural references of spooky bats (Halloween, dark caves, scary movies).

Extension—In China, bats are perceived as good luck (not spooky). Prompt students to rewrite the first paragraph for a Chinese audience by revising words or phrases the author used. Words that suggest spookiness should be replaced with words that suggest luckiness.

Going Batty *(cont.)*

Phase 1—Hitting the Surface

Who Reads	Annotations (See page 63.)		
❑ teacher	☑ highlight main points	❑ underline key details	❑ write questions
☑ students	❑ circle key vocabulary	❑ arrows for connections	☑ other: draw visualization

Procedure

1. Explain the purposes (from page 209) before students read.
2. Have students read the text independently. As they read, have students annotate their copies of the text to answer the questions *What is this text about? What does the author want readers to know?*
3. Throughout each phase, as students read, circulate to observe their work, and provide scaffolds as guides for those who need assistance. These might be additional layered questions, prompts to encourage them to reflect on a certain part of the passage, or cues to remember related information. Insights you gain through this formative assessment can also influence the next questions to be asked of the whole group.
4. **Partners**—After students have read and annotated the text once, pairs can share their thinking as related to the initial questions.
5. **Whole Class**—Regroup as a class, and display the text for all students. Ask students to share their responses to the question regarding what the text is about. Have them support their responses with their annotations. If possible, record student annotations on a displayed copy of the text.

Going Batty *(cont.)*

Phase 2—Digging Deeper

Who Reads	Annotations (See page 63.)		
❑ teacher	☑ highlight main points	❑ underline key details	☑ write questions
☑ students	☑ circle key vocabulary	☑ arrows for connections	❑ other: ________

Procedure

1. Before students read the text a second time, say, "Now, let's reread to find answers to the questions *What text features do you notice in this passage?* and *How do they help you understand information in this passage?* Mark the text with your thoughts by circling helpful features and by writing notes and questions in the margins."
2. **Partners**—After reading, have student pairs share their annotations and thoughts about the two text-dependent questions.
3. **Whole Class**—Have students share with the whole group. Make sure to ask them to support their responses with their annotations. If possible, record student annotations on a displayed copy of the text.
4. If needed, ask additional layered/scaffolded questions, such as:
   - Why did the author use numbers instead of bullets or indenting for each step?
   - The number of illustrations is different from the number of steps. Which illustrations go with which steps? Connect each illustration to a step.
   - How is the writing in the first paragraph different from the writing in the steps?
5. During the next close read, direct students to circle the various forms of the word *bat* and add notes and/or questions in the margins.
6. If students need more layered/scaffolded questions, ask:
   - In the first paragraph, why did the author say "get majorly batty" instead of "have fun"?
   - Why did the author use the word *flittermice*? Does she know most readers will not know that word?
7. **Partners**—Allow time for students to share their annotations and thoughts with their partners.
8. **Whole Class**—Lead a class discussion in which students support their responses with their annotations. If possible, record student annotations on a displayed copy of the text.

Going Batty *(cont.)*

Phase 3—Digging Even Deeper

Who Reads

- ❑ teacher
- ☑ students

Annotations (See page 63.)

- ❑ highlight main points
- ❑ underline key details
- ☑ write questions
- ❑ circle key vocabulary
- ❑ arrows for connections
- ❑ other: ____________

Procedure

1. Distribute square sheets of black paper and scissors. Ask students to reread the passage and follow the steps to create origami bats.
2. Direct students to review their annotations from previous readings to remember how text features were used in this passage. How did the text features help you as you followed the directions to create an origami bat?
3. Ask students to consider how the text would be different if the text features were not used. Have students complete the *Poof!* activity (page 215) to discuss and record their ideas.
4. **Partners**—Provide time for students to share their ideas and revise their responses with partners.
5. **Whole Class**—Have student pairs share their responses, supported by annotations, with the whole class. If possible, record student ideas on a displayed copy of the text.

Performance Assessment

1. Assign the performance assessment *Write the Instructions* (pages 216–217). Provide square sheets of paper for students to use to create their original origami shapes. Students can refer to their annotated "Going Batty" passage as they use similar text features to explain how to make their origami shapes.
2. Explain that students' assignments will be graded based on the *Write the Instructions Scoring Rubric* (page 218). The scoring rubric is for both students and teachers to guide and score work.

Name: ______________________ Date: ______________

Going Batty

How batty can you be? You can get majorly batty by making these fun and easy origami bats and hanging them in creepy corners. It takes a steady hand and a steadier heart to surround yourself with a cloud of flying flittermice. (That's an old English word for bats!) Just follow these steps.

1. Get paper and scissors. You will need an 8-inch square of black paper that is easy to fold.
2. To make one bat, fold a sheet of paper in half to make a triangle. Be sure to make a good crease on the fold.
3. Fold down the top two inches of the triangle at its longest side.
4. Fold in the side flaps along the inside dotted lines, shown in the picture.
5. Fold out the side flaps along the outside dotted lines, shown in the picture. This makes the bat's wings stand out from its body.
6. Cut out a notch between the wings as shown. This will make the bat's ears.
7. Flip the bat over, and fold along the bottom dotted line, shown in the picture. This will give the bat's body some shape.
8. Attach string to your bat, and hang it anywhere you like. Hang a bunch of them for an even battier look!

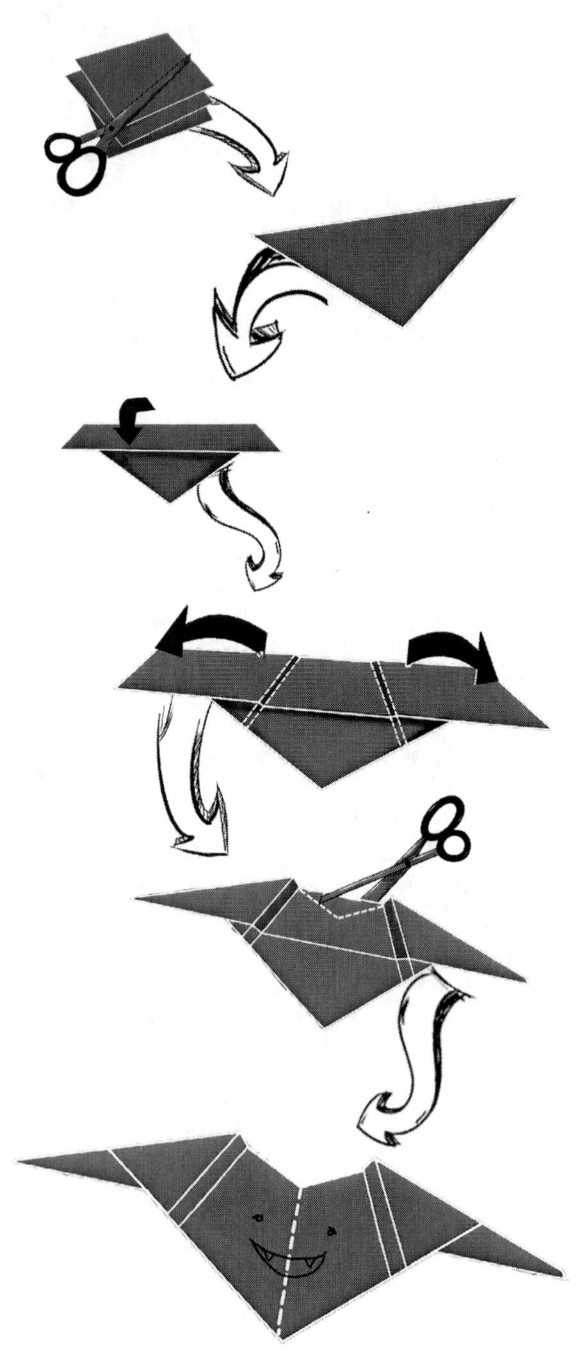

Name: ______________________ Date: ____________

Poof!

Directions: Imagine reading the text as described in each prompt. Finish the sentence to describe how you would read the text differently.

What if the text features that helped you make sense of "Going Batty" disappeared? How would that change the way you read the text?

Poof! The numbers disappear. The text is written as two paragraphs.

If the text looked like this, I would

____

Poof! The illustrations disappear. The text is a numbered list of steps.

If the text looked like this, I would

____

Poof! The numbered steps disappear. The text is a list of illustrations.

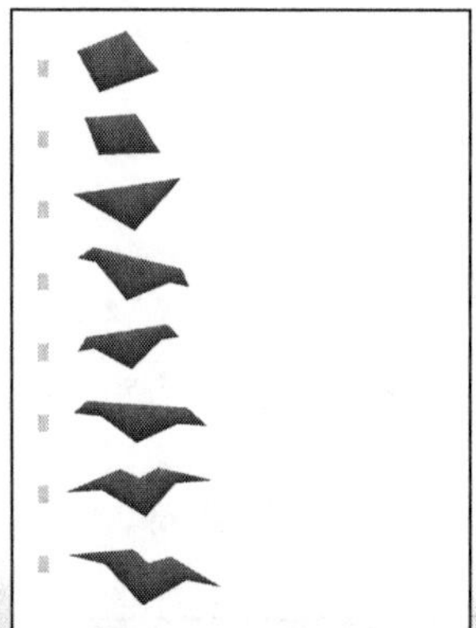

If the text looked like this, I would

____

Name: ______________________________ Date: ________________

Write the Instructions

Directions: Make your own origami, and teach someone how to make it.

1. Create a simple folded piece of art. It can be an animal or an interesting shape.
2. Write the step-by-step instructions describing how someone else can make your folded art.
3. Draw illustrations that help show how to follow your instructions.

Name:______________________ Date:____________

Write the Instructions *(cont.)*

Name: ______________________________ Date: ________________

Write the Instructions Scoring Rubric

Directions: Complete the self-assessment section of this rubric. Then, turn this in with your completed *Write the Instructions* activity. (4 means "I strongly agree." 1 means "I do not agree.")

Self-Assessment

	4	3	2	1
The sequence of my instructions is clear and logical.				
I used illustrations appropriately.				
By following the steps, a careful reader could create my folded art.				
I chose words and phrases that paint a picture in the reader's mind.				

Additional comments: ______________________________

____

____

____

Teacher Assessment

	4	3	2	1
The sequence of instructions is clear and logical.				
The writer used illustrations appropriately.				
By following the steps, a careful reader could create the folded art.				
The writer chose words and phrases that paint a picture in the reader's mind.				

Additional comments: ______________________________

____

____

____

Rubric based on work by Lapp, D., B. Moss, M. Grant, & K. Johnson (2015)

Digestion in Depth

Purpose

WHAT: Use scientific language to explain the main ideas and details of an informational text.

HOW: Write an e-mail explaining the process of digestion.

I CAN: I can use scientific language to explain an informational text.

Standards

- **Reading:** Refer to details and examples in a text when explaining what the text says explicitly and when drawing inferences from the text.
- **Writing:** Use precise language and content-specific vocabulary to inform about or explain the topic.
- **Language:** Acquire and use accurately grade-appropriate academic and content-specific words and phrases, including those that signal precise actions, emotions, or states of being.
- **Science:** Construct an argument that plants and animals have internal and external structures that function to support survival, growth, behavior, and reproduction.

Performance Assessment

- Students will write using precise language and content-specific vocabulary to explain the process of digestion.

Text Selection

- "Digestion in Depth"
- Text is organized in paragraphs.

Materials

- *Digestion in Depth passage*, one copy per student (page 224; digestion.pdf)
- *School Talk Using Super Science Words* activity (page 225)
- *Flow Chart for Food* activity (page 226)
- *Digesting a Blueberry* activity (page 227)
- *Digesting a Blueberry Scoring Rubric* (page 228)

Text-Dependent Questions (See pages 44–48 for more information.)

- What is this text about? What does the author want readers to know?
- How does the author help you to understand the meaning of the word *digestion*?
- What clues help you predict the meaning of the word *feces*?
- Why do you think the author recommends chewing each bite 20 times before swallowing and drinking lots of water?

Digestion in Depth *(cont.)*

Areas of Complexity

	Measure	Explanation
Quantitative	Lexile Level	680L
Qualitative	Meaning or Purpose	The information includes complex ideas and extensive details.
	Structure	The text organization identifies the sequence of the digestive process. It is very explicitly described. The visual supports comprehension.
	Language Features	The vocabulary is academic and scientific.
Reader/Task	Knowledge Demands	The content addresses technical information. Students must use technical vocabulary to complete the performance assessment.

Text Synopsis

The text describes the digestion process using content-specific vocabulary. The author wants the reader to understand that how long the digestion process takes depends on the type of food and that digestion moves food through the body. The visual clarifies the variation in time needed to complete digestion based on the type of food shown.

Differentiation

Additional Support—You may want to provide a diagram of the digestive system.

Students can transfer their knowledge about digestion to the *Flow Chart for Food* activity (page 226) as they reread the text.

If needed, guide students to focus on the last paragraph. Ask, "What happens if you eat too fast? What are the benefits of drinking water? Why might a person want to drink water and chew longer when eating a hamburger?"

Extension—Have students write about the digestive system from the point of view of the food being eaten.

Digestion in Depth *(cont.)*

Phase 1—Hitting the Surface

Who Reads	Annotations (See page 64.)		
❑ teacher	❑ highlight main points	☑ underline key details	☑ write questions
☑ students	❑ circle key vocabulary	❑ arrows for connections	❑ other: ____________

Procedure

1. Explain the purposes (from page 219) before students read.
2. Have students read the text independently. As they read, have students annotate their copies of the text to answer the questions *What is this text about? What does the author want readers to know?*
3. Throughout each phase, as students read, circulate to observe their work, and provide scaffolds as guides for those who need assistance. These might be additional layered questions, prompts to encourage them to reflect on a certain part of the passage, or cues to remember related information. Insights you gain through this formative assessment can also influence the next questions to be asked of the whole group.
4. **Partners**—After students have read and annotated the text once, pairs can share their thinking as related to the initial questions.
5. **Whole Class**—Regroup as a class, and display the text for all students. Ask students to share their responses to the question regarding what the text is about. Have them support their responses with their annotations. If possible, record student annotations on a displayed copy of the text.

Digestion in Depth *(cont.)*

Phase 2—Digging Deeper

Who Reads

- ❑ teacher
- ☑ students

Annotations (See page 64.)

- ☑ highlight main points
- ❑ underline key details
- ☑ write questions
- ☑ circle key vocabulary
- ☑ arrows for connections
- ❑ other: ____________

Procedure

1. Before students read a second time, say, "Now, let's reread to find responses to the question *How does the author help you to understand the meaning of the word* digestion? Annotate the text to show where you find ideas to support your thinking. Write your notes and questions in the margins so when you return to these, you'll remember what you were thinking."
2. **Partners**—After reading, have student pairs share their annotations and thoughts about this text-dependent question.
3. **Whole Class**—Have students share their ideas with the whole group. Make sure to ask them to support their responses with their annotations. If possible, record student annotations on a displayed copy of the text.
4. If needed, ask an additional layered/scaffolded question, such as:
    - How does the author help you to understand the path food takes as it travels through the body?
5. Before students return to the text, say, "The author uses many science words in the text. What clues help you predict the meaning of the word *feces*?"
6. If students need more layered/scaffolded questions, ask:
    - How do you think the idea of "foods spending time rotting in the intestine" connects to the science word *feces*?
7. **Partners**—Allow time for students to share their annotations and thoughts with their partners. Have partners complete the *School Talk Using Super Science Words* activity (page 225) to practice using the science words from the text.
8. **Whole Class**—Lead a whole class discussion in which students support their responses with their annotations. If possible, record student annotations on a displayed copy of the text.

Digestion in Depth *(cont.)*

Phase 3—Digging Even Deeper

Who Reads	Annotations (See page 64.)		
☐ teacher	☑ highlight main points	☐ underline key details	☐ write questions
☑ students	☐ circle key vocabulary	☑ arrows for connections	☐ other: ____________

Procedure

1. Before students return to the text, ask, "Why do you think the author recommends chewing each bite 20 times before swallowing and drinking lots of water?" Encourage students to refer to specific information from the text in their responses.
2. If students need more layered/scaffolded questions, ask:
   - Look at paragraph two. How does the time it takes for certain foods to digest compare to how hard they are to digest?
   - Based on the illustration, which takes longer to digest: a hamburger or broccoli?
   - Which is harder to digest, a hamburger or broccoli?
3. **Partners**—Allow time for students to share their annotations and thoughts with their partners.
4. **Whole Class**—If time allows, lead a whole class discussion on the text-dependent question. Have students support their responses with their annotations. If possible, record student annotations on a displayed copy of the text.
5. After the class discussion, have students complete the *Flow Chart for Food* activity (page 226) to record their understanding of the passage.

Performance Assessment

1. Assign the performance task *Digesting a Blueberry* (page 227). Students can refer to their annotated "Digestion in Depth" texts as they write RAFTs (Role, Audience, Format, and Topic), using appropriate science words (such as *digestion*, *intestine*, *nutrients*, and *feces*) to explain the process of digestion. You may have students write their RAFTs individually or with partners.
2. Explain that students' assignments will be graded based on the *Digesting a Blueberry Scoring Rubric* (page 228). The scoring rubric is for both students and teachers to guide and score work.

Name: ______________________ Date: ______________

Digestion in Depth

1 No one can deny that humans love to eat. We eat many different kinds of foods, and we each have our favorites. But when it comes to digestion, there are certain things every human has in common. It takes us between 5 and 30 seconds to chew a bite of food. It takes about 10 seconds to swallow. When the food reaches our stomachs, it can slosh around for three to four hours. Food travels through the small intestine for three hours. Then, it visits the large intestine to dry out. It could be in there up to two days!

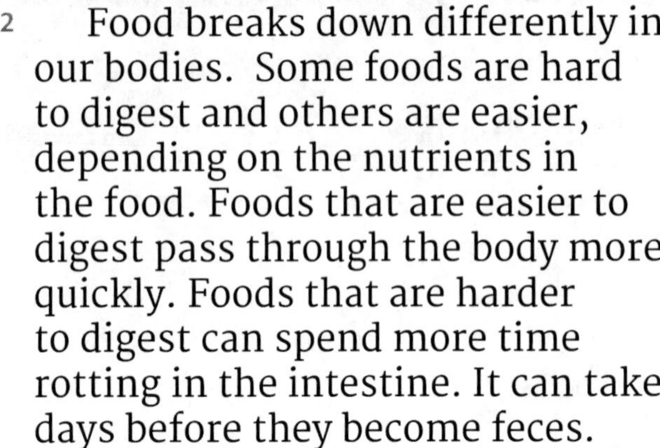

2 Food breaks down differently in our bodies. Some foods are hard to digest and others are easier, depending on the nutrients in the food. Foods that are easier to digest pass through the body more quickly. Foods that are harder to digest can spend more time rotting in the intestine. It can take days before they become feces.

3 No matter what you eat, there are some easy ways to help your digestion. Drink lots of water. That will help keep the digestive system moving. Exercise also helps speed up digestion.

4 Running is a great way to keep your intestines healthy. But sometimes, we also need to slow down. Eating quickly can cause gas and bloating. Try to eat slowly. You may even want to count the number of times you chew each bite—20 is a good number!

Name:______________________________ Date: ________________

School Talk Using Super Science Words

Directions: Create a list of science words from the text. Share and compare lists with a partner, adding words to your own list. With your partner, write a sentence for each word using the sentence frames.

Science Words

Our Sentences

At first, ______________________________.

The next step ______________________________.

We've learned that ______________________________.

The text states ______________________________.

The process includes ______________________________.

Later on, ______________________________.

Finally, ______________________________.

In the end, ______________________________.

Based on what we read, we know ______________________________

____

____

Name: ______________________ Date: ______________

Flow Chart for Food

Directions: Complete the digestion flow chart by writing a brief description of each illustration.

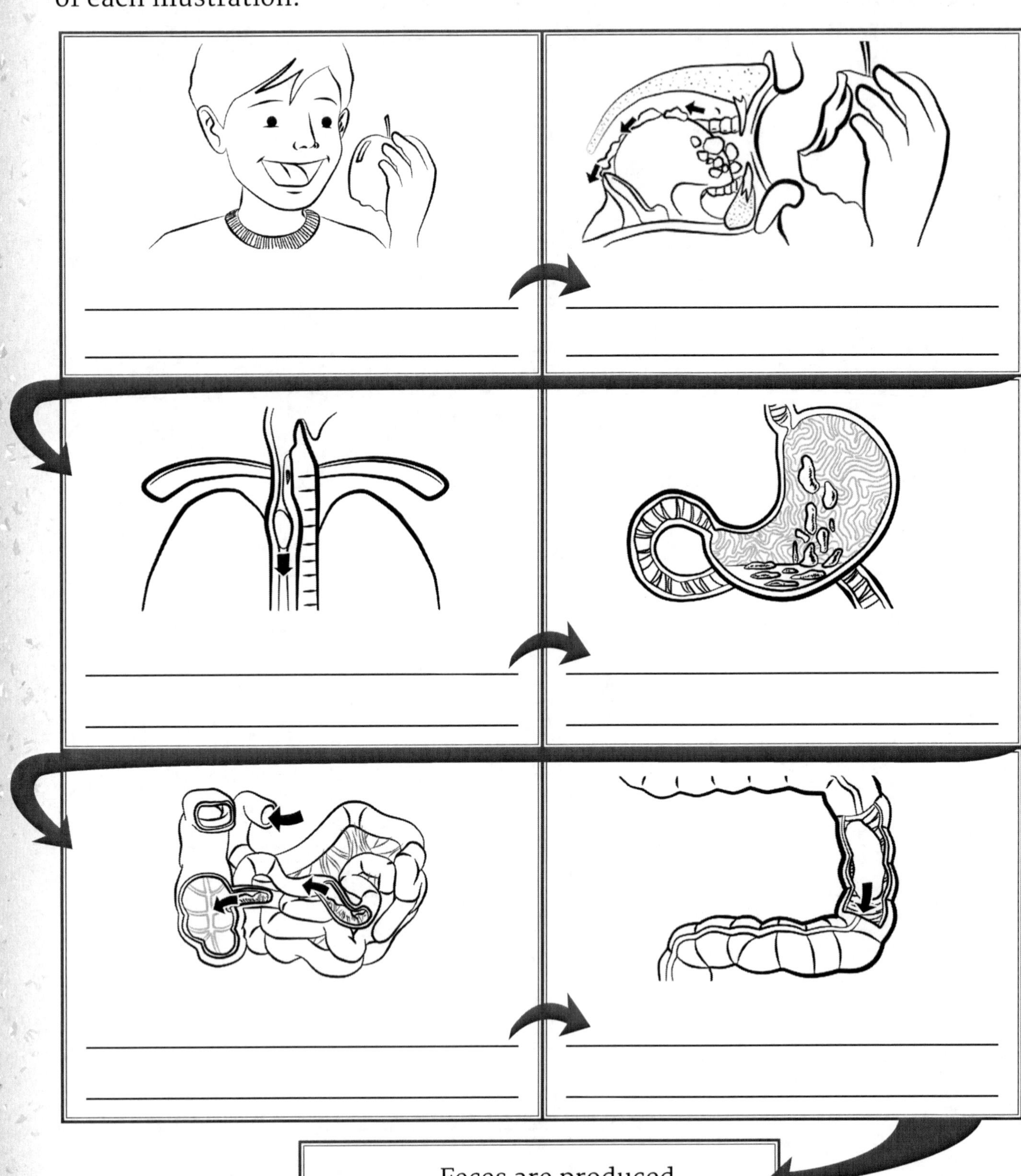

Feces are produced.

Name:______________________________ Date: ______________

Digesting a Blueberry

Directions: Write a RAFT (Role, Audience, Format, and Topic) using appropriate science words (such as *digestion*, *intestine*, *nutrients*, and *feces*) to explain the process of digestion.

R—a blueberry

A—a person who is going to scoop you up and eat you

F—an email

T—how your body will digest me

Name: ______________________________ Date: ______________

Digesting a Blueberry Scoring Rubric

Directions: Complete the self-assessment section of this rubric. Then, turn this in with your completed *Digesting a Blueberry* activity. (4 means "I strongly agree." 1 means "I do not agree.")

Self-Assessment

	4	3	2	1
My RAFT begins with a salutation (greeting).				
I describe the digestive process from the mouth (chewing) to the end (feces).				
I use science words such as *digestion*, *intestine*, *nutrients*, and *feces*.				
I use science talk, such as *This can cause*______; *I know this*_______ *because*______; and *When I read, I learned* ______.				
My email ends with a closing and my blueberry signature.				

Additional comments: ____

____

____

Teacher Assessment

	4	3	2	1
There is a salutation (greeting).				
There is a detailed description of the digestive process from the mouth (chewing) to the end (feces).				
The RAFT includes science words.				
The RAFT includes academic language (science talk).				
There is a closing and blueberry signature.				

Additional comments: ____

____

____

Rubric based on work by Lapp, D., B. Moss, M. Grant, & K. Johnson (2015)

Trapped for 69 Days

Purposes

WHAT: Assess how word choice affects the tone of a text.

WHAT: Interpret words and phrases in a sequenced text.

HOW: Write a series of e-mails using appropriate word choice.

I CAN: I can use word choice to set the tone of a text.

Standards

- **Reading:** Describe how a narrator's point of view influences how events are described.
- **Writing:** Produce clear and coherent writing in which the development and organization are appropriate to the task, purpose, and audience.
- **Language:** Use knowledge of language and its conventions when writing, speaking, reading, or listening.

Performance Assessment

- Students will write a series of emails that include the most important updates on the miners' situation. Word choice will be used to set an appropriate tone.

Text Selection

- "Trapped for 69 Days"
- Text is organized in paragraphs with an accompanying time line.

Materials

- *Trapped for 69 Days* passage, one copy per student (page 234; trapped.pdf)
- *Line It Up* activity (page 235)
- *Word Power* activity (page 236)
- *Email Updates* activity (page 237)
- *Email Updates Scoring Rubric* (page 238)

Text-Dependent Questions (See pages 49–53 for more information.)

- What is this text about? What does the author want readers to know?
- How does the author present the sequence of events?
- How much time passes between each event?
- What tone or feeling does the author's choice of words create?

Trapped for 69 Days *(cont.)*

Areas of Complexity

	Measure	Explanation
Quantitative	Lexile Level	790L
Qualitative	Meaning or Purpose	The information is presented explicitly with dramatic nonfiction narrative elements.
Qualitative	Structure	The time line is presented in chronological order, while the text slightly varies its chronology by presenting the basic scenario at the outset, in an effort to build tension.
Qualitative	Language Features	There are both technical terms and Spanish words included in the text.
Reader/Task	Knowledge Demands	The text requires that students have a very basic, general understanding of digging underground for resources. Students must infer the needs of ancillary figures (the miners' families) to complete the performance assessment.

Text Synopsis

This presents the real-life drama of a group of miners that were trapped underground for 69 days. The men survived on their own for several weeks before rescuers could reach them. They then received food and gifts from family and friends, and rescuers worked to free them. The men became famous after the world watched them emerge from the mine alive.

Differentiation

Additional Support—Students who have trouble following the specific sequence of events in the text may benefit from using the *Line It Up* activity (page 235) to organize their understanding on the first or second read. If needed, review the meaning between similar words. Have students define words that have nearly the same meaning but that set different tones. Provide access to dictionaries and other reference resources.

Extension—Have students change the word choice in the text to set a different tone. Different words can make the text more appropriate for a tabloid magazine, a safety manual, or a dramatic novel.

Trapped for 69 Days *(cont.)*

Phase 1—Hitting the Surface

Who Reads	Annotations (See page 64.)		
❑ teacher	☑ highlight main points	☑ underline key details	☑ write questions
☑ students	❑ circle key vocabulary	❑ arrows for connections	❑ other: ___________

Procedure

1. Explain the purposes (from page 229) before students read.
2. Have students read the text independently. As they read, have students annotate their copies of the text to answer the questions *What is this text about?* and *What does the author want readers to know?*
3. Throughout each phase, as students read, circulate to observe their work, and provide scaffolds as guides for those who need assistance. These might be additional layered questions, prompts to encourage them to reflect on a certain part of the passage, or cues to remember related information. Insights you gain through this formative assessment can also influence the next questions to be asked of the whole group.
4. **Partners**—After students have read and annotated the text once, pairs can share their thinking as related to the initial questions.
5. **Whole Class**—Regroup as a class, and display the text for all students. Ask students to share their responses to the question regarding what the text is about. Have them support their responses with their annotations. If possible, record student annotations on a displayed copy of the text.

Trapped for 69 Days *(cont.)*

Phase 2—Digging Deeper

Who Reads	Annotations (See page 64.)		
☑ teacher	❑ highlight main points	❑ underline key details	☑ write questions
❑ students	☑ circle key vocabulary	☑ arrows for connections	☑ other: number the events in order

Procedure

1. Before students read a second time, explain to them that authors can use sequence (the order of events) to tell a story. Reread "Trapped for 69 Days" (page 234) to answer the text-dependent question *How does the author present the sequence of events?* Have students number the events the author describes and circle the words that help them follow the sequence.
2. **Partners**—After students have read and annotated the text, pairs can share their thinking as related to the text-dependent question.
3. Have students to annotate the text further in response to the question *How much time passes between each event?* Say, "Annotate the text to show where you find ideas to support your thinking. Write your notes and questions in the margins so when you return to these, you'll remember what you were thinking."
4. If needed, ask additional layered/scaffolded questions, such as:
   - When were the men first trapped?
   - How many days have passed when this event happened?
   - How can you mark how much time has passed?
5. **Whole Class**—Regroup as a class, and display the text for all students. Ask students to share their responses to the question regarding how much time passes. Have them support their responses with their annotations. If possible, record student annotations on a displayed copy of the text.
6. **Partners**—Guide student partners to use their annotated text to complete *Line It Up* activity (page 235).

Trapped for 69 Days *(cont.)*

Phase 3—Digging Even Deeper

Who Reads	Annotations (See page 64.)		
☐ teacher	☐ highlight main points	☐ underline key details	☐ write questions
☑ students	☑ circle key vocabulary	☐ arrows for connections	☐ other: ________

Procedure

1. Before returning to the text, have students consider the text-dependent question *What tone or feeling does the author's choice of words create?* Say, "As you reread the text, look for words that make you feel something. Is the author being serious, silly, dramatic, sympathetic, angry, or something else?"
2. If needed, ask additional layered/scaffolded questions, such as:
   - In paragraph one, what is the impact of the word *saga*?
   - In paragraph one, what is the impact of the phrase *buried alive*?
   - In paragraph two, what is the impact of the phrase *feared the worst*?
   - In paragraph four, what is the impact of the phrase *devised a plan*?
   - In paragraph five, what is the impact of the word *superstars*?
3. **Whole Class**—Regroup as a class, and display the text for all students. Lead a discussion of the author's word choice. Have students support their ideas with their annotations. If possible, record student annotations on a displayed copy of the text.
4. Work together as a group, in partners, or individually to complete the *Word Power* activity (page 236).

Performance Assessment

1. Assign the performance task *Email Updates* (page 237).
2. Explain that students' assignments will be graded based on the *Email Updates Scoring Rubric* (page 238). The scoring rubric is for both students and teachers to guide and score work.

Name: ______________________ Date: ______________

Trapped for 69 Days

1 For 69 days in 2010, people around the world wondered if the 33 miners trapped in a mine in northern Chile would ever make it out alive. The saga began August 5th, when the entrance to the San José gold and copper mine collapsed. The men, ranging from 19 to 63 years old, were buried alive.

2 During the first 17 days, there was no contact from the men. Their families and friends feared the worst. But just as hope was waning, good news came from the rescue team: All 33 men were alive!

3 The group had found an emergency shelter off one of the mine's tunnels. Despite the heat and darkness, the group remained in good spirits. For those first 17 days, the men drank water from radiator tanks. They shared food that was meant to only last for 48 hours. Once they were located, rescuers drilled small holes and sent down tubes with food, water, clothes, and other supplies. The men received letters from their families, a TV, an MP3 player, and games.

4 But how would they get out? Rescuers devised a plan to build a tunnel that could transport a 13-foot capsule down 2,041 feet. It would be sent down to retrieve the men, one by one. On October 13, the first miner was rescued, soon followed by his 32 colleagues. It was the longest time anyone had ever survived being trapped underground.

5 The crowd cheered as the men emerged. Some became superstars. Many had trouble adjusting to their new life. But all were glad to be alive.

0 days - 69 days

A boulder seals the exit.	The miners survive 17 days without contact from above ground.	Experts from around the world race to save the miners.

Trapped - Rescued!

Name:______________________ Date: ______________

Line It Up

Directions: Each tick on the time line represents one day. Extend the lines for important days, and label them with events described in "Trapped for 69 Days." The first one has been done for you.

Day 0: entrance to the mine collapsed

Name: ______________________ Date: ______________

Word Power

Directions: Replace the underlined word with a more powerful synonym. Then, describe the tone or feeling your sentence creates.

1. I walked to the front of the class to get my award.

____

2. Jules walked into the cold, dark cave.

____

3. Frankenstein's monster walked through the village.

____

4. Min got so mad, she walked out in the middle of dinner.

____

5. Ten dancers walked across the stage.

____

Name:_________________________ Date: ______________

Email Updates

Directions: Pretend you are the director of the rescue team working to save the miners. Write three emails to send to the miners' families. Choose three important dates from the text, and include important details to update the families about what has happened to the miners on those dates. Make sure to choose words that set the appropriate tone for worried families.

To: **Date:**

From:

____

____

____

____

To: **Date:**

From:

____

____

____

____

To: **Date:**

From:

____

____

____

____

Name: ______________________________ Date: ________________

Email Updates Scoring Rubric

Directions: Complete the self-assessment section of this rubric. Then, turn this in with your completed *Email Updates* activity. (4 means "I strongly agree." 1 means "I do not agree.")

Self-Assessment

	4	3	2	1
I chose three important dates from the text.				
I included important events from the text.				
My words create an appropriate tone.				
My writing is clear and easily understood.				

Additional comments: ______________________________

____

____

____

Teacher Assessment

	4	3	2	1
The writer chose three important dates from the text.				
The writer included important events from the text.				
The writer's words created an appropriate tone.				
The writing is clear and easily understood.				

Additional comments: ______________________________

____

____

____

Rubric based on work by Lapp, D., B. Moss, M. Grant, & K. Johnson (2015)

Legless, Fearless

Purpose

WHAT: Identify cause and effect relationships.

HOW: Write a letter highlighting the cause and effect relationship between Aimee Mullins' attitude and achievements.

I CAN: I can identify cause and effect relationships in a text.

Standards

- **Reading:** Describe the logical connection between particular sentences and paragraphs in a text (e.g., comparison, cause/effect, first/second/third in a sequence).
- **Writing:** Develop the topic with facts, definitions, and details.
- **Language:** Use sentence-level context as a clue to the meaning of a word or phrase.

Performance Assessment

- Students will write informative pieces, showing the cause and effect relationships between challenges and successes.

Text Selection

- "Legless, Fearless"
- Text is divided into paragraphs.

Materials

- *Legless, Fearless* passage, one copy per student (page 244; leglessfearless.pdf)
- *What's the Relationship?* activity (page 245)
- *Please Explain* activity (page 246)
- *Role Model Assembly* activity (page 247)
- *Role Model Assembly Scoring Rubric* (page 248)

Text-Dependent Questions (See pages 40–43 for more information.)

- What is this text about? What does the author want readers to know?
- What are the cause and effect relationships?
- How do the facts fit together?
- How does the author help you understand the term *prosthetic leg*?
- How is Mullins described in the text and illustration?
- How does Mullins describe what her legs do for her?
- What is the difference between being a fashion model and being a model for living well?

Legless, Fearless *(cont.)*

Areas of Complexity

	Measure	Explanation
Quantitative	Lexile Level	770L
Qualitative	Meaning or Purpose	The text is used as a way to inspire readers to achieve things despite challenges.
	Structure	The text is organized by paragraphs that develop the story. Aimee Mullins' life and accomplishments are presented in chronological order.
	Language Features	Technical terms and general academic vocabulary may impede comprehension. There is a mix of formal and informal language. Some words have several possible meanings that can only be fully understood in context.
Reader/Task	Knowledge Demands	The main character's achievements are easily understood. The details of her challenges and her tools are described with technical details. Students must understand cause and effect relationships to complete the performance assessment.

Text Synopsis

The story is about a girl whose legs had to be removed as a child. Despite this challenge, the girl uses prosthetic legs and has become a top athlete, fashion model, and public speaker.

Differentiation

Additional Support—You may need to assist students with identifying cause and effect relationships to ensure success with the writing activity. As needed, students can transfer their annotations to the *What's the Relationship?* activity (page 245).

Extension—Instruct students to identify the relationship between challenges and success in the life of inspirational figures they know.

Legless, Fearless *(cont.)*

Phase 1—Hitting the Surface

Who Reads

☐ teacher

☑ students

Annotations (See page 63.)

☑ highlight main points ☐ underline key details ☑ write questions

☑ circle key vocabulary ☐ arrows for connections ☐ other: ____________

Procedure

1. Explain the purposes (from page 239) before students read.
2. Have students read the text independently. As they read, have students annotate their copies of the text to answer the questions *What is this text about? What does the author want readers to know?*
3. Throughout each phase, as students read, circulate to observe their work, and provide scaffolds as guides for those who need assistance. These might be additional layered questions, prompts to encourage them to reflect on a certain part of the passage, or cues to remember related information. Insights you gain through this formative assessment can also influence the next questions to be asked of the whole group.
4. **Partners**—After students have read and annotated the text once, pairs can share their thinking as related to the initial questions.
5. **Whole Class**—Regroup as a class, and display the text for all students. Ask students to share their responses to the question regarding what the text is about. Have them support their responses with their annotations. If possible, record student annotations on a displayed copy of the text.

Legless, Fearless *(cont.)*

Phase 2—Digging Deeper

Who Reads

- ❑ teacher
- ☑ students

Annotations (See page 63.)

- ❑ highlight main points
- ☑ underline key details
- ❑ write questions
- ☑ circle key vocabulary
- ☑ arrows for connections
- ☑ other: notes in the margin

Procedure

1. Before students read the text a second time, say, "Now, let's reread to identify the structure of this text. How is this text organized? Don't forget to mark the text with underlining and arrows, and write notes in the margins so you'll remember what you were thinking."
2. If needed, ask additional layered/scaffold questions, such as:
   - What are the main facts?
   - How do the facts fit together?
   - What are the cause and effect relationships?
   - What things happened that caused other things to happen?
3. **Whole Group**—After students have read and annotated the text, lead a discussion about text structure. Encourage students to refer to their annotations in their responses.
4. Say, "Find the word *prosthetic* in multiple places in the text. How does the author help you to understand the term *prosthetic leg*? Mark the text to show your thinking."
5. If needed, ask additional layered/scaffolded questions, such as:
   - What does this sentence tell you about prosthetic legs?
   - According to the text, what is unique about prosthetic legs?
6. **Partners**—After students have read and annotated the text, pairs can share their understanding of prosthetic legs. Have each student think of a sentence about Aimee Mullins that uses this new word.

Legless, Fearless *(cont.)*

Phase 3—Digging Even Deeper

Who Reads

☐ teacher
☑ students

Annotations **(See page 63.)**

☑ highlight main points
☑ underline key details
☐ write questions
☐ circle key vocabulary
☐ arrows for connections
☐ other: ____________

Procedure

1. Have students return to the text to add additional thoughts and ideas about Aimee Mullins. Ask, "How is Mullins described in the text and illustration?"
2. If needed, ask additional layered/scaffolded questions, such as:
   - How does Mullins describe what her legs do for her?
   - What is the difference between being a fashion model and being a model for living well?
   - How is the illustration helpful?
   - How does the illustration grab the reader's attention?
   - What can be learned from the illustration that is not included in the text?
3. **Partners**—After students have read and annotated the text, pairs can share their thinking about Mullins' personality traits and her achievements.
4. Prior to the performance task, have students think about the passage individually by completing the *What's the Relationship*? activity (page 245).

Performance Assessment

1. Assign the performance task *Role Model Assembly* (page 247).
2. Explain that students' assignments will be graded based on the *Role Model Assembly Scoring Rubric* (page 248). The scoring rubric is for both students and teachers to guide and score work.

Name: ______________________ Date: ______________

Legless, Fearless

1 Some professional athletes return to peak fitness after being hurt, while others struggle to maintain their performance level with bodies that some might deem limited. Aimee Mullins is one such athlete. Mullins's legs were amputated below the knee when she was a baby as a result of being born without fibular (fibulae) bones. Unlike the bones in her legs, Mullins was strong, and she used her strength and confidence to overcome this obstacle. Fitted with prosthetic legs made from metal and other materials, she learned to walk. With her new legs, Mullins became a top track and field athlete.

2 Mullins now works as a fashion model. You can find her walking the runway in today's top fashion shows or in magazines donning the latest makeup trends.

3 Many people admire Mullins and her story. If you want to know more about her drive and tenacity, she is more than happy to tell. She gives motivational speeches and helps people see what they can achieve. Mullins explains that her legs give her "superpowers." She doesn't see her legs as a hindrance; she sees them as a great gift. In fact, she has many different pairs of legs. She chooses a different pair each day depending on what she wants to do!

4 Mullins is not *only* a fashion model. She is not *only* an athlete. She is also a model for living well.

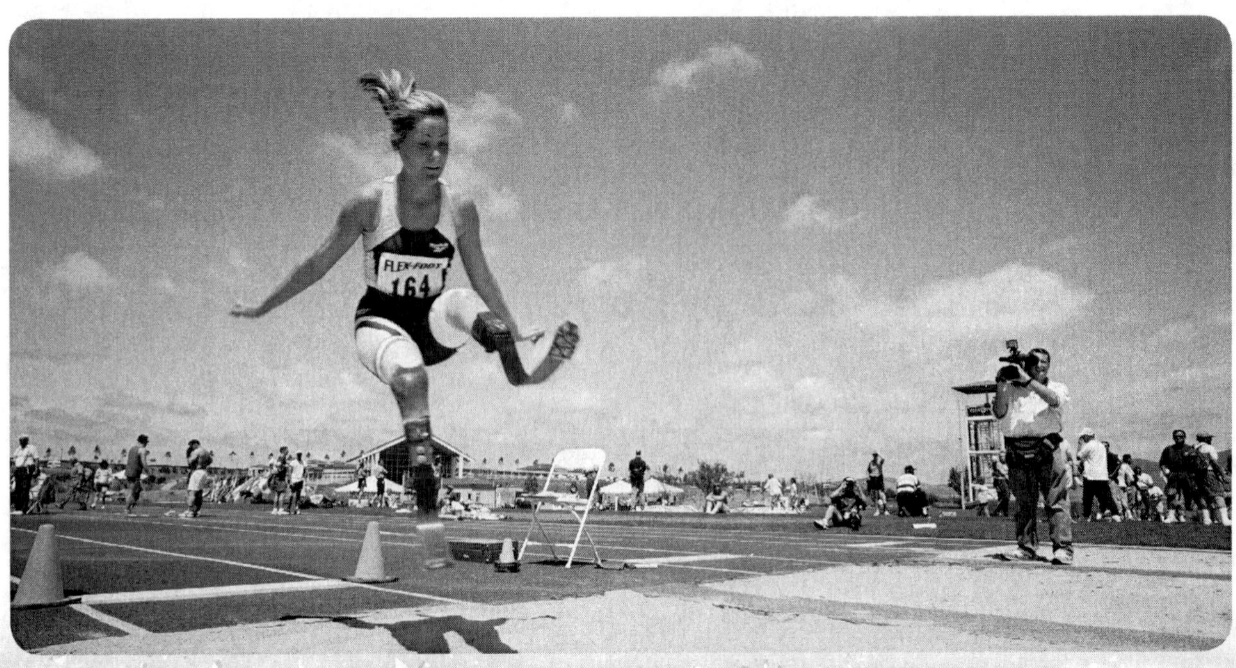

Name:______________________________ Date: ______________

What's the Relationship?

Directions: Use the relationship words in the word bank to describe how one element from the text was affected by another.

Mullins's legs removed as a baby — **prosthetic legs**

____

____

Mullins's attitude — **Mullins's ability**

____

____

Mullins's story — **people who hear Mullins's story**

____

____

Cause-and-Effect Words		
caused	will cause	because
affected	affects	will affect

Name: ____________________ Date: ____________

Please Explain

Directions: Refer to the passage "Legless, Fearless" to define words and phrases a reader may not understand.

Challenging Word(s)	Clues from the Text	Definition
admire		
prosthetic		
peak fitness		
speeches		
fashion model		
model for living well		

Name:______________________________ Date: ______________

Role Model Assembly

Directions: Write a letter to your principal to recommend inviting Aimee Mullins to speak at a school assembly. Use facts from the text to explain the cause and effect relationship between Aimee Mullins' attitude and achievements. Also, predict the effect Mullins' speech would have on students.

Name: ______________________________ Date: ______________

Role Model Assembly Scoring Rubric

Directions: Complete the self-assessment section of this rubric. Then, turn this in with your completed *Role Model Assembly* activity. (4 means "I strongly agree." 1 means "I do not agree.")

Self-Assessment

	4	3	2	1
I suggested my principal invite Mullins to speak at an assembly.				
I explained the cause and effect relationships between Mullins' attitude and achievements.				
I predicted the effect of Mullins' speech on students.				
I included facts from the text to support my recommendation to the principal.				

Additional comments: ______________________________

____

____

Teacher Assessment

	4	3	2	1
The writer suggested the principal invite Mullins to speak at an assembly.				
The writer explained the cause and effect relationships between Mullins' attitude and achievements.				
The writer predicted the effect of Mullins' speech on students.				
The writer included facts from the text to support the recommendation to the principal.				

Additional comments: ______________________________

____

____

Rubric based on work by Lapp, D., B. Moss, M. Grant, & K. Johnson (2015)

It's the Law! But Why?

4th Grade

Informational
Integration of Knowledge and Ideas

Purpose

WHAT: Integrate details in a text.

HOW: Write a summary.

I CAN: I can integrate details in a text to form a summary.

Standards

- **Reading:** Explain how an author uses reasons and evidence to support particular points in a text.
- **Writing:** Combine details into larger statements.
- **Language:** Choose punctuation for effect.

Performance Assessment

- Students will write summaries using punctuation for effect.

Text Selection

- "It's the Law! But Why?"
- Text is divided into paragraphs.

Materials

- *It's the Law! But Why?* passage, one copy per student (page 254; itsthelaw.pdf)
- *Gather the Details* activity (page 255)
- *Express Yourself!* activity (page 256)
- *World's Shortest Summary* activity, (page 257)
- *World's Shortest Summary Scoring Rubric* (page 258)

Text-Dependent Questions (See pages 44–48 for more information.)

- What is this text about? What does the author want readers to know?
- What does *kookiest* mean in this text?
- How do the sentences in the text relate to each other?
- What does the text communicate about how police officers prioritize their work?
- What makes laws less powerful?

It's the Law! But Why? *(cont.)*

Areas of Complexity

	Measure	Explanation
Quantitative	Lexile Level	660L
Qualitative	Meaning or Purpose	The text communicates fun, factual information about silly laws that exist in certain states.
	Structure	The author begins with a statement about the importance of laws. Then, the author lists several silly laws. The author concludes about how silly laws are handled today.
	Language Features	The language is accessible.
Reader/Task	Knowledge Demands	It is assumed that readers will understand the concept of laws.

Text Synopsis

The text is about the silly laws that exist in many states. These laws have been on the books for many years, and they do not seem to make sense today. No one really knows why they were ever created.

Differentiation

Additional Support—You may need to assist students' comprehension by allowing them to discuss the text in pairs.

As needed, students can transfer their annotations to the *Gather the Details* activity (page 255). This graphic organizer supports students as they reread the text.

Extension—Instruct students to write about reasons they think certain silly laws were originally created.

It's the Law! But Why? *(cont.)*

Phase 1—Hitting the Surface

Who Reads	Annotations (See page 64.)		
☐ teacher	☐ highlight main points	☑ underline key details	☑ write questions
☑ students	☐ circle key vocabulary	☐ arrows for connections	☐ other: ________

Procedure

1. Explain the purposes (from page 249) before students read.
2. Have students read the text independently. As they read, have students annotate their copies of the text to answer the questions *What is this text about? What does the author want readers to know?*
3. Throughout each phase, as students read, circulate to observe their work, and provide scaffolds as guides for those who need assistance. These might be additional layered questions, prompts to encourage them to reflect on a certain part of the passage, or cues to remember related information. Insights you gain through this formative assessment can also influence the next questions to be asked of the whole group.
4. **Partners**—After students have read and annotated the text once, pairs can share their thinking as related to the initial questions.
5. **Whole Class**—Regroup as a class, and display the text for all students. Ask students to share their responses to the question regarding what the text is about. Have them support their responses with their annotations. If possible, record student annotations on a displayed copy of the text.

It's the Law! But Why? *(cont.)*

Phase 2—Digging Deeper

Who Reads

- ☐ teacher
- ☑ students

Annotations (See page 64.)

- ☐ highlight main points
- ☐ underline key details
- ☐ write questions
- ☐ circle key vocabulary
- ☑ arrows for connections
- ☐ other: ________________

Procedure

1. Before students read the text a second time, say, "Now, let's reread, looking for connections between sentences. How do the sentences in the text relate to each other? Draw arrows to connect sentences that support each other." (Example: It's almost always a good idea to obey the law. Laws keep people safe.)
2. If needed, ask additional layered/scaffolded questions, such as:
   - What sentence supports the sentence in paragraph 4, "It's generally a good idea to obey the law."?
   - What other sentence adds clarity to this sentence?
   - What other sentence provides an example to support this sentence?
3. **Partners**—After students have read and annotated the text, pairs can share their thinking about connections in the text.
4. Say, "What do you notice about the punctuation in this text? Mark the text to show how the punctuation is used."
5. If needed, ask additional layered/scaffold questions, such as:
   - How many periods do you see?
   - How many question marks do you see?
   - How many exclamation points do you see?
   - How do the periods affect the text?
   - How do the question marks affect the text?
   - How do the exclamation points affect the text?
6. **Partners**—After students have read and annotated the text, pairs can share the punctuation they have marked and the effects they have noted.
7. **Whole Class**—Regroup as a class, and display the text for all students. Ask students to share their ideas about how punctuation is used for effect. If possible, record student annotations on a displayed copy of the text.

It's the Law! But Why? *(cont.)*

Phase 3—Digging Even Deeper

Who Reads

- ☐ teacher
- ☑ students

Annotations (See page 64.)

- ☑ highlight main points
- ☑ underline key details
- ☑ write questions
- ☐ circle key vocabulary
- ☐ arrows for connections
- ☐ other: ____________

Procedure

1. Have students return to the text to identify the significance of the information in the second paragraph.
2. If needed, ask additional layered/scaffolded questions, such as:
   - What reasons does the author provide to support the usefulness of most laws?
   - Why might there be a law about not singing at night?
   - Why might a police officer choose to ignore or enforce this law?
   - How do laws relate to people living peacefully?
3. **Whole Class**—Regroup as a class, and display the text for all students. Ask students to share their responses to the question regarding the second paragraph. Have them support their responses with their annotations. If possible, record student annotations on a displayed copy of the text.
4. Prior to the performance task, have students think about the passage individually by completing the *Gather the Details* activity (page 255).

Performance Assessment

1. Assign the performance task *World's Shortest Summary* (page 256).
2. Explain that students' assignments will be graded based on the *World's Shortest Summary Scoring Rubric* (page 257). The scoring rubric is for both students and teachers to guide and score work.

Name: ______________________ Date: ______________

It's the Law! But Why?

1 Laws keep people safe and help us live together peacefully. But sometimes, there are laws that defy logic. Many laws were written hundreds of years ago, making some of them outdated, odd, or just downright silly!

2 Did you know that in Alabama, you can go to jail for wearing a fake mustache in church? Make sure you've taken your singing classes because in North Carolina, it's against the law to sing off key. Speaking of singing...in Kansas, you could be penalized for singing at night!

3 In Maryland, it is unlawful to take a lion to the movies (this one seems rather obvious). In Ohio, it's illegal to dye chickens. You could be arrested if you ride a camel in Nevada. And you can't eat ice cream on Sunday in Oregon. Who knew?

4 Some of these laws are very old. So it's hard to know under what circumstances they were written and even harder to enforce many of them. But we can't ignore every law. It's generally a good idea to obey the law. Laws are only powerful if we obey them. What will you do the next time you find a strange law?

Ohio State Code 926.62
5 **Dyeing Rabbits and Chicks**
No person shall dye or otherwise color any rabbit or baby poultry, including, but not limited to, chicks and ducklings. No person shall sell, offer for sale, expose for sale, raffle, or give away any rabbit or baby poultry which has been dyed or otherwise colored.

Name:____________________ Date: ____________

Gather the Details

Directions: Group the details from "It's the Law! But Why?" into categories. Write a statement to describe each category. The details should support the statement by making it more clear or by providing examples.

Statement: ____________________
Detail:____________________
Detail:____________________
Detail:____________________
Detail:____________________

Statement: ____________________
Detail:____________________
Detail:____________________
Detail:____________________
Detail:____________________

Statement: ____________________
Detail:____________________
Detail:____________________
Detail:____________________
Detail:____________________

Name: ______________________ Date: ______________

Express Yourself!

Directions: Circle the punctuation marks in the two paragraphs from "It's the Law! But Why?" Take turns reading a paragraph aloud to a partner. Change your voice to emphasize the punctuation marks.

Partner 1:

Did you know that in Alabama, you can go to jail for wearing a fake mustache in church? Make sure you've taken your singing classes because in North Carolina, it's against the law to sing off key. Speaking of singing...in Kansas, you could be penalized for singing at night!

Partner 2:

In Maryland, it is unlawful to take a lion to the movies (this one seems rather obvious). In Ohio, it's illegal to dye chickens. You could be arrested if you ride a camel in Nevada. And you can't eat ice cream on Sunday in Oregon. Who knew?

Name:______________________________ Date: ________________

World's Shortest Summary

Directions: Combine three to four key details from "It's the Law! But Why?" into a few big ideas. Summarize the entire text in 30 words or less. Use punctuation for effect. Make sure each detail from the text connects to your summary. (Multiple details can connect to the same sentence.)

____

____

____

____

____

____

____

____

Name: ______________________ Date: ______________

World's Shortest Summary Scoring Rubric

Directions: Complete the self-assessment section of this rubric. Then, turn this in with your completed *World's Shortest Summary* activity. (4 means "I strongly agree." 1 means "I do not agree.")

Self-Assessment

	4	3	2	1
My summary included 3–4 key details from the text.				
I combined multiple details into a few big ideas.				
I used 30 words or less in my summary.				
I used punctuation for effect.				

Additional comments: ______________________

____

____

____

Teacher Assessment

	4	3	2	1
The summary included 3–4 key details from the text.				
The writer combined multiple details into a few big ideas.				
The writer used 30 words or less in the summary.				
The writer used varied punctuation for effect.				

Additional comments: ______________________

____

____

____

Rubric based on work by Lapp, D., B. Moss, M. Grant, & K. Johnson (2015)

Emergency Alert Text: Earthquake Update

Purpose

WHAT: Use information from more than one text to recount an event.

HOW: Write a summarizing text using information from a text alert and a journal entry.

I CAN: I can use information from two sources to recount an event.

Standards

- **Reading:** Integrate information from several texts on the same topic in order to write or speak about the subject knowledgeably.
- **Writing:** Use precise language and domain-specific vocabulary to inform about or explain the topic.
- **Language:** Use a comma to separate an introductory phrase from the rest of the sentence.

Performance Assessment

- Students will write texts, integrating information from two different sources.

Text Selection

- "Emergency Alert Text: Earthquake Update"
- Text is divided into paragraphs.

Materials

- *Emergency Alert Text: Earthquake Update* passage, one copy per student (page 264; emergency.pdf)
- *Gathering Information* activity (page 265)
- *Be Precise* activity (page 266)
- *Rewrite It* activity (page 267)
- *Rewrite It Scoring Rubric* (page 268)

Text-Dependent Questions (See pages 49–53 for more information.)

- What are these texts about? What does the author want readers to know?
- What important information is provided in each account of the earthquake?
- How are the texts different and/or the same?
- Which account of the earthquake was personal, and how can you tell?
- What information in the first account of the earthquake would be helpful for local residents?
- What details are added by the introductory phrases?

Emergency Alert Text: Earthquake Update *(cont.)*

Areas of Complexity

	Measure	Explanation
Quantitative	Lexile Level	710L
Qualitative	Meaning or Purpose	The purpose of the text is to provide two accounts of the same story. One is factual and comprehensive. The other is personal.
	Structure	The text is organized in two ways. The first is shown on a cell phone as an emergency alert text. The second is an entry from a girl's diary.
	Language Features	Language in the emergency alert text is stilted and abbreviated. The diary entry includes informal language and irrelevant details.
Reader/Task	Knowledge Demands	Words such as *aftershock* and *consulted* may be unfamiliar to students. Students must integrate details from two texts to complete the performance task.

Text Synopsis

The text provides two accounts of the same event. The first account is in an emergency alert text, informing the public about an earthquake. Information is provided about when it happened and what is being done as well as where residents can get help. The second account is a diary entry from a girl telling about what she saw and what she did when she woke up and realized she was experiencing an earthquake.

Differentiation

Additional Support—You may need to assist students with unfamiliar words (*aftershock, consulted*) in order to increase comprehension.

As needed, students can transfer their annotations to the *Be Precise* activity (page 266). This chart supports students as they reread the text.

Extension—Instruct students to tell about a personal experience in the form of a news broadcast.

Emergency Alert Text: Earthquake Update *(cont.)*

Phase 1—Hitting the Surface

Who Reads

- ❑ teacher
- ☑ students

Annotations (See page 64.)

- ☑ highlight main points
- ☑ underline key details
- ☑ write questions
- ❑ circle key vocabulary
- ❑ arrows for connections
- ❑ other: ____________

Procedure

1. Explain the purposes (from page 259) before students read.
2. Have students read the text independently. As they read, have students annotate their copies of the text to answer the questions *What are these texts about? What does the author want readers to know?*
3. Throughout each phase, as students read, circulate to observe their work, and provide scaffolds as guides for those who need assistance. These might be additional layered questions, prompts to encourage them to reflect on a certain part of the passage, or cues to remember related information. Insights you gain through this formative assessment can also influence the next questions to be asked of the whole group.
4. **Partners**—After students have read and annotated the text once, pairs can share their thinking as related to the initial questions.
5. **Whole Class**—Regroup as a class, and display the text for all students. Ask students to share their responses to the question regarding what the texts are about. Have them support their responses with their annotations. If possible, record student annotations on a displayed copy of the text.

Phase 2—Digging Deeper

Who Reads

- ❑ teacher
- ☑ students

Annotations (See page 64.)

- ❑ highlight main points
- ☑ underline key details
- ❑ write questions
- ❑ circle key vocabulary
- ❑ arrows for connections
- ☑ other: notes in the margin

Procedure

1. Before students read the text a second time, say, "Now, let's reread to identify the use of precise language to explain the topic. What important information is provided in each account of the earthquake? What details are included? Underline the words and phrases that are precise and helpful for understanding what happened."

Emergency Alert and Earthquake! *(cont.)*

Phase 2—Digging Deeper *(cont.)*

Procedure *(cont.)*

2. If needed, ask additional layered/scaffolded questions, such as:
    - How strong was the earthquake?
    - How long was power and water shut off?
    - How many people died?
    - What happened to Lily's windows?
    - What happened to the books in Lily's room?
3. **Partners**—After students have read and annotated the text once, pairs can share their thinking related to the use of precise language.
4. Prior to the performance task, have students think about the passage individually by completing the *Gathering Information* activity (page 265).

Phase 3—Digging Even Deeper

Who Reads	Annotations (See page 64.)		
❑ teacher	❑ highlight main points	❑ underline key details	❑ write questions
☑ students	❑ circle key vocabulary	❑ arrows for connections	☑ other: circle commas used to separate introductory elements of sentences

Procedure

1. Before students return to the text, ask, "How are the texts different and/or the same?" Mark the text to show your thinking.
2. If needed, ask additional layered/scaffolded questions, such as:
    - What details are in one text and not the other?
    - Which details are essentially the same in both texts?
    - Which account of the earthquake was personal, and how can you tell?
    - Which account of the earthquake would be helpful for local residents? What details make it helpful?

Emergency Alert and Earthquake! *(cont.)*

Phase 3—Digging Even Deeper *(cont.)*

Procedure *(cont.)*

3. **Partners**—After students have read and annotated the text, pairs can share their annotations.
4. Ask students to focus on the sentences with introductory phrases. Say, "What details are added by the introductory phrases?"
5. If needed, ask additional layered/scaffolded questions, such as:
   - What does *at first* tell you?
   - What does *when I opened my eyes* tell you?
   - What does *finally* tell you?
   - What does *immediately* tell you?
   - What category describes the details you gathered from the introductory phrases?
6. **Whole Class**—Regroup as a class, and display the text for all students. Ask students to describe the introductory phrases in the text. If possible, record student annotations on a displayed copy of the text.
7. Before assigning the performance task, have students complete the *Be Precise* activity (page 266).

Performance Assessment

1. Assign the performance task *Rewrite It* (page 267).
2. Explain that students' assignments will be graded based on the *Rewrite It Scoring Rubric* (page 268). The scoring rubric is for both students and teachers to guide and score work.

Name: ______________________________ Date: ________________

Emergency Alert Text: Earthquake Update

1 **September 27, 5:22 a.m.**

2 5.6 earthquake confirmed Tuesday morning. Aftershocks lasted nearly 24 hours. No power or water services for two hours. Several buildings were damaged. County offices are coordinating response. No deaths have been reported. Many taken to the hospital for care (infants and elderly). Assistance available at local libraries.

Earthquake! Excerpted from the Diary of Lily Winkler

September 27–

1 At first, I thought it was a bad dream. One minute I was
2 flying through imaginary clouds, and the next the entire room
was in motion. When I opened my eyes, the clock read 5:22
a.m. My bed was shaking. The windows were rattling. The
long purple curtains were swaying against them. Immediately,
I wanted Mom and Dad to pick me up and tell me everything
was okay like they used to do when I fell down or scraped an
elbow. But this was different. It seemed something was wrong
with the whole world.

I felt like I was surfing. But I was trying to ride waves on
3 the ground instead of waves in the ocean. Books leapt from
my shelf to the carpet with a stream of thuds in the darkness.
Finally, the shaking began to slow. And, at last, it came to a
stop. After what seemed like hours, I finally heard my Mom
calling for me. She, Dad, and I calmed each other down and
had an early breakfast in front of the television news.

4 It turns out, the house was fine. The whole neighborhood
was fine. Dad went to check on Old Mr. Atherton. Mom got
called in to help volunteer at the library. I went with her and
helped coordinate clean up of a few damaged buildings and
hand out supply kits.

Name:______________________________ Date: ________________

Gathering Information

Directions: Use the text "Emergency Alert Text: Earthquake Update" to complete the chart. Write information gathered from the news story and information gathered from the diary entry.

Text Message	Diary Entry

Name: ______________________________ Date: ______________

Be Precise

Directions: The authors of "Emergency Alert Text: Earthquake Update" use precise language to help us understand what happened. Complete the chart by writing words from the text that indicate *who*, *what*, *where*, *when*, *why*, and *how*.

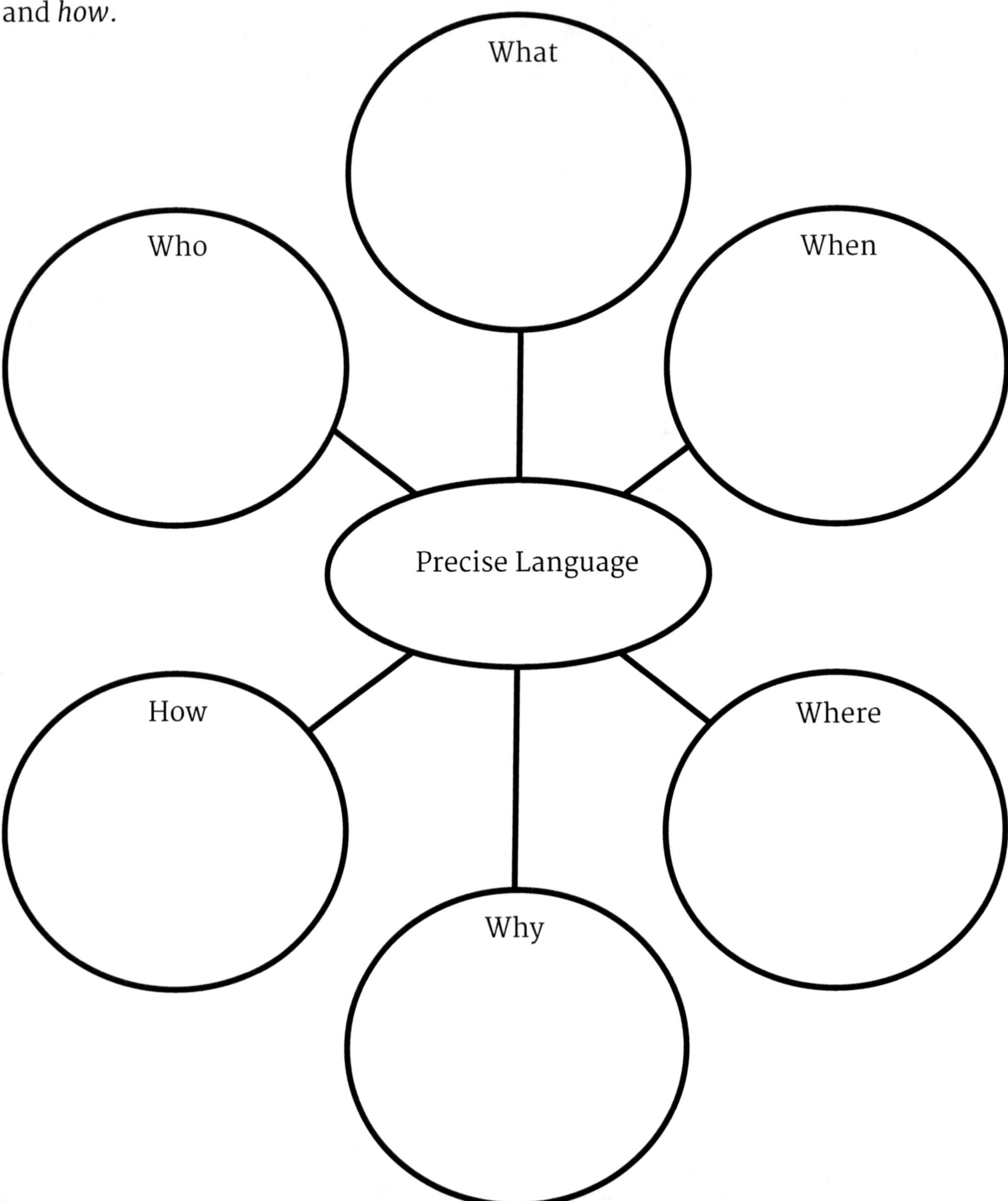

Name:______________________________ Date: _______________

Rewrite It

Directions: Choose another form of writing to retell the details of the earthquake described in the texts. Pull details from both sources to provide details about the event. Make sure to use precise language and to use commas to separate parts of the sentence that indicate time and place.

Forms of Writing

- letter to an out-of-state family member
- speech at a news conference
- page from a biography
- other:________________________

Name: ______________________________ Date: ____________________

Rewrite It Scoring Rubric

Directions: Complete the self-assessment section of this rubric. Then, turn this in with your completed *Rewrite It* activity. (4 means "I strongly agree." 1 means "I do not agree.")

Self-Assessment

	4	3	2	1
I included important details about the earthquake.				
I provided both objective and personal information.				
I used precise language to help the reader understand the event.				
I used introductory phrases to indicate time and place.				

Additional comments: ______________________________

____

____

____

Teacher Assessment

	4	3	2	1
The writer included important details about the earthquake.				
The writer provided both objective and personal information.				
The writer used precise language to help the reader understand the event.				
The writer used introductory phrases to indicate time and place.				

Additional comments: ______________________________

____

____

____

Rubric based on work by Lapp, D., B. Moss, M. Grant, & K. Johnson (2015)

Try It!

Directions: Use the passage below and the planning forms that follow (page 270–271) to plan a close reading lesson.

Racing Rocks

Sailing stones or sliding stones, roving rocks or racing rocks—no matter what name they're given, they remain a mystery.

The sliding rocks first puzzled visitors to Death Valley over a hundred years ago. And it seems scientists are just as confused by the spectacle.

Stretching out for miles, spectators see nothing but desolate, cracked earth and sand in the dried-up lakebed called Racetrack Playa. Nothing, that is, except stones of varying sizes. When people are present, the rocks stay put, exactly as one would expect. However, they are traveling. We know because they leave grooved tracks in their wake. Some rocks move only a few inches, others have traveled close to 3,000 feet (0.91 km). Some trails are straight and even, others are coiled and curly. It appears that a few rocks prefer to travel in pairs, but most go on solo excursions.

It's fairly easy for a rock to get kicked about by people or pushed by wind or water. But the stones we're talking about aren't pebbles. They're boulders, weighing as little as one pound (0.45 kg) but go up to 700 (317.5 kg)! It would take a wind speed of 150 miles (241.4 km) per hour or more to move them, yet wind on the playa tops out at around 70 miles (112.7 km) per hour.

Gravity and earthquakes would provide simple explanations, but neither is the culprit here. Scientists have ruled out plenty of other theories as well. For example, some thought the rocks might be made of a special material. However, inspection reveals they're common dolomite from the mountain highlands.

Perplexed, investigators started looking for answers not in the rocks themselves but in the dry lakebed where they landed. They thought perhaps the friction might be reduced by water. The clay doesn't get slippery when moist, though. Water, however, takes other forms.

It snows in the mountains above the desert during winter. And when water melts and runs downhill, it collects in the playa and freezes overnight. Scientists posit that sheets of ice could move rocks in pairs. For solitary stones, an ice collar could keep a rock partially afloat. If the wind were to move the water around it, the heavy rock would shift as well.

The ice theory seems to hold real water, although it's yet to be proven. To this day, no one has witnessed a racing rock move.

Planning for Close Reading

Planning Chart for Close Reading

Planning

Date: ____________ Grade: ________ Discipline: ____________________

Purpose(s): ____

Standard(s): ____

Text Selection (literary or informational): ______________________

Performance Assessment: ______________________________________

Materials: ____

Text Selection

Title: ____

Author: ____

Page(s) or section(s): ______________________________________

How should this text be chunked? ______________________________

____

Areas of Complexity

Lexile Level: ____

Meaning or Purpose: ______________________________________

Structure: ____

Language Features: ______________________________________

Knowledge Demands: ______________________________________

Text-Dependent Questions

1. ____
2. ____
3. ____
4. ____
5. ____

Performance Task

____
____
____
____

Differentiation

Additional Support: ______________
____

Extension: ______________________
____

Teaching Close Reading

Teaching

Limited Frontloading ❑ yes ❑ no

Describe:

First Read

Who Reads? ❑ teacher ❑ student

Student Resources

❑ graphic organizer ❑ group consensus form

❑ note taking guide ❑ summary form

Second Read

Who Reads? ❑ teacher ❑ student

Student Resources

❑ graphic organizer ❑ group consensus form

❑ note taking guide ❑ summary form

Additional Reads

Who Reads? ❑ teacher ❑ student

Student Resources

❑ graphic organizer ❑ group consensus form

❑ note taking guide ❑ summary form

Extension	**Reteaching**

References Cited

ACT. 2006. "Reading Between the Lines: What the ACT Reveals About College Readiness in Reading." https://www.act.org/research/policymakers/pdf/reading_report.pdf.

Airasian, Peter W., Kathleen A. Cruikshank, Richard E. Mayer, Paul R. Pintrich, James Raths, and Merlin C. Wittrock. 2001. *A Taxonomy for Learning, Teaching, and Assessing: A Revision of Bloom's Taxonomy of Educational Objectives (Complete edition)*. Edited by Lorin W. Anderson and David R. Krathwohl. New York: Longman.

Boyles, Nancy. 2012. "Closing in on Close Reading." *Educational Leadership (Association for Supervision and Curriculum Development)* 70 (4): 36–41.

Coleman, David, and Susan Pimentel. 2012. *Revised Publishers' Criteria for the Common Core State Standards in English Language Arts and Literacy, Grades 3–12.*

Common Core State Initiative. *Common Core State Standards for English Language Arts, Appendix A (Additional Information)*. NGA and CCSSO.

Fountas, Sue, and Gay Pinnell. 2012. "F&P Text Level Gradient." *Heinemann*. http://www.heinemann.com/fountasandpinnell/handouts/FP_TextLevelGradient.pdf.

———. 2015. "Instructional Grade-Level Equivalence Chart." http://www.fountasandpinnel.com/shared/resources/FP_FPL_Chart_Instructional-Grade-Level-Equivalence-Chart.pdf

Lapp, Diane, Barbara Moss, Maria Grant, and Kelly Johnson. 2015. A Close Look at Close Reading: Teaching Students to Analyze Complex Texts, Grades K–5. ASCD.

National Governors Association Center for Best Practices & Council of Chief State School Officers. 2010. *Common Core State Standards for English Language Arts and Literacy in History/Social Studies, Science, and Technical Subjects*. Washington, DC: Authors.

Partnership for Assessment of Readiness for College and Careers. *PARCC Model Content Frameworks: English Language Arts/Literacy Grades 3–11*. http://parcconline.org/resources/educator-resources/model-content-frameworks.

Plant, E. Ashby, K. Anders Ericsson, Len Hill, and Kia Asberg. 2005. "Why Study Time Does Not Predict Grade Point Average Across College Students: Implications of Deliberate Practice for Academic Performance." *Contemporary Educational Psychology* 30.

Rusch, Elizabeth. 2014. *The Next Wave: The Quest to Harness the Power of the Oceans.* New York: Houghton Mifflin Harcourt.

Webb, Norman. *Research Monograph Number 6: Criteria for Alignment of Expectations and Assessments on Mathematics and Science Education.* Washington, D.C.: CCSSO.

Williamson, G. L. 2006. "Student Readiness for Postsecondary Endeavors." American Educational Research Association (AERA). San Francisco: MetaMetrics, Inc.

Glossary of Reteaching Ideas

character profiles: Write key information about a character from the text onto a graphic organizer. Details might include age, gender, nationality, relationships to other characters (mother, brother, friend, enemy, or boss), physical characteristics, personality, strengths and weaknesses, and education.

character web: Write the character's name in a square in the middle of the paper. Draw ovals around the square with branches out to a series of ovals. Draw a line to connect each oval to the square. In the ovals, write words or phrases to describe the character.

claim/evidence/analysis: Make a claim about a text. Use evidence from the text to support the claim. Analyze the evidence and share reader's interpretation of the evidence.

For each activity marked with a computer icon, a template or graphic organizer is provided in the Digital Download. See the contents on pages 274–276.

concept maps: Use graphic organizers to demonstrate and organize knowledge of a subject. Begin with a concept enclosed in a box or circle. Draw branches out from the box or circle, showing how the concept can be broken down into smaller parts, each with their own branches.

connect two: In this game, two lists of words are posted. Players make connections between a word on the first list and a word on the second list, explaining the reason for the connection (e.g., synonyms, antonyms, or parts of speech).

essential questions: Ask questions that dig down to the issues we struggle with or consider throughout our lives. They are not easily answered through a single text or exercise, such as "What defines life?", "Is art a matter of taste or skill?", "Can war be just?", "What makes a person a good friend?", or "How do we know what really happened?"

flip-flop: Rewrite or retell an existing story with a new tone (e.g., make something scary, funny; make something silly, sad).

Frayer cards: Divide a note card or piece of paper into fourths. Quadrant 1 houses a challenging vocabulary word. Quadrant 2 includes the definition. Quadrant 3 contains a picture of it. Quadrant 4 uses the word in a sentence. An alternative version integrates a synonym or antonym, too.

Freytag's Pyramid: Create a visual representation of a literature text's structure. Label a flat line at the bottom of the page with *Exposition* or *Beginning*. Add steeply angled line on the left labeled *Rising Action*. Label the top *Climax*, and the steep line down the right side *Falling Action*. Complete the pyramid with another flat line at the bottom labeled *Denouement* or *Resolution*. Add details from a current text to each part of the line.

Gimme 5: Write five key details from a text on a sheet of paper.

Glossary of Reteaching Ideas *(cont.)*

graphic organizers: Use visual shapes that help readers organize and analyze concepts and content from their reading.

hash tags: Write a hash tag that whittles down complex concepts into a single word or phrase.

inquiry charts: Gather information from several sources and compile it on a grid. Across the top, label the columns with topic-appropriate questions. The final two columns are labeled *Other Interesting Facts* and *New Questions*. Label each row is labeled with a separate source. Label the final row *Summary*.

newspaper headlines and story titles: Use headlines and titles to illuminate texts' main ideas.

personal dictionaries: Create dictionaries that contain vocabulary terms. They can be subject specific or alphabetical, English-only or bilingual, and contain synonyms and antonyms.

plot skeletons: Create a bare-bones description of a literature text's plot. Use a graphic organizer shaped like a skeleton, identifying the main character, his or her needs (obvious and/or hidden), causes, resulting complications, how these inform the decision that is made, and the resolution.

signal terms: Use or create lists of signal words to denote various text structures, such as chronological order, cause/effect, description, compare/contrast, and problem/solution.

Somebody Wanted But So Then (SWBST): Use this framework for creating summaries that is completed during reading. Write a summary sentence from the accumulated information.

song lyrics: Use song lyrics to provide accessible sources of figurative language.

storyboards: Create a series of images that depict the elements of a text.

story maps: Use these graphic representations to record and organize key information about a text. Story maps typically include sections for information about the setting, characters, and problem and solution. Sometimes other information, such as sequence of events, title, author, and main idea, are included.

story summary graphic organizers: Use these graphic organizers provide visual spaces to record key information needed to summarize a text.

task cards: Create reusable cards containing one activity or question per card, breaking down a potentially overwhelming task into manageable pieces.

T-chart: Draw a two-column chart that enables readers to make comparisons, such as between words, characters, or concepts.

text feature BINGO: Fill in squares with various text features to reinforce concepts.

Glossary of Reteaching Ideas *(cont.)*

text feature checklist: Use a checklist as a student-friendly way to search texts to find text features.

Toulmin Model of Arguments: Use this model to break down arguments into six parts: claim, evidence, warrant (the connection between the claim and evidence), backing (justifying the warrant), counterargument/rebuttal, and qualifier (additions to the claim that counter rebuttals).

tweet the main idea: Limit writing to 140 characters. This concise format requires authors to whittle down complex concepts.

Visual Thinking Strategies (VTS): Use a set of art-based techniques that use open-ended questions, neutral paraphrasing, requests for evidence, and linking of participant observations to help participants develop observational and analytic skills.

vocabulary matrices: Write one set of vocabulary words across the top of a grid and another down the first column. For each place where the row of one word intersects the column of another, write a sentence that correctly uses both words.

word associations: Lead a discussion about how words are connected, such as synonyms vs. antonyms or examples vs. non-examples.

word maps: Draw graphic representations that connect vocabulary words to other concepts in various ways and include developing a definition, synonyms, antonyms, and a picture for a particular vocabulary word.

word sorts: Write categorized words on card stock, such as negatively connotative words versus positively connotative words.

words in context: Highlight surrounding words that provide clues to the meaning of unknown words.

Contents of the Digital Download

Digital Download

The following documents are designed to help with the planning and implementation of close reading lessons. For details about how to locate and download, see page 14.

Page Number	Title	Filename
17	Incorporating Close Reading	incorporatingclosereading.pdf
56	Planning Close Reading	planningclosereading.pdf
63–64	Annotation Ideas	annotationideas.pdf
67	Teaching Close Reading	teachingclosereading.pdf

Incorporating Close Reading

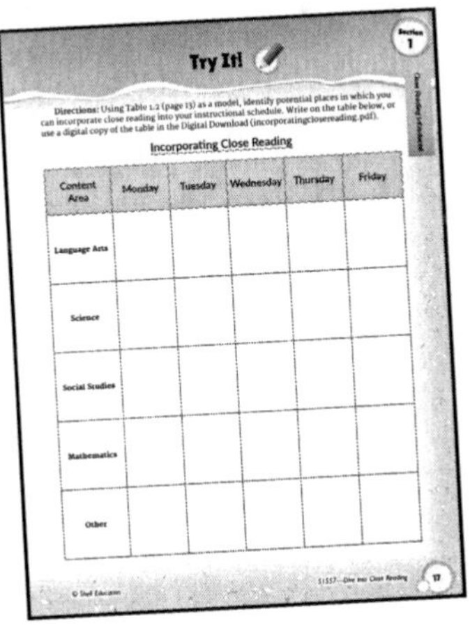

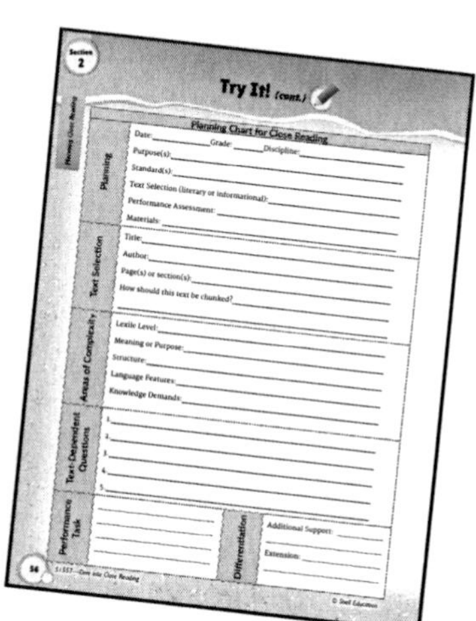

Planning Close Reading

Annotation Ideas

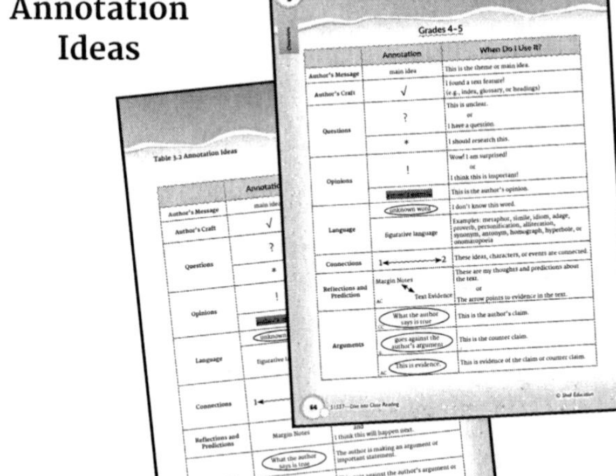

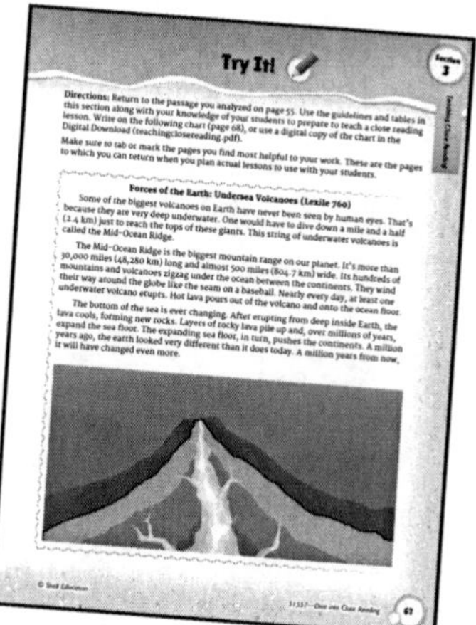

Teaching Close Reading

Contents of the Digital Download *(cont.)*

The following passages can be used to implement the sample lessons. See pages 83–268 for details.

Page Number	Title	Filename
88	The Fox and the Crow	foxandcrow.pdf
98	A Cry for Help	cryforhelp.pdf
108	Slimy	slimy.pdf
118	My Life: The Fruit Fly's Story	fruitflysstory.pdf
128	From 613 King Street to Room 4F	kingstreet.pdf
138	The Pup	thepup.pdf
148	Did You See?	didyousee.pdf
158	Plastic Panic	plasticpanic.pdf
168	A Royal Prisoner	royalprisoner.pdf
184	Lincoln's Hat	lincoln.pdf
194	Underwater Architect	underwater.pdf
204	Blood, Sweat, and Tears	bloodsweattears.pdf
214	Going Batty	goingbatty.pdf
224	Digestion in Depth	digestion.pdf
234	Trapped for 69 Days	trapped.pdf
244	Legless, Fearless	leglessfearless.pdf
254	It's the Law! But Why?	itsthelaw.pdf
264	Emergency Alert Text: Earthquake Update	emergency.pdf
n/a	Standards Correlation for all sample lessons	standardscorrelations.pdf

Contents of the Digital Download *(cont.)*

The following reteaching resources are designed to be used with the reteaching ideas listed in Appendix B (pages 274–276).

Page Number	Title	Filename
274	character profiles	characterprofiles.pdf
274	character web	characterweb.pdf
274	concept maps	conceptmaps.pdf
275	inquiry charts	inquirycharts.pdf
275	plot skeletons	plotskeletons.pdf
275	story maps	storymaps.pdf
275	story summary graphic organizers	storysummarygraphicorganizers.pdf
275	T-chart	tchart.pdf
275	text feature BINGO	textfeaturebingo.pdf
276	text feature checklist	textfeaturechecklist.pdf
276	Toulmin Model of Arguments	toulminmodel.pdf
276	vocabulary matrix	vocabularymatrix.pdf
276	word maps	wordmaps.pdf

Notes